M

"A heartfelt, honest, at times harrowing, and inspiring memoir that reminds us of the indomitable human spirit."

—Rabbi Nechemia Coopersmith, Chief Editor, Aish.com

"Miranda Portnoy tells a compelling story of how she emerged from a toxic family, which nearly destroyed her, forged a turbulent, troubled young adulthood to arrive as a devoutly religious woman, married to a wonderful man and living with her family in Jerusalem. She is a gifted writer who has written a psychologically sophisticated, gut-wrenching memoir of courage and determination. As a clinical psychologist, I was privileged to witness many individuals recreate themselves and move on to live better and more productive lives. It is rare, however, to find such a gifted writer who can bring her reader so palpably close to the pain of family trauma and the challenges that lie along the path of recovery. Her story gives hope to every human being who strives to emerge from psychological despair and spiritual darkness to a more tranquil, meaningful life."

—Yisrael Levitz, PhD, clinical psychologist, Founding Dean, The Family Institute of Neve Yerushalayim and Professor Emeritus, Yeshiva University

"A truly inspiring life story that illustrates that one not only needs clarity in life, but also unlimited determination. A must-read for anyone who ever had a door slammed in their face, and instead of giving up, got in through the window."

—Lori Palatnik, author, international speaker, Founding Director of Momentum

"*Cinder-oy-la!* is an authentic, eye-opening personal journey of a victim of child abuse determined to survive and strive toward a healthy and meaningful life. She takes us on her journey candidly; we can feel her joys and sorrows as she climbs, falls, and climbs again. This is a story of hope, determination, and redemption. A must-read for anyone wanting to understand the struggle for and process of recovery from childhood abuse."

—Chaya Weisberg, Co-Director, Heritage House, www.heritage.org.il

"Each of us has a past. Some of us are lucky enough to use it to propel us forward to achieve great accomplishments. In so doing, we carry along with us all of those who nurtured and guided us through our formative years. Others of us are not so lucky. Our past was painful, lonely, and at times terrifying. It clings to us accusingly, reminding us each moment that we are nothing and will never amount to anything. And that's when we need, if we can, to embrace courage. With renewed faith and conviction, we can turn the darkness into light, and the despair into hope. Miranda Portnoy has accomplished this phenomenal feat, and I salute her."

—Tova Mordechai, author of *To Play with Fire*

CINDER-OY-LA!

How a Jewish Scapegoat
Becomes a Princess

A Memoir by Miranda Portnoy

BookLocker
Saint Petersburg, Florida

Copyright © 2021 Miranda Portnoy

Print ISBN: 978-1-64718-877-1
Epub ISBN: 978-1-64718-878-8
Mobi ISBN: 978-1-64718-879-5

Published by BookLocker.com, Inc., St. Petersburg, Florida.

Printed on acid-free paper.

BookLocker.com, Inc.
2021

First Edition

Library of Congress Cataloguing in Publication Data
Portnoy, Miranda
CINDER-OY-LA! How a Jewish Scapegoat Becomes a Princess by Miranda Portnoy
Library of Congress Control Number: 2020916295

Scripture quotations are modified from The Holy Scriptures According to the Masoretic Text, published by the Jewish Publication Society in 1917.

Translations of the Siddur (Jewish prayer book) are modified from public-domain translations available at Sefaria.org.

Dedicated to my beloved husband, whose wisdom, courage, and love made this story and everything else possible

The national history of the Jewish people unfolds in the personal life of the Jewish mystic.

—Zohar

All Jews are responsible for one another.

—Babylonian Talmud, *Sanhedrin* 27b

Table of Contents

Preface

L ong ago, when the Jewish people left Egypt and stood before the sea that parted for their passage, Sages say the lowliest maidservant had a vision of Divine Providence as vivid as the greatest prophet. The revelation of God's hand in *my* life could not be meant just for me, in a world so needy of God's love. Though I am no Scheherazade, the patient reader will be rewarded with a true tale of psychological and spiritual emancipation, a quintessentially Jewish parable, with misfortune lost and transcendence gained.

Author's notes: Whereas the events to the best of my recollection took place precisely as described, all names of persons and places have been changed for confidentiality; the actual university in question was not Harvard.

Whenever I speak of God as He or Him, I honor convention, and my own experience of God as a Father, though God has no gender.

Part One

In the Bosom of Family

And you shall eat the fruit of your own body, the flesh of your sons and of your daughters whom the Lord your God has given you...if you will not observe to do all the words of this law that are written in this book...

—Deuteronomy 28:53, 58

Chapter 1

"*W*<i>hich</i> Turovs are you?"
Everywhere I go in the holy city of Jerusalem I am asked, from which branch on this celebrated family's tree did you emerge? My married name conjures towering figures of Orthodox Jewish learning and refined conduct. The Turov dynasty spawned several English-speaking Torah giants in the twentieth century with innumerable descendants devoted to the cause. Hailing from Belarus, where their family combined European culture and erudition with the highest standard of fealty to ancient Jewish law, the Turovs are revered like royalty in the Torah world—which respects lineage.

But I carry an amusing secret. Estelle, the irritable, overbearing mother of George Costanza on the 1990s TV series *Seinfeld*, more closely resembles my kin. Yet Estelle Costanza was much more benign than my mother was.

As fate would have it, my mother happened to have borderline personality disorder *and* narcissistic and histrionic personality disorders. But she didn't come shrink-wrapped and labelled. Nor did we get her at a discount. In fact, I only found out about her diagnoses as a grown woman when the scars she had left on me could no longer be ignored. Clinical depression is like that. When one falls apart at the picnic because the roasted hotdog fell on its way to the bun and lies in the dirt—when this releases a torrent of tears and self-recrimination of the kind Stalin doesn't deserve to suffer—one comes to the attention of a psychiatrist. That's what happened to me when I was eighteen and a freshman at an Ivy League university. Until then, I suffered. But I didn't take it lying down. I fought as though my life depended on it.

I don't remember a time when I wasn't fighting with my mother. My earliest, vaguest memories are of violence accompanying my decision to wear the green playsuit rather than the pink one she had laid out for me.

My mother was indeed a pushy woman. When she picked me up from a friend's home, she would blow the car horn nonstop until I came out the front door, deafening wildlife within miles. When we ate in restaurants, she would inevitably request menu substitutions.

"I'd like a beverage instead of my second vegetable—a coffee, please."

"I'm sorry, ma'am, we can't do that. You can have applesauce, peas and carrots, or corn."

"I'll have a hot tea, then."

"Ma'am, we don't substitute beverages for vegetables."

"Well, I suggest you tell the manager that he ought to allow menu substitutions. I'm on a special diet for diabetics, and I can't eat too many vegetables."

Cringing behind my menu, I knew what was coming next.

"Did you know that my daughter got a 96 on her math test in school last Friday?"

I copied the answers from Peggy Calhoun, I thought to myself— *tell him that too, okay?*

"That's very nice."

"She's a very good student."

"That's very nice."

"She was reading before she was walking."

"How nice. I'll bet she ate her vegetables."

Cinder-*oy*-la!

Growing up with Evelyn Portnoy for a mother was like walking around with a thumbtack in my shoe.

My mother knew what her assets were and how to accentuate them. *My name is Evelyn Portnoy, and I'd like you to meet my décolletage.* After work, she usually wore dyed skinny jeans on her short, stacked frame, with high-heeled pumps. Her hair and lips sported a matching shade of atomic tangerine, her cropped hair the texture of Rumpelstiltskin's straw from too many trips to the beauty parlor. Encrusted with chunky gold rings as big as brass knuckles, her small hands were transformed into prizefighter's fists.

A high school star who married at eighteen, my mother dedicated herself to the most conventional path to glory open to women of her 1950s generation: vicarious accomplishment through her husband and children. Convinced that doctors were an uber-race of demigods—holding the key to life and death in their hands—she determined that her children would gain admission to this exalted sect, intoxicated by their power. She uttered the words *residency, internship,* and *fellowship* many, many times a day with the holy reverence due a biblical hymn.

With a twelfth-grade diploma and mere secretarial skills, my powerless mother waged her power over us with uncompromising control. Driven by an emptiness too vast to fill, she would crush us like candy between her teeth for failing to gratify her outsized ambitions. Promised paradise or threatened with annihilation—depending on whether I acquiesced to her desperate fantasies—I would come downstairs in the morning and lay my head on the vinyl placemat, listening to the whoosh of the kitchen faucet with an already quickened heartbeat, knowing that at any moment, my mother's harsh voice would summon me to a new day.

Nevertheless, I credit my mother with the birth of my scruples. As early as I could remember, I recoiled from her contemptuous slurs against African Americans and Gentiles. I shrank from her obsession with money and her worship of doctors, who epitomized the social prestige she craved. She *was* the caricature of the Jewish mother. With her greed so naked, I had no choice but to embrace the opposite values. We drew battle lines early: I shaped my identity in a firing kiln. My social-climbing mother gave birth to an artsy, bohemian daughter determined to bring compassion to Madonna's material world. Born with a surfeit of conscience, I remember crusading as a tot through my grandparents' littered Roxbury, Boston neighborhood with a placard taped to a yardstick on which I had scrawled, "Don't Plute [pollute]!" I won a place in the county newspaper for banding together girls to collect for the SPCA with cat and dog-shaped coin banks, instead of hustling candy at Halloween.

Along the margin of the popular clique, but attractive enough not to be excluded entirely, I made my mark as an early reformer, sticking up for the awkward girls that were picked on. Serving as the resident pincushion for the popular set, I was the perennial victim of the malicious bull sessions of the kind in which fifth-grade girls excel. The two blonde queens would go around the circle of girls sitting Indian style and gleefully roast every member to her face. Only my turn was distinguished by an added ritual: they would repeat my nickname over and over, shaking their heads disdainfully, "Miri, Miri, Miri, *Miri*," as though they just couldn't stomach reciting *my* shortcomings. Then they would declare me the source of the resurgence of childhood polio.

Forsaking my mother's dreams of a B'nai B'rith Girls' princess—complete with a surgical nose and frosted hair—I defied even my generation and became a feminist-socialist-Zionist, clad in blue work shirt and Wallabees, long after it was fashionable. Alone on a Habonim summer camp stage at fourteen, I strummed Ralph McTell's "Streets of London" and John Prine's "Hello in There" on my guitar—mournful, cathartic folksongs—to an audience much more interested in adolescent debauchery than I was.

Habonim Dror—in English, "the builders of freedom"—was a group founded in 1929 by European Jewish Marxist Zionists. We were dedicated to purging society of everything hypocritical and bourgeois, and to establishing a utopian socialist society modeled after the Israeli kibbutz. We championed the ideals of the American sixties—which I considered myself fortunate to be touched by, despite coming of age a decade too late. Needless to say, my participation in Habonim was nothing less than vexing to my mother, for whom the term *social justice* meant eugenics.

Owing to the increasing tension at home, I suffered debilitating insomnia in junior high school. I would lie awake from midnight until morning, sleeping only for a few hours after school each day. On the less stressful weekends, I took special joy in sleeping until ten in the morning. Faced with my conscientious objection to her daughter-improvement program, my mother deployed more subtle tactics to induce my submission.

Her favorite maneuver was to charge through my door at seven o'clock on Saturdays, snap up my window shade in a cacophony of noise, and yell, "RISE AND SHINE, MIRANDA! TIME TO WAKE UP! THE WHOLE DAY IS ALMOST OVER!" If I failed to open my eyes, she would throw back the blanket and slap the bottoms of my bare feet. Next, she would blast the radio—shattering my dreams of a world without mothers with ear-splitting WBZ news.

When I would oversleep during the week and miss the school bus, we would ride to school in frenzied silence, my mother tapping her inch-long, pink plastic fingernails on the steering wheel—TAP! TAP! TAP! TAP! TAP!—inhaling and exhaling so loudly and forcefully, I feared the dashboard would catch fire.

How a Jewish Scapegoat Becomes a Princess

At about age ten, I became acquainted with my older brother's best friend, Shawn Dougherty. Shawn was a gentle, sweet guy eight years older than I was who lived across the street and occasionally gave me guitar lessons. He knew—as did the whole neighborhood—that my mother tormented my brother Richard and me, and he sensed that beneath my withdrawn shyness, I was very unhappy. If Richard wasn't home when he stopped by, Shawn would convey a big-brotherly sympathy in the few words we spoke.

By the time I was twelve, I was passionately infatuated. As is typical of twelve-year-olds, however, I became increasingly dumbstruck in his presence and hid in my room whenever he came over. I confessed my feelings only in a notebook I stashed among old magazines and schoolbooks in a box on my closet shelf. In that notebook, I sketched out elaborate fantasies of the day during a guitar lesson when Shawn's eyes would get misty, he would lean close, take the guitar from my hands, and whisper, "I want you, Miranda," and give me a warm, juicy kiss.

My mother, however, detested Shawn: He wasn't Jewish. He wasn't going to be a plastic surgeon. He was a dangerous influence on my brother and me.

When I was fourteen, we moved away, and Shawn and my brother drifted apart. I rarely saw Shawn anymore. Yet I still thought of him, trying to accelerate my growth so he would no longer be too old for me.

One day, at fifteen, I was sitting in my mother's room, talking animatedly on the phone with my friend Julie. Fiddling absentmindedly with the phonebook on her night table, I knocked some papers tucked between the pages onto the floor. Retrieving the material, I immediately recognized my own handwriting. I felt the blood surge to my face as a siren blasted off between my ears. The pages were photocopies of my fantasies about Shawn Dougherty, clipped to an envelope addressed to him.

I was mortified: my shock, humiliation, and utter fury at the invasion of my privacy were so overwhelming that I flew out of the apartment and ran over three miles, propelled by pure emotional energy. Julie—who lived upstairs in the apartment building—followed me to the high school football field. She sat with me while I vented hours of unrelenting tears in an outpouring of shame.

My mother, when confronted with this violation, merely inverted the truth: she blamed *me* for being secretive. "I have every right to determine with whom you associate, by whatever means you *force* me to use," she accused. I could only presume she was sending a letter along with my diary musings, threatening an indifferent, unaware, and astonished Shawn Dougherty to keep away from me. I felt my sense of control over my life and welfare completely dissolve in the face of my mother's intransigence. During my entire childhood and adolescence, I never heard her say the words "I'm sorry."

Before long, my overactive conscience, initially occupied with righting the wrongs outside my family, turned inward upon saving myself and my father and brother from the corrosive force in our own home. I fell instinctively into the role of my older brother's savior and my parents' therapist—trying to preserve harmony and promote détente between the ever-shifting factions. Here and there, I abandoned diplomacy to double as a pint-sized bouncer, breaking up my parents' brawls.

In the early years, my father and I forged a subversive alliance against my mother; we both needed protection. Berating him mercilessly for his weaknesses—whether social, financial, or sartorial—she goaded him to defend his fractured masculinity.

In one moment's lapse in her vigilance, my mother offered a compliment of my father, which I forever cherished: in contrast to her friends in their role-segregated early 1960s marriages, *she* never had to press her husband to spend time with his children. In childhood, my father was my hero, releasing me from detention at the kitchen table by inviting me to unload my soggy unfinished peas onto his plate while my mother was behind the refrigerator door. I remember him reading to me as a child and teaching me to ride my first two-wheeled Raleigh bike. My father liked little children and pets, creatures who could be both pacified and manipulated by treats and pats on the head. As long as I was naive and worshipful, he was gentle and tender with me.

Yet I remember my father's red face, wet with tears, his body beaten after a particularly bruising battle with my mother: "Miranda," he exclaimed, "I just can't take it anymore." When he moved out, life got worse, and no less dramatic. Instead of the fights erupting between my parents in our den, my father broke into our house every so often to vent his rage at my mother's outlandish legal gambits in their bitter divorce. Once he managed to twist the steering wheel of my mother's car into a pretzel before he even crossed the threshold of the front door. The police knew about the Portnoy family. We aroused the sleepy suburban police of Medway, Massachusetts with the occasional distress call.

Unfairly, in retrospect, I blamed my mother for fostering the estrangement between my father and me. Although my mother would come home several times a week with Loehmann's shopping bags under each arm and had two walk-in closets stuffed with clothes, purses, and shoes, she never had money for her children's needs. When I would ask her for milk money or change for a school trip, she would snarl, "I haven't got it. Ask your ignoramus *father*—that %$#$&@# hasn't sent a penny in months!" Every day she would rail about the heinous things *my* father had done.

My father's weekly visits provoked scuffles between my mother and me: I would have to wrestle her to get outside to see him, her fists pummeling me while she blocked the door. "Good, go and don't come back!" she would shout, as I pulled out of her grip. I would wait with trepidation until the end of our visit before sheepishly bleating, "Dad, Mom won't give me milk money 'cause she says you're not sending any—is that true?" My father began to treat me like an accomplice and hold me responsible for my mother's behavior, as she exploited me to do battle on her behalf.

When my mother would become particularly violent, I would call my father for help. He would call the police. After they would summon me to confirm I was still breathing, the police would reprimand *me* for pitting one parent against the other. (We lived in the suburbs, and parents don't beat their children in the suburbs.)

However, I came to realize that the idealized savior of my childhood dreams is a much more ambiguous and shadowy figure. My father disappeared from my life in adolescence without a backward glance, only to usher in critical traumas later on. I maintained a stubborn loyalty to my father for longer than he deserved—reluctant as I was to part with comforting illusions. Realizing that flattering my father was the only route to preserving some connection with him, I found his neglect eventually snuffed out what remained of my gratitude.

After building a new life with his second wife, Theresa, my father reappeared for a cameo in my early twenties when he was going through another divorce. He was warm, attentive, and apologetic. After a few congenial phone calls, he asked me for a letter for the judge declaring that he had sent me a sizable monthly sum for support all these years. "I'll have more money for you," he claimed. "No," I told him. "I'm not going to lie." "C'mon, you never liked Theresa anyway." This paper is too pristine to print the language my father hurled at me before hanging up, when his plan to bilk a second wife out of alimony encountered resistance. His new offer to contribute to my college tuition—had I even believed it—would not persuade me. I clung like a leech to morality that was decidedly absent from my upbringing: it was my only insurance that I would not meet my parents' fate.

As an adult looking back, I once shed a rare tear of self-compassion in utter perplexity: my brother and I were both—by anyone's objective standards—good kids. We were both bright children; administrators placed us in the academically talented track early in our schooling. I remember proudly marching up the aisle in Hebrew school to claim all six of the honors given out to the first-grade class. As teenagers, we were neither promiscuous nor profane. We managed to sidestep delinquency, drugs, and drink, despite being caught in the crossfire of a hellish divorce. In truth, our parents had reason to be grateful that we displayed strength and self-possession amidst a chaotic family life.

Yet I am struck dumb when I remember my mother's foul-mouthed tirades, day after day, moment by moment, because I wouldn't salt my eggs or change into a freakish green lounging robe at dusk, or memorize a medical school anatomy workbook when I was a child longing to finger paint. My mother's blistering rages, along with my father's creeping abandonment—so inconsistent with my actual transgressions—left me feeling guilty and *bad* beyond what I deserved. Faced with the contradiction between my self-image and my parents' reflection—and the subsequent cognitive dissonance—I leveled the gap by accepting the projection of their sins. A child needs her world to make sense, and her parents to be sane, if she is to feel protected at all in the world.

My mother was whipped about between two forces: a terrifying emptiness and an unparalleled entitlement. I was buffeted between the currents of her mercurial moods, one moment clutched to her chest like a suckling babe, the next receiving the *thwack* of her hand full force across my face.

When I was a small child, hours after a savage attack, she would come into my darkened room and scoop me up—limp from wailing—and rock me in her arms: "Ah, ah, baybee, ah, ah, baybee," she'd soothe. My mother's secret lure was her touch. The tenderness of her hugs and kisses almost made up for the horror that preceded them. Her uncanny ability to switch effortlessly from the most ardent idealization to the most eviscerating demonization left me hurtling like a pinball between withering curses and grasping praise. My mother could careen so impetuously from rage to pathos and back again that in time, I had no choice but to flee from her whirlwind and forfeit the warmth I cherished so much. The misplaced ambition transformed her love into domination, yet she claimed to love me.

Had my mother been solely rejecting and cruel, I might have detached sooner. Instead, I was tempted by her kindness to chase after her love. Daughters of borderlines are driven, like all daughters, by dependency. We cannot forsake our mothers without imperiling ourselves.

A social worker whom I saw as an adolescent explained to me that she had once had a patient whose mother was schizophrenic. Because the patient's mother was so clearly and incontrovertibly crazy, the daughter adapted by seeking support and succor from others in her life, withdrawing any expectations from her mother. Because my mother had some veneer of sanity and professed to love me in language almost lyrical, I never stopped hoping that one day my plaintive cries would reach her heart and mind. With the spectacle of her adolescent daughter, tears streaming down her cheeks, pleading for mercy from her merciless tirades, she might finally cease her degradation. But the sight of me, reflecting her own powerlessness, only seemed to enrage her further: "Are you *finished* yet?" she'd demand, refusing to look at me—her crossed leg shaking as fast as a jackhammer—"I haven't got time to listen to your *G-d-d-mn-d* psychological *bullsh—t!*"

Her abject lack of compassion, the viciousness with which she shamed and humiliated me, forever stains my memory of her. And the utter denial, the feigned innocence—casting herself as the unappreciated martyr, who lived only for her children's happiness—is what purges my heart of all sympathy.

A narcissistic borderline's abuse is different from an average hypercritical parent's scrutiny. It's like growing up in a blender with Julia Child on speed. Moments after you perform thoughtful gestures, you'll be accused of always thinking only of yourself. Innocently mentioning a new acquaintance brings instant accusations that "You only live for *her*. Only *her* you love. Heaven forbid you should ever think of your own mother. You wouldn't care if I drove off a bridge. Yeah, that's what I'm gonna do. I'll drive off a bridge. Then you'll realize what I meant to you. You've never appreciated a %@$&%$# thing I ever did for you, but after I'm gone, you're gonna be sorry!" Remember those Looney Tunes' cartoons with Elmer Fudd's face being clobbered from side to side so fast it's blurry? That's what it's like, except you look into the eyes of your tormentor to find yourself, or to find pity and compassion, and you can't find either and can't figure out who you are.

My mother once offhandedly mentioned that when I was a young child, I formally petitioned her with a list of demands. First on the list was "my right to be myself." Although she missed the poignancy in that appeal, I felt vindicated. Learning I had so long contested her oppression confirmed that it was real and not a self-serving fabrication.

To this day, I do not know how I survived the insanity of a mother who regarded normal separation and individuation as a betrayal. Nothing would have made her happier than if I had crawled back into her belly where she could possess me forever. I defined myself in a climate where every autonomous step was an inadvertent declaration of war.

Memories of my mother are plagued by the sound of her shrieking and the image of her lips drawn around pointed teeth tearing into my sensitive soul with a brutal tongue. The daily punches were trivial by comparison. Old enough no longer to be a fool, I would threaten, "If you hit me again, I'm hitting you back."

Hearing "I'll smash your face in, you little $%@&#!" as the refrain of my lullaby was especially hard in that my mother had the borderline's knack for knowing where and with whom to unleash her fury. Being secretly savaged by my mother, while she carried on a thin veneer of normalcy with the rest of the world, meant I was left to wage self-defense unassisted and suffer the self-doubt and guilt that accompany any child who dares to truly battle a parent.

That I resisted the scorn my mother heaped upon me—yet hurled it down upon myself in her absence—would be her pyrrhic victory. Instead of priding herself on having two content and healthy children who were able to separate from her, my mother preferred her children depressed and debilitated if only *malleable.*

I witnessed this firsthand when I suffered my beloved older brother's first clinical depression *with* him, after he dropped out of Syracuse University in his first year. Richard lay on the living room couch in a fetal curl, mumbling about suicide—his greasy hair matted against his forehead by the pillow he clutched for months.

I never saw my mother so alive and so elated. She positively exulted in wishful fantasies. Richard would go back to school to study medicine. He would drop his "cockamamie" friends. He would start dressing like a go-getter. All he had to do was listen to her, and she would chart his path to stardom. "He could have been reconstructing the Boston skyline like Donald Trump by now, instead of painting houses for money, if only he'd listened to me," she rapturized.

In his pathetic state, my brother couldn't resist her. He put up no fight. She dressed him and spoon-fed him like a gargantuan infant. That he was unable to bring himself to bathe did not dissuade her.

Finally responding when lithium was added to his third course of antidepressants, Richard got up off that couch to resume his former life. And that's when she descended upon him in a panic, hissing into his ears all the vile epithets he had muttered about himself for those many months when severe depression distorted his thinking: that's how desperate she was to restore his lifeless surrender. Few spectacles highlighted her insanity as boldly as this.

Then I did what I always did when faced with my family's dysfunction. I protected my brother; I defended him and I pleaded helplessly for his mercy. And got abused in the melee, by both of them. But my brother's real abuse would only come later. At that age, I was still no threat to his ego. I myself was a withdrawn little creature who barely occupied the psychic space of a flea. I was busy every waking moment perpetuating the same relentless self-reproach that would eventually consume me as it consumed my brother.

Some mothers forever remain larger than life. She cast a pall across family borders and down generations. Her only brother, Isaac, would fall into dark, brooding moods whenever my mother crossed his path. Isaac's wife, Vivienne, once confessed to me in my late twenties—by way of apology for their abandonment—"Miranda, if I had allowed our family to stay in contact with your family, it would have been the end of my marriage." Because of my mother's theatrics, we were shunned by relatives, so I had no one to validate my perceptions nor help me shed the shame that I carried for being a bad child and responsible for her rage.

A child of working-class Eastern European Jewish immigrants who sweated for prosperity in the New World, my mother lost her father early in her own marriage, and her mother a few years later. Perpetually lionizing them as paragons of devotion, she claimed to be the product of a perfect harmony. Her pathology belied this fantasy, yet her family's secrets were buried along with her parents.

My own brother, driven to skepticism and wrung dry of compassion by a mother who played for sympathy too often, became an angry, selfish brute, jealously protecting his meager territory. After a lifetime of coming to his aid, I turned to him once when afflicted with severe gastroenteritis, begging him to bring me some Imodium so I could get myself to the doctor without soiling myself the whole way there. He declared, "Get it yourself—I'm too busy," and hung up the phone, though he lived only a few blocks away. By the time my roommate returned a few days later and took me to the emergency room, I was admitted for dehydration, seeing stars.

Later, my mother's newly second but soon-to-be-ex-husband Albert—frustrated by my refusal to cocreate the *happy family* illusion with him—exploded at me, "You're just like your mother. She pretends to be so loving and inviting, but try to get close to her on a Friday night and she just pushes you away. She wants you to *crawl*."

My uncle, my father, my brother, Albert—anyone who came into my mother's orbit—was so traumatized as to punish me because they couldn't punish her.

What does a good girl do—full of normal, filial feelings—in quarantine with a feral mother? No matter how she protests, she blames herself. My utter inability to penetrate the heart of this primitive creature left me feeling helpless and exquisitely inadequate.

Instinctively, I chose gentleness in a bid not to become like the woman who raised me. Yet her abuse left its mark. Increasingly fearful of criticism from teachers—expecting from all subsequent authority my mother's persecution—I performed poorly, though I was believed to be gifted. My mother's excessive pressure for me to perform put me at odds with my own ambition: To achieve was to gratify this insatiable tyrant. To fail was to vindicate her derision, restoring her place of authority and the natural order.

Two incidents emerge from the blur of my final year under my mother's roof. Not having her talent for the pointed and cruel, I meekly defended myself with "I hate you" when my mother would tear into me, to which she would respond, "I hate you, too!" But once, I said something nasty—I can't even remember what it was, though it was richly deserved, *whatever* it was. My mother spun around, yanked open a kitchen drawer, and the next thing I knew, she was brandishing a steak knife at me with venom in her eyes. Not knowing what to do, I flung the glass of milk I was holding into her face. She stood there, mouth agape, with milk dripping into her cleavage. For once, I had rendered her speechless.

The night before my college entrance exams, I went to the movies with my friend Julie. Carelessly forgetting the train schedule, we found ourselves stranded without a way home. I called my mother, who refused to pick us up, in pique. Arriving home tired, despondent after a two-hour walk, and anxious about the next morning's exam, I found an unwelcome surprise: my bedroom door refused to give way. Forcing it open, I found my room a shambles. In front of me lay devastation wreaked by a human hurricane. Drawers were overturned and shelves spilled in an exhausted heap: books, papers, clothes, records, pictures torn from the walls. I stared in horror at my mother's misguided vengeance on her own child. My anger swelled impotently—I knew how useless it was. Good luck on your SATs, Miranda!

By the grace of my then unacknowledged God, I was offered the chance to spend my senior year in high school living and working on an Israeli kibbutz, in culmination of my years in the Zionist youth movement Habonim Dror. Given permission to graduate high school a year early in order to do so—on condition that I pass two English classes at a university before my departure—I seized the opportunity to flee what would have become my asylum.

I remember the morning of my flight, banging on my mother's bedroom door, begging her to open it so I could say goodbye with a hug and a kiss. I was just sixteen. No matter how we fought, she was my mother and I was her only daughter. But she refused, tearfully cursing me for leaving from the other side of the door...until the last calculating moment.

The feelings lingering for my mother ran all the way from intense hatred to bitter dislike. Like a barren scarecrow, I was filled with straw where feelings should be. The six thousand miles between us would not be far enough.

Chapter 2

It was many years before I began to understand what made my mother push me so hard, why she (and countless Jewish mothers like her) would have given my father's kidney if I would become a doctor. And why I was unwilling to quit academia and join the stenography pool despite a decade failing to finish my college degree.

What makes a Jewish mother?

The answer is right there in God's testimony, the Hebrew Bible. The Jews have a unique role and destiny, on which the entire world's redemption depends.

Why are the Jews, a tiny tribe, responsible for so much benevolence? Why is a Jew more likely to choose a service profession than, say, a career as a professional boxer, sailor, or big game hunter? Why do we give more charity,[1] volunteer more

---

[1] Stephen D. Isaacs, *Jews and American Politics* (New York: Doubleday, 1974), 6, 119–20, quoted in Dennis Prager and Joseph Telushkin, *Why the Jews? The Reason for Anti-Semitism* (New York: Touchstone, 2003), 36.

time?[2] Why are we madly overrepresented in the fields of medicine, social work, education, law[3]—anything that heals, sustains, and uplifts the human race? It's because we can't get service out of our bones, no matter how far we've strayed from Sinai.[4]

Yet when we try to replace spiritual, transcendental achievement with finite substitutes such as academic laurels or financial reward, they cannot fill the void.

My mother sat preening while I read *The Omnivorous Cockroach* fluently, sitting on the lap of my first-grade principal, Mr. Pellet, as my fellow pupils stumbled over *Fun with Dick and Jane* in the classroom next door. Mr. Pellet wanted me transferred to the brainy track in our suburban public school, predominantly filled with other Jewish kids and Asians. This would be the beginning of my catapult to fame, powered by my mother, who would bask in my reflected glory. Instead, her pushing ignited

---

[2] A study of the effect of religion on volunteerism found that "Jews were more likely to volunteer than any others." John Wilson and Thomas Janoski, "The Contribution of Religion to Volunteer Work," *Sociology of Religion* 56, no. 2 (1995): 137–152, https://digitalcommons.unomaha.edu/cgi/viewcontent.cgi?article=1058&context=slcestgen.

[3] Amy Chua and Jed Rubenfeld, *The Triple Package: How Three Unlikely Traits Explain the Rise and Fall of Cultural Groups in America* (New York: Penguin, 2014), 52–53.

[4] Sinai refers to the modest mountain in the desert peninsula between ancient Egypt and Canaan where the Jewish people, present and future, accepted upon themselves a covenant with God to fulfill the Torah revealed there and become His treasured nation, in the Hebrew year 2448 (1312 BCE).

my rebellion—her competitiveness repelling my sensitive Jewish conscience.

I maintain that my mother's estrangement from the wisdom and mandate of our Jewish heritage gave birth to her bottomless hunger and my own dogged ambition. As I came to understand over the ensuing years, through the journey revealed in these pages, the Jewish desire for accomplishment and influence is not a cultural eccentricity, a defense against millennial persecution, or a persistent pathology. If we're indeed chosen to serve the Creator of the world—obliged to embody a piety that will inspire the entire human race to forsake its corruption and fulfill its spiritual potential—then our need for significance is inborn. Glory is our birthright. Anything less will never be enough.

In the meantime, the land of milk and honey evidently supplied just the nutrition my body needed, as I left America at sixteen a prepubescent beanpole and returned from Israel with my mother's voluptuous figure ten months later. Under siege at home, I might as well have had a clinical case of "failure to thrive," healed by the nurturing time spent in Israel with my peers.

Despite my inconsistent academic record from high school, pulling two As in two Ivy League university English courses the summer before I left for Israel allowed me to sneak into the Cambridge, Massachusetts' institution through the back door when I returned.

Although my father had vowed to pay my tuition if I would attend college in Boston, unsurprisingly, he reneged *after* I relinquished my dream of studying as far away from home as possible. Taking out student loans to cover the sizable tuition bill, I eventually adopted an atypical undergraduate rhythm, working during the day and taking one or two classes a semester in the evening division.

Whereas I was happy to be starting college, I schlepped more baggage than freshman jitters to the preppy, entitled atmosphere of—let's call it—Latham University, in the 1980s. I had a restless mind and guarded a trove of insecurity while keeping my feelers out for other vulnerable spirits like me. With my beat-up Guild guitar, Joni Mitchell records, and macramé plant holder, I was still clinging to a kinder, gentler era as my trendy roommates were hustling in fishnet stockings to fraternity house keg parties. In the winter of my freshman year, I spent the holiday break at a Habonim Dror camp in the Berkshires where an unlikely debut became the gateway to a fateful transition.

In the *tenuah*, which means "the movement," we were frugal socialists who provided ourselves homemade entertainment in the form of amateur plays. Farm foreclosures featured in the news because of roundly condemned Reagan-era agricultural budget cuts. Someone wrote a treacly tearjerker about a farm widow and, in a bit of intuitive casting, assigned me as the tragic heroine. My solo finale, in which I upbraided an uncaring establishment for precipitating my farmer husband's suicide, opened the floodgates of my tightly held anguish and grief—which I allowed to flow in service of the drama.

At the end of my soliloquy, I found myself the sudden recipient of a great deal of adulation. Right and left, I was congratulated on my moving performance. I caught the eye of a fellow Latham University student who attended our movement's winter camp for the first time with his older brother, a veteran. I was thrust from the shy sidelines right onto center stage. This crest of goodwill and good fortune lifted me out of my usual morbid preoccupations. I began dating the young man when we both got back to Latham. All this fanfare was important because it laid the noose that shortly closed around my neck.

I still believed I was fundamentally flawed, fatally faulty, damaged, defective, and doomed. How could I believe otherwise with parents and a sibling who had so poisoned my self-image? The sudden praise and the doting boyfriend simply paved the road on which I knew I would stumble. In anticipation of the very rejection I believed to be inevitable, I slid preemptively into a clinical depression severe enough to bring me psychiatric attention for the first time.

In the spring of my freshman year, my familiar self-contempt came dangerously close to delusion. My lifelong insomnia became so severe I no longer bothered to get in bed at night. Returning often from the computer room at three in the morning, my roommate would find me sitting in the dark. My reflexes slowed down—the scenery unfurled around me like a slow-motion picture. I felt as if sticky honey coated my cerebellum, clogging up my brain and drowning signals in the muck. My emotions cut loose from my voluntary control: I cried at the slightest provocation and increasingly, for no reason at all. Respecting no etiquette, the tears flowed during classes, on the campus thoroughfare, at the supermarket. Drowning my head in a toilet bowl of insults such as *morose, worthless, boring, stupid, trite, maudlin, dull, self-indulgent, ugly,* and *paranoid,* I had a vicious Siamese twin attached to me, torturing and taunting me.

Toward summer, I dropped several pounds as I lost the will to eat. I felt increasingly hopeless about my future and contemplated giving up entirely.

Because these feelings were merely an amplification of what I had felt throughout my adolescence, I didn't realize for far too long that I wasn't having typical college adjustment trouble. A wise guidance counselor told me that I needed to see a psychiatrist.

The first one I contacted invited me to join a "double blind" research study where I would receive a daily placebo, vitamin C, an antidepressant, or valium, for six weeks. Neither of us would know which one I'd receive. Dissolving in a puddle of tears at his feet, I revealed I could not accept the quarter chance I'd get what I needed.

The second doctor, Eugene Sherman, asked me, "What do you like about yourself?" I didn't have to struggle with this question: I had had the same answer for years. "Sensitivity" was the only asset I could claim. I knew I was sensitive because if someone else stubbed her toe, I started to cry. That's all it took.

After thirty more questions, Dr. Sherman told me to relax, that he'd seen dozens of people like me. "After six weeks on antidepressant medication," he claimed breezily, "you'll be skipping out of my office." He armed me with an explanation for the madness I felt. I had what therapists call "double depression": a constant baseline of dysphoria punctuated by an episode of acute clinical depression.

Although I knew I was unhappy growing up, I never considered that I might have something found in a psychiatrist's desk reference. I never imagined there could be a biological explanation for what I knew essentially as my character. I had been this way for as long as I could remember.

While I was neither as rapidly nor as easily cured as kind Dr. Sherman had predicted, my symptoms did eventually yield to pharmacological repair several years later when I tried an old-fashioned tricyclic antidepressant called Sinequan. An unpopular drug because of its anticholinergic side effects, Sinequan causes fatigue and dries out the body. Yet I learned that it helps those whose depression is complicated by post-traumatic stress disorder as mine evidently was. Before I found my blue and white capsule, I depended entirely on the two hours a week I spent in my new therapist's office.

What transpired there was a slow revolution in my way of thinking. Prodded by a talented, dedicated young psychologist named Charlotte Brenner, I gradually released my grip on convictions about myself I had held since the womb. Refusing to mimic my negative distortions, she became the mirror in which I saw my true self emerge. Together we took a rotting head of lettuce and peeled away every limp, brown, gooey layer until we found the unspoiled root at its core.

According to Dr. Brenner, my main prophylactic prescription was to scale back my enmeshment with my deranged and despotic mother. Dr. Brenner recognized the presence of severe personality disorders such as borderline personality and narcissism in my mother's raging abuse, which she witnessed firsthand and heard about in my recollections. She was the first of many to urge me to sever ties with my mother if I was to escape emotionally intact. Although it would take years for me to break away fully, asserting a coherent, authentic identity in my mother's shadow became my urgent mission.

I remember the day my rebirth took root. I had been a patient of Dr. Brenner's for two years. I hadn't yet found my pharmacological cure, and I was still bearing too much pain. I complained that she and Dr. Sherman had promised that I'd be better after six weeks and then again, after another two months, while I tried yet another antidepressant: "Why am I not better?" I demanded.

Dr. Brenner lost her patience with me for the first time. She returned my insistent stare and declared, "Miranda, if you're going to get better, it's going to be up to *you*." Her rebuke came at precisely the moment I was prepared to hear it. She had nurtured me well enough that I was ready to assume responsibility for myself. I left her office feeling oddly empowered.

The very same evening, back at the dormitory, I began taking risks, sharing a kind word or an amusing anecdote instead of silently yearning to be noticed. I felt like an infant waddling around in diapers, trying out brand-new reflexes. I discovered at age twenty that I had an operable sense of humor—that I could make someone laugh instead of groan in exasperation and boredom. Freed from self-conscious worry, I could respond to others with spontaneity. With the relief of distance and detachment, I wrote a truly cathartic send-up of my mother for a nonfiction writing class at Latham University, which won me my first attention as a writer. My social life took a quantum leap forward.

Displaying their signature loyalty, my parents continued to profit at my expense throughout my undergraduate career. Though they could both afford to help, they denied me financial support in college. Yet they also refused to provide their tax returns to the university proving that they weren't claiming me as a dependent. Three guesses as to why not. As a result, the university would not evaluate me for financial aid as an independent student either, without corroboration. But the burden of supporting myself turned out to be a blessing, as I performed better on the job than I did in my studies.

I still carried a deep confusion about my intellectual talent. Although I placed exceptionally in standardized tests, and my written work displayed a sophistication that set me apart from my peers, I nearly always fumbled longer writing assignments, exhibiting a grave attraction to the grade of "incomplete." A vast discrepancy persisted from my childhood between my potential and my performance.

Attempting to forestall the inevitable criticism I expected from all university teachers—stand-ins for my brutish parents— I caught the perfection infection. Fearing my academic work had to be flawless, I became immobilized. Procrastination became my defense against the anticipated rejection.

Prone as I was to amateur self-analysis, I attributed my academic self-sabotage to a stubborn need to deprive my mother of precisely the gravy she lived for. No matter that I rejected her social values; I conceded that academic achievement was the measure of my self-worth. Paralyzed with fright when my opening lines didn't display genius, I echoed the idealization and demonization of my borderline mother for whom I was never myself, warts and all, but either an imbecile or an Einstein, depending on her mood.

In my heart lurked the shy person's longing to tell her story. For as long as I could remember, I yearned to be able to write. Yet I was deeply skeptical of my own talent. Acknowledging my implacable stage fright, I concluded that the analytical bent born of my brutal childhood would lend itself to clinical psychology. Through my responsibility as in-house family analyst, I was able to feel needed, in control, and superior. Aspiring to be a psychotherapist, I chose to commercialize my role as savior and healer. (Seeking to make myself indispensable to the needy, I sought to banish my orphanhood by professionally succoring others.)

With the benefit of hindsight, I view that ambition as the stirring of codependence. But recovering from double depression with a good therapist reinforced my career goal, once I stopped dabbling in studies just to please my parents. My father, an accountant and stockbroker, implicitly communicated the edict: don't dare rise above me. So I took a requisite year of economics, and premed biology and chemistry for my mother, before admitting to myself that I was not to win their love this way.

As a psychology major, I breezed through the introductory courses. I excelled in the procrastinator's gift for memorizing all the material under the pressure of the eleventh hour. However, college lays a trap for dilettantes like me. In higher-level courses requiring long, complex papers, my sprinter's engine sputtered. I would start big projects in a flourish of creativity and passion to prove an original thesis, only to drown in an ocean of three-by-five cards filled with copious research findings. When I collected more incompletes than grades, the university insisted I take a leave of absence until I finished my courses. Meanwhile, my friends moved on to graduate school and began establishing families, while I still yearned for my first breast from which to nurse.

Like a squirrel that forages for food and refuge for the winter when the daylight diminishes in the fall, I had the dormant seeds of various future traumas within me just waiting to sprout. While my fellow Latham graduates were experimenting with formal commitments, trying on personas and professions, the contours of my protracted undergraduate life were to be carved by men: my father, his father, and someone whose resemblance in character to my own mother and father would make him singularly compelling.

Chapter 3

Abraham Portnoy, my paternal grandfather, was the exception in my family. He was a tender man whose mercy extended to everyone and everything: neighborhood children who received two dollars on their birthdays, stray cats in the Navy Yard where he worked, and withered vines in the craggy backyard that yielded supple yellow roses under his touch. Abe's tenderness was anchored by a deep sense of loyalty. When my grandmother Miriam went blind from glaucoma near the age of sixty, my grandfather dutifully assumed her role. Learning to cook roast chicken tastier than hers, he bathed, dressed, and fed her until the day she died. He mended the pants and jackets of a widowed friend who drove him to the ballroom dances he loved. It was foreign to Abe's calculus to take without giving, and his whole life was marked by quiet acts of gratitude.

Then why did I avoid my grandfather? Why does a person deny herself good? I remember the moment I made the decision. I was about six years old, sitting in my grandparents' kitchen at a battered Formica table on a yellow chair mended with silver duct tape. My grandfather and I were singing the Hebrew folk song "Ba'shanah Haba'ah" with childlike gusto. I felt the tenderness and love in my grandfather's eyes as he gazed at me, a fellow connoisseur of sentimental tunes. He was smiling broadly. I thought to myself, "He is old. He is going to die soon."

The legal separation of my warring parents already felt like having my heart ripped out of my chest without anesthesia. I knew I could not survive any more loss. From that moment on, I walled myself off from a source of warmth I would only rediscover many years later.

In truth, avoiding my grandmother was reason enough. Although the dusty glass candy dish full of peppermint Chiclets beckoned me, as soon as we were alone together, Miriam would launch into sordid tales of my mother's decadence—insisting that my mother was the tinder for the domestic inferno into which I was born, rather than her son. I naturally recoiled from her tales, no matter how much I disliked my own mother.

But the real reason I avoided my grandfather was the promise of love he offered me. I felt unworthy, undeserving. I didn't know how to receive it or how to return it. I was already a shattered vessel, unable to hold a drop of moisture.

How did Providence grant me a second chance? Some sixteen years later, when my grandmother was about eighty-two and my grandfather eighty, Mom-Mom caught pneumonia. Hospitalized nearby, she was fretful with the unfamiliar cafeteria food. Pop-Pop, ever the caretaker, took four buses every day to visit her and bring her his home cooking wrapped in wrinkled tin foil. After two weeks of faithful care and an encouraging forecast from the doctor, one morning he didn't come. He bolted for a few hours on a round-trip bus to Cape Cod, to refresh his weary spirit with ocean breezes and cool water in a sweltering July. On that first morning without him and his home cooking, she died.

My grandfather was beside himself with guilt. He sat in his chair in the dark weeping and lamenting, "I just saw her last night. She was fine. They said she was almost better. She could come home soon. Mammele, Mammele! How could it be? Why did I go?" I felt such pity for him. He was inconsolable. He was so lonely and so lost with no one to care for. And I was the little match girl without a home. I stepped into the breach, and a new alliance was born.

My grandfather, Abraham Portnoy, was an unlikely mix of stoic peasant and genteel Renaissance man. Born in a village outside Kiev in Russia, he had little secular education. He was forced to quit *cheder*, religious Jewish elementary school, to help support his ten orphan siblings after his mother's sudden death. Learning the trade of paperhanging in America after making his way there alone at twelve, eventually he was compelled to hustle supplies for the American military among cussing sailors in the Charlestown Navy Yard during the Great Depression, when no one could afford wallpaper. Yet my grandfather was drawn throughout his life to refined pursuits: gardening, cooking, ballroom dancing, and chanting the Hebrew prayers as his synagogue's cantor.

The reconciliation with my grandfather developed swiftly because we were spiritual as well as physical kin. The will to give that distinguished my grandfather survived in me. I began to visit my grandfather on Sunday afternoons, taking a Massachusetts Bay Transportation Authority (MBTA) bus and the "T" subway to his frugal row house at 409 Townsend Street in a Roxbury, Boston slum.

The neighborhood had been rich with industrious Jewish immigrants at the turn of the twentieth century, but now only a few Jewish seniors remained as their prospering children fled for the suburbs, and the neighborhood demographics shifted to an African American population. The decoratively wrought *P* in my grandfather's aluminum screen door reflected a trace of pride, but the "9¢" cut out from a grocery store circular and pasted next to the ancient numerals 4 and 0 on the brick house on Townsend Street revealed his essential thrift.

My grandfather's row house was tiny, stuffed with too much furniture and too many TVs. Because he couldn't bring himself to throw anything out, new TVs were perched on top of the old ones when the picture tubes burst, in a precarious, avant-garde glass tower.

After the week of shivah mourning, my grandfather's first initiative was to repaper the house, an ambition my grandmother forbade him while she was alive. Setting up scaffolding and repapering the house was not the safest way to purge his grief, but my grandfather was determined. The walls of his home now boasted fresh velvet flocking common to suburban homes in the 1950s. Since his sight was ailing, he put gold flocking on one wall, green on another, and black and white on a third, reflecting the assortment of remnants he had in the basement. The work was impeccably done all the way up to the cornices, and I marveled at this feat of exertion by a grieving octogenarian.

My visits to Pop-Pop's house had a predictable rhythm. I would walk the few blocks from the Jackson Square subway station through the seedy neighborhood with tense determination, climb the high cement steps, and knock hard on his weathered screen door. Slowly he would unlock the inner vestibule door and his bespectacled, round face would appear, bobbing behind the Plexiglas window, smiling a smile of unabashed delight.

"Mireleh, come in!"

"Hi, Pop-Pop. How are you?"

Learning to talk with my grandfather was an exercise in Zen simplicity. There was no exchange of angst, no mutual probing. I discovered in our rapport the joy and liberation of communicating with someone who didn't speak psychobabble. We talked about the weather, what was on sale at the supermarket, what he'd done the past week. He would tell me the same several jokes again and again from week to week.

Before long, he would usher me into the kitchen. He would open the ancient white refrigerator, with the chrome handle hinge that clicked, and begin to prepare me an omelet or reheat some cold roast chicken in a blackened frying pan, its grip reattached with the ubiquitous silver duct tape.

My grandfather never asked why I took a sudden interest in him. He simply received me with grace and bestowed his humble nurture. Somehow I knew that I was making a pilgrimage to a holy man—and in the most mundane exchanges of food, conversation, and companionship, I was giving myself a chance to heal.

In time, my Pop-Pop and I forged a bond of love and interdependence that was unprecedented in my life. Whereas my mother and I were long estranged, I had a remote relationship with my father, who would join my grandfather and me with corned beef sandwiches from B & D Deli on Jewish holidays.

In one strange month, I managed to lacerate my cornea twice, once with my fingernail and once with the edge of a rolled-up newspaper accidentally pulled with acute force right into my eye. After the second incident, I had to have both eyes patched for a few days because I disturbed the healing cells of my wounded eye while tracking with my good eye. Living alone, I was helpless with both eyes patched. (I had long before moved out of a college dormitory to save money.) I begged my father to bring me from Cambridge to his home in Cape Cod to look after me, but he refused. With nowhere else to turn, I had my friends take me in a cab to my grandfather's house.

Pop-Pop was my Florence Nightingale. He took me on two buses every day to Massachusetts Eye and Ear Infirmary so they could irrigate and salve my eye, and he kept me fed, safe, and calm. I slept in the small back room, which had been the children's bedroom. I only went home when the clinic uncovered my eyes.

In return, about a year later, when my grandfather began complaining of chest pains and nausea, I brought him to a cardiologist. I had better paying work by then as a Hospital of Latham University administrative secretary, and I knew the good doctors. Dr. Ron Itzkowitz determined that my grandfather had already had a silent heart attack and recommended a pacemaker. But my grandfather was so petrified that he refused to go through with the operation. Exercising any leverage I could, I persuaded Ron to let me into the operating room—the only condition under which my grandfather would submit to the procedure. While my father and his sister took no part in their father's care, I donned hospital scrubs and held his hand as the doctors administered the anesthesia.

I felt so close to my Pop-Pop by this time that I suggested he convalesce with me instead of in his lonely hovel, yet he insisted on going home alone. I clung to my grandfather like a rhesus monkey in a Harry Harlow experiment.

Pop-Pop was always active, whether ballroom dancing, swimming, gardening, or shopping. Although he was heavy, his abundant exercise granted him longevity. After his surgery, two drugs that treat congestive heart failure—digoxin and the diuretic Lasix—kept the fluid from building up in his lungs. My grandfather's health mercifully returned to normal, and we continued building our bond. Our relationship resumed its gentle rhythm with my Sunday visits.

About this time, at the age of twenty-seven—while I was still fitfully pursuing a bachelor's degree in the social science of psychology—I enrolled in an elective Latham University course that would prompt a change in my life's direction. The class was called "Introduction to Classical Judaism," taught by a Modern Orthodox professor named Gabriel Rakover. The course was a comprehensive introduction to biblical and rabbinic Judaism—

which informs and guides the practice of today's Orthodox Jews.[1] Although the college sported seven thousand undergraduates, only three more could be found that semester who wanted to study the religion with the greatest impact on Western civilization—to my good fortune, as I tended to be shy in large groups.

I found that Judaism, refreshingly, turned conventional wisdom on its head. In addition to affirming ideas patently rejected by modern secular humanism—such as the existence of God, divine revelation, and the potential for human relationship with God—Judaism posited that idealism was insufficient to motivate virtue, given human weakness. Therefore, God had issued commandments to mankind. Judaism was a biblically mandated system for cultivating *kedushah* (holiness) by prescribing virtuous deeds and proscribing iniquitous ones. Within these divine laws—fulfilled freely by human will—a Jew was to attain holiness and make a home for God within herself and her community. Choosing to perform deeds commanded by a just, benevolent God gave one's whole character a divine imprimatur.

Learning that Judaism also mandates the Jewish day of rest from labor for a Jew's non-Jewish employees and beasts of burden appealed to my universalist sympathies. The weekly Sabbath's brake on the unfettered accumulation of capital and the command to provide for the needy awakened my socialist roots. That a Jew was obliged to feed his pets and farm animals before satiating his own hunger concretized mercy. Learning that

---

[1] I reluctantly use the term *Orthodox* in this book, because it is a misnomer. Orthodox Jews are simply practicing *Judaism* as codified in the Talmud over fifteen hundred years ago.

Torah Sages urge a man to marry to fulfill his emotional needs and a woman to marry to satisfy her sexual needs suggested to me an enlightened investment in gender balance and harmony. I sometimes wept with the beauty of what I was learning.

But what I loved most about the class was grappling with the moral messages of the Jewish Bible. Our teacher required us to probe the Torah text, mining it for our own gold. In our first assignment, we were asked to analyze the famous Torah portion called the "Binding of Isaac," in which God commands the first Jewish patriarch, Abraham, to take his only son by his wife, Sarah—progeny for whom he has waited one hundred years—and offer him as a sacrifice to God on a distant mountain.

To understand this frightful ordeal, I looked back to the Garden of Eden story to place the relationship between Abraham and God in a context. A theory emerged for me that God corrected His overindulgence of Adam and Eve—by tempting them through the guise of the serpent—in order to forge a new relationship with human beings based on mutual giving and sacrifice, embodied by a covenant. God cultivated Abraham's faith and righteousness over a period of trial and testing—which elicited Abraham's reliance and trust—confirmed by Isaac's redemption for the ram.

Still tied in knots by insecurity, I took two weeks longer than my classmates did to turn my own paper, but I turned in a personal best. I had anticipated ancient Jewish Sages' understanding of the biblical text at several junctures, and I'm still proud of my analysis to this day. Yearning for the righteousness and compassion that eluded my family, I was captivated by the teachings of the Torah.

Professor Rakover became a mentor as well as a teacher, enriching his performance with the Jew's mandate to engage in *chesed* (kindness). He encouraged my potential despite my being an anguished older undergraduate who didn't know where to pin her sights in academia. In the end, I failed to turn in my final paper, a vast assignment that overwhelmed me—garnering another in my trail of incompletes. At the end of the semester, our teacher invited all his students for brunch at his home in the suburbs, and I got a glimpse of a close-knit, Torah-observant Jewish family whose refinement beckoned me yet seemed so far beyond my ken.

During the early years my parents still lived together, my mother had encouraged a token form of religious observance— limited to the lighting of a Chanukah menorah and a perfunctory Passover Seder—driven by her bloated Jewish pride. My own Jewish identity was cultivated by the years in Habonim Dror, which fostered a patina of Hebrew-speaking social justice, carefully excised from its religious roots. The chaos in my upbringing robbed me of the luxury of dwelling on spiritual questions, leaving me, at best, with the distinct feeling that if there was a God, He had cast His shadow over my family, particularly.

Walking home one afternoon after attending our final lecture on the Talmud, I suddenly recalled that I myself used to pray the Shema prayer before bed to a personal God, as I had been taught as a small child in Hebrew school. Remembering the comfort and security it gave me, I longed for that simple faith in a divine protector, which had been shattered along with my family. Faith that wasn't shaken by mental illness and divorce had been hijacked by trendy religious skepticism, becoming a blind atheist dogma along the way.

Although my soul yearned to come close to God through the time-tested deeds of our ancestors, my heart was filled with fear that a great big *family*, which an Orthodox Jewish community represented, would only be the scene of further humiliation. Yet I was never quite so moved as when I was studying and writing about the Torah. I wondered whether taking up the academic study of Judaism rather than psychology might free me from the curse of my tragic family history and the gravitational pull of others' family problems. While I did not yet know how or when, the transcendental seeds of hope planted during this single college course would ultimately blossom into a completely new way of life.

Part Two

The Snake Charmer and the Sleepwalker

Now the serpent was more sly than any beast of the field that the Lord God had made.

—Genesis 3:1

Chapter 4

Finishing my final exam for Gaby Rakover's course two years later, I found my desire to build a Jewish family rekindled through the effort and study. I pinned my hopes for deliverance on the Harbor Fellowship Synagogue singles mixer taking place the coming Sabbath eve. That night, an unexpected snowfall blanketed the streets of Downtown Boston a virgin white, but I was not about to let six inches of snow defeat me. Slush and Friday night revelers seeking the satisfactions of the city snarled public transportation. I marched through the snow the whole twenty-one blocks to the synagogue with a self-righteous piety that left me ripe for exploitation.

A small crèche of souls huddled in the vast auditorium, the speaker's voice echoing through the emptiness. Rabbi Shuster didn't even try to unify his flock at the close of the evening. Clothed in a faded turquoise and purple alpaca sweater and snow boots, face shorn of makeup, I looked as naive and needy as I was. Gathering afterwards in the vestibule, donning our coats, each of us searched timidly for some reason to address one another and find the reason for our common assembly.

I noticed Simon immediately, so elegantly dressed, handsome, and tall. We were yin and yang: he swelled where I withdrew, abundant where I was withered. He wore a light blue cotton button-down tucked into a black leather belt with a brushed silver buckle, wool slacks, and leather loafers. He wrapped himself in what I would come to call his "Schindler coat"—a grey houndstooth that evoked Liam Neeson in *Schindler's List*. He glanced in my direction and asked, "Would anyone like a ride home?" I grasped the bait. Simon escorted me to a silver Saab, which only enhanced his tasteful appearance.

On the way home, he asked if I'd like to stop for a drink. Sitting in an elegant corner café, we sipped exotic coffee, the kind I never bought myself. When Simon revealed he was an aspiring movie director, with one independent film under his belt already, we bonded over our favorite French, Spanish, and Dutch cinema. How could a man who appreciated *Breaker Morant*, *My Life as a Dog*, and Pedro Almodóvar possibly break my heart? I met him in *synagogue*, for Christ's sake. Something vulnerable about Simon attracted me from the beginning. I cannot explain my weakness for him, but it had something to do with sensing a need in him that I could fill.

Simon called me on Monday evening, opening with the disarming line, "I was planning a Wednesday call." I welcomed his pursuit like a Canada lily opening to the hummingbird. I was twenty-nine and deliriously in love. He was Jewish, he was handsome, and *he went to synagogue*. He loved a compatible genre of music and the same kind of offbeat, foreign movies—which I took for similar values. With our prodigious appetites for giving and taking, we were inseparable within weeks.

When we weren't together, we spent countless hours on the phone cooing to each other in a smoochy language, which I could only call the music of the *spheres*. Having irresistible, mutual moon-rising sign conjunctions, we were tipsy with the illusion of being each other's ideal loves. With Simon's materialism and the selfishness he would come to display, he counterbalanced my social conscience, my frugality, and my obsession with virtue.

Simon wanted my company all the time. He wanted my opinion about home furnishings, my ideas on his latest script, my warmth in his bed. Why is it that under those conditions, a woman thinks marriage? Isn't that what society still raises us to believe: meet, fall in love, get married, have children—in that order?

Despite the poor example from my own home, I clung to the security of the traditional family, rejecting outright the possibility of single motherhood. Establishing a family had been a secondary consideration in my twenties when education and fostering a career were uppermost in my mind. As I neared my thirties, considerations of marriage and motherhood began to weigh upon my heart.

Despite my explicit stake in a future, Simon's present needs established the agenda for our relationship. I was recruited to recast his life, for as much as it appeared glamorous on the surface, it was deeply decayed.

Simon spent a lot of time going to the gym, shopping, and watching television. He had directed one feature film from an original script after college, and retained a movie agent, but hadn't accomplished anything in years. He was ostensibly doing research with all that television watching. He was suffering malaise only mildly camouflaged by his conspicuous consumption.

After many months together, I watched his first film with trepidation, quite certain that it would never impress me. Yet it did. He had captured some poignancy in his characters' relationship. I set about, with his solicitation, tightening up his next script as he set off for the gym or the mall. I failed to notice how often I was solicited for services—writing, consulting on every decision, giving backrubs and other delights—and otherwise dismissed to my hovel.

I was working nine to six as an administrative secretary to a Hospital of Latham University division chief. Although my work lacked status, it was better paying than my research jobs in the mental health field had been and afforded me tuition benefits, one course at a time. But I was living an itinerant hobo's existence on the cusp of my thirties. My one-bedroom rental apartment was furnished with secondhand wicker and flea market chintz, my most exclusive appliance, an espresso machine given to me as a gift by friends. Simon lived in a newly purchased, spacious condominium filled with the latest culinary devices, original fine art, sophisticated audiovisual equipment, and three different types of bicycles mounted on a wall. His wardrobe was the envy of any woman, his walk-in closet a retail shop with stacks of color-graded clothes.

The lack of balance in our relationship showed itself in where we spent our time. Simon refused to spend time in my apartment. When I would complain, he would invoke the poverty of my quarters, and I felt I couldn't argue. Simon wanted my company and perspective in decorating his condominium. Initially flattered, I spent countless hours shopping with him and helping him to furnish his flat. After a year and a half together, begging and pleading, I finally procured his help one time to hang a picture on the wall of my apartment. He resentfully left a pile of plaster dust on top of everything on my desk.

Simon's parents, to whom he introduced me right away, were a study in contrasts: his father a short, bookish legal professor and his mother a tall, fashionable Mrs. Robinson. She seemed to disdain her husband Sidney, while milking his adoration. I had a good relationship with them, though I was wary of his mother, whose appetite for glamour reminded me of my mother's and was therefore suspect. I went out of my way to be endearing because I reckoned I was in their family for keeps. In my estimation, marriage was the only answer to such an irresistible need. This is what love felt like, or so I thought.

With Simon's thirtieth birthday approaching, I seized the opportunity to declare my love by planning an elaborate surprise birthday party. Apparently fated to be involved with a loner, I scrambled to find any of Simon's friends, forced to grasp at the waitress at our favorite diner or his bicycle mechanic. His mother and I collaborated enthusiastically on the venue and the menu. I didn't notice how reluctant Simon was to be seen with me among his friends, most of whom turned out to be women. Looking back, I realize Simon was probably still sleeping with many of the guests. I was content to be behind the scenes facilitating everyone else's good time. Simon wrote me a lovely thank-you card afterwards, clearly touched by my gesture.

The following day, Simon began to mope and brood. I urged him to confide in me, and he dropped the bomb that exploded my fragile emotional security. "My parents want me to break up with you," he said. I was devastated. I felt so betrayed and used after his mother and I had worked so closely together to pull off such a successful party for her son. What had I done wrong?

Gallingly, Simon sought comfort from me for his parents' decision, completely oblivious to the pain he had caused me in revealing their feelings. I was bidden never to expose to them that I knew. His disclosure hurt me so deeply that within a matter of weeks, I slid into a clinical depression again; I had to resume taking Sinequan with all of its undesirable side effects.

My panic subsided when I saw that Simon didn't intend to fulfill their wishes, but I felt a deep-seated unease with his family ever after. Our frequent visits to his parents' home were fraught with unbearable tension, as I had to be cordial and poker-faced even as I knew they found me unsuitable as a future wife for their son. I regularly moaned to Simon about the injustice of it all.

Two years later, I found out the truth, when Michelle—fiancée of Simon's brother, Jeremy—picked me up on the street in her car. I took advantage of our private moment to confide my pain at her soon-to-be in-laws' rejection of *me*. She told me, "That's not what they said, Miranda. I'm so sorry he misled you."

Jeremy had told Michelle exactly what his parents had said, because they had shared their decision with Jeremy, too. Their message after Simon's birthday party had been this: "*If you're not going to marry her*, then we want you to break up with her. She's far too nice a girl and too devoted to you for you to string her along, only to hurt her in the end." His parents were actually looking out for my welfare, while I remained the clueless victim of Simon's unconscionable selfishness. Simon allowed me to suffer bodily harm from the pain of their "rejection," rather than concede that he was using me.

Meanwhile, the love and gratitude I felt for Simon's companionship inspired me to give. For instance, I treated him to a Valentine's Day feast and ballroom dance at a ritzy Park Square hotel overlooking the Charles River. In an effort at solidarity, Simon's mother chided me, "Save your money, Miranda. Let him spend it on you!" But I was liberated, and I was unaccustomed to being cared for materially. Money turned out to be the most vexing commodity in our relationship.

Simon lived a double life from which he excluded me, his steady girlfriend. With sizable student loan payments that devoured everything besides essentials, I couldn't afford to eat in fancy restaurants, enjoy expensive entertainment, or travel. Therefore, Simon responded by doing these things without me. Our life together revolved around Victoria's Diner, where five or seven dollars of my own money could procure me a tasty feast of black beans and rice with gumbo soup, alongside him.

As an acolyte of Habonim Dror, I still believed in the socialist credo "to each according to his need, from each according to his ability." I believed that partners in a committed relationship should decide together what they wanted to do for recreation, and each should contribute financially according to his or her means. I expected the love Simon claimed to feel for me to manifest in a desire to give. Only it didn't. I wasn't expecting him to treat me entirely, but his unwillingness to spend anything on me even as he feted himself seemed so unfair. Simon continued to spend lavishly on himself while insisting we go Dutch treat at the diner. I put up with it. Since my parents had resented every nickel they ever spent on me, Simon's repudiation of anything I might cost him was as familiar as worn, comfortable slippers.

Simon refused to introduce me to his New York agent or his friends, because I didn't have "the right clothes." He contrived to shame me, knowing that, effectively demoralized, I would never make demands upon him. After years of ridiculing my clothing, he took me once to Bloomingdale's to buy something that met his standards that he knew I couldn't afford. In line at the register, right before the saleslady took us, he asked me "Are you getting this?"

I felt so low and worthless that I allowed him to treat me with contempt. I didn't recognize how degrading the relationship was.

I regarded money warily as the source of inevitable acrimony. My parents had played mortal hide-and-seek games with money during the years of their divorce court battle—games in which an expensive, jointly owned beach house suspiciously burned down, and plenty of bruises were sustained. After I was already out on my own supporting myself, my mother would send me lists of the occasional paltry sums she spent on me if I refused to fulfill her designs—the cords attached to her miserly "gifts" transparent. With even less of a conscience, my father simply walked away from me. I felt undeserving of even minimal sustenance from God or anyone else.

But I also faced existential worries as a woman on her own with sizable college debt and an unidentified impediment to getting my degree. Simon plucked a chord that had been bred into my very constitution: Who was I to have wants or needs? Of course I should give yet be denied myself, the only formula I knew for a relationship.

What seemed to matter most to Simon was finding funding for his next movie. I solved that problem for him too. I suggested the idea of attending business school to obtain an MBA. Along with learning the actual mechanics of fundraising, he could look forward to a lucrative job that would fund his artistic projects. He liked this option and favored even more my willingness to fulfill all the necessary requirements. I wrote his undergraduate professors for letters of recommendation and his business school application essays. I didn't question the propriety of doing for my lover what he could reasonably be expected to do for himself. I was already trained to take care of those who relinquished their responsibilities. I had flattered my father and only brother for crumbs and had rescued my brother from lifelong, self-made crises. I believed if I made myself indispensable, Simon would marry me. I perceived being needed by him as a mark of security. Giving was a claim on the receiver in my emotional arithmetic. But it was not in his.

I trusted the love letters I received, the endless time together, and the exquisite, profound need we seemed to share for each other. I felt sure all this would yield to its natural romantic end, in time. I wasn't coy about my wish to get married. Simon participated in these rhapsodies about when, where, and how soon. He never declared that he wouldn't marry me. He never said, *I'm just in this for fun, or for what I can get out of it, ya know.* After we would vividly envision our wedding, Simon would come over to me, stick his finger into the corner of my mouth, and inspect my gums and teeth as if I were a crippled horse for sale. Never was the word *love* bandied about more liberally or betrayed more deliberately. Hypnotized by the piper's flute, I fell in step like a toy soldier.

Cinder-*oy*-la!

We were living a contradiction: Simon professed his love in speech, in writing, in his appetite for my company, affection, and support. Yet he drew the line at his currency and commitment. I failed to realize that Simon was loving as long as the terms remained in his favor. As long as I gave and cost him nothing but time, he was by my side with an uncommon warmth and tenderness. If I so much as challenged the ethics of this 1990s version of courtship, Simon posed the question that aroused my feelings of worthlessness: "What makes *you* think you're entitled to anything?"

As a glorified secretary with no college degree, I didn't feel like much. The superficial details may have been different, but the feelings were the same as those my parents evoked: shame, neglect, deprivation, humiliation. Driven to redress the wounds of childhood, in the process—in my numbness—I was becoming victimized again.

What was the attraction between Simon and me? Why did I stay? Simon participated in a fantasy that was so alluring and so gratifying that my hopes were enough to convince me of their realization. He attended synagogue with me virtually every Friday night since we met, but he insisted we sit apart from the congregation and leave before any socializing. I attributed his aloofness to Simon's fear or shyness and encouraged him to share with others. I persuaded him of the rewards of giving and connection. He listened to my sermons on friendship and community, while I assured myself that he just needed patience and encouragement to let down his guard.

Simon was always confessing bitterness and resentment over others' slights, complaining of the futility of his efforts because unspecified nefarious forces were arrayed against him. I was the perpetual Pollyanna providing benign rationalizations. His outlook was dark and cynical, and mine was light and spiritual, despite my Dickensian upbringing. In his receptiveness to and interest in my words, I perceived his transformation. In his attraction to me, I convinced myself that he wished to evolve from a loner to a more wholesome social character.

Yet Simon had a criminal's habit of confessing from across the room in words I failed to hear. "You're a wonderful person, and I'm gonna burn in hell someday," he'd say.

"What did you say, Simon?"

"Oh, nothing. Never mind."

We shared an undeniable chemistry, but what that chemistry was made of still baffles me. His principal gift to me was that he helped me laugh at myself. He used to mimic my "I care for the state of your soul" with the silliest expression, allowing me to climb down from my soapbox and hear my own earnest inanity. He brought me mirth, yet there was tribute in his teasing. He mirrored my own sweetness in the countless pet names he used to call me. I honestly believe he appreciated me because I was so genuine, so earnest, and so vulnerable.

Our asphyxiating symbiosis was relieved only by Simon's addiction to travel. He was always on the move—to New York, Alaska, Europe, or Israel. He would announce his departures shortly before he took them and endure the discomfort of a couple of days of my brooding. Although my pride was hurt by his refusal to invite me on these escapades, I gradually relaxed in the days after he left and reclaimed my solitude with an unacknowledged relief.

With the exception of one male married friend, all Simon's friends seemed to be ex-girlfriends. At least that is what he led me to believe. Some of his trips involved visits to these former loves, some were check-ins with his erstwhile New York agent, and most were pure adventure.

I felt tension and resentment before his leaving, but I felt powerless to protest. He had female friends; I had male friends. Who was I to deny him friendship with an ex-girlfriend he claimed to pity—*so I would feel sorry for her too and not deny her his company,* I mused to myself. But once, something inside propelled me to search for clues—it didn't feel right. While Simon was out, I rummaged through his drawers. And I found it: a recent letter from Amanda. I scanned the large, girlish script, stopping at the first inkling of trouble. I didn't need to read further: "I can't wait to lick your stomach," she wrote.

Simon only had to turn the tables on me to shut me up: "How *dare* you touch my drawers? How *dare* you violate my private things!" he bellowed. I relinquished the evidence like a guilty schoolgirl. It never occurred to me to declare who was violating whom. Like a ballerina in a young girl's music box, I was so wound up by family trauma that I responded with an unstoppable twirl once the fated perpetrator opened the box.

When Simon wasn't traveling, he took me faithfully to my grandfather's house every Sunday on his way to the racquetball court, yet never stayed beyond a perfunctory hello. My grandfather was suspicious of my boyfriend who usually appeared in bicycle pants: "Why does he always wear such short pants?" my grandfather would ask, pegging Simon for the playboy that he was.

Eventually, I insisted that I share in some of the recreation that consumed Simon's hours, days, and weeks. Facing an ultimatum, Simon agreed to take me along for two consecutive weekend voyages to New Hampshire to see the fall foliage. He insisted we sleep in the car, a standard of lodging put in place only when I was along for the ride. However, my protest and its modest victory unexpectedly opened up a second front in my battle to win decency and dignity for myself and those I loved.

Chapter 5

E ver since my grandfather's first discharge from the hospital after his pacemaker implant, I arranged his medications in a weekly pill dispenser every Sunday during my visit. Knowing that I would not see my grandfather for two consecutive Sundays, I bought him a monthly pill dispenser, and filled each day's compartment with Lasix and digoxin to keep his congestive heart failure at bay. Pop-Pop bade me goodbye with a hug and a kiss. I felt relaxed about my travel knowing that my grandfather wouldn't suffer for my absence.

What I saw on my return three Sundays later was unspeakable. My grandfather was breathing heavily, complaining of chest pains, and couldn't smile despite our happy reunion. We went into the kitchen and sat at his table. I took out the pill dispenser from the plastic Stop & Shop bag and saw that it was empty. I didn't understand what could be wrong. It suddenly occurred to me to check the original pill vials. Incomprehensibly, the monthly vials were as full as if newly purchased, yet they were the very vials I had emptied before my trip. All the little white pills were back in one container and all the little yellow pills were back in the other.

My grandfather's thick fingers could not carefully separate the pills and restore them to their respective containers. And I doubted that with his failing eyesight, he could even distinguish the tiny yellow pill from the white.

The macabre truth hit me with a jolt.

"Pop-Pop, did Daddy take away your pills?" I asked.

"Mirileh, he tells me I don't need them."

"Pop-Pop, of course you need them. Look at you!"

When I consider all that transpired afterwards, I realize how strange it is that I stayed calm and unemotional despite the sinister discovery. I have come to learn that childhood trauma freezes one's feelings. I knew what I had to do and I knew it would be a fight, but I don't remember weeping.

That evening with a trembling but determined voice, I confronted my father on the phone.

"Dad, why did you take away Pop-Pop's medication?"

"Miranda, he's lived a long life. Leave him alone. You have no business interfering. It's none of your business." And he hung up the phone on me, repeatedly.

The next day, I called the Jewish Family & Children's Agency in Boston and made an appointment with a social worker. Three times over the next two and a half years, I sought the help of social workers, hoping that a professional would help me protect my grandfather. When I opened the cases, each listened to me patiently and with concern. Yet every time, the extraordinary happened: my father convinced the social workers that I was the threat to my grandfather. Each time, initially sympathetic social workers bought my father's claims, which they repeated to me, that I was a drug addict who was hitting up my grandfather for money. They then proceeded to close the cases instead of stepping in to protect my grandfather. Later, I met one of these social workers at Friday night services in the Harbor Fellowship Synagogue. She glared at me contemptuously, refusing even to acknowledge that we had met.

Unbeknownst to me at this stage, I was poised between two smooth-talking, self-absorbed rogues—my father and my lover—who could convince themselves and others of their virtue while committing fraud, larceny, even murder.

Simon took a back seat to the drama unfolding within my family. In some ways, my life with him was still a welcome reprieve. Despite my simmering discontent with his refusal to commit to me, we shared a great deal of physical affection and laughter, which nourished me. He affirmed my goodness amidst a family of thieves, and I found this terribly validating.

Meanwhile, my Pop-Pop, in his weakness and vulnerability, was not prepared to declare to the authorities that his son was harming him. Although I didn't understand any of the details, I knew that my father had been collecting my grandfather's generous pension checks from the US military for years, ostensibly in order to provide for his father in his old age. Since my father had been an accountant, stockbroker, and securities manager (until fraudulent practices had cost him his licenses), it must have felt natural for my grandfather to trust his son to manage his financial affairs. This was all the more likely because my naive grandfather probably didn't know about his son's occupational misconduct, which I had learned about via my mother. My grandfather was beholden to the very son who was now sabotaging and stealing from him.

My grandfather was the type to spend his two-week vacation from the Navy Yard repapering his children's homes or riding the "T" to swim at Revere Beach. He owned the same car for thirty years and never moved out of the first tiny row house he bought as a bachelor in 1926.

When the Great Depression forced him to give up the paperhanging trade, my grandfather procured supplies for the Charlestown Navy Yard with the US military through the Second World War, winning awards for his dedication. He was known to be so honorable that the captains invited him to the officers' balls to keep their wives entertained on the dance floor while they gambled and got drunk. He had no vices that I was aware of. Collecting coupons and green stamps all his life—with a navy pension and few expenses—he shouldn't have had to worry about solvency. But my father had control over his money. So he would complain to me, but not to the social workers.

I didn't like to remind my grandfather of the sorry state of our family or the sins of his son. The dismal truth brought both of us despair. Therefore, I tried my best to care for my grandfather myself and did not pressure him to speak out against his son. I knew that blowing the whistle on my father with law enforcement would plunge the whole family into chaos and cause my grandfather great shame. If only I could keep my grandfather healthy and continue to enjoy his precious company and love, I would be satisfied.

Although my father succeeded in convincing the social workers of his innocence, at least I had made it clear that he could not tamper with my grandfather's medication with impunity. Whereas I resumed primary medical responsibility for my grandfather, my father continued to pressure him to abandon his treatment.

A disgraceful pattern revealed my father's mercenary motives. Outpatient medication did not always hold my grandfather's symptoms in check, after one heart attack left him with chronic heart failure. Eventually his condition would worsen, and he would wake up breathless in fright to reach for the sublingual nitroglycerin. Approximately once a year, his heart doctor would recommend hospitalizing him to drain the accumulated fluid from his lungs.

By my grandfather's side in the emergency room of St. Elizabeth's Medical Center, I heard my father try to talk Dr. Burchard, the cardiologist, out of hospitalizing him. Failing that, he went to work on my grandfather: "You don't have a heart condition. You don't need pills. You didn't need a pacemaker.

Why do you listen to Miri? She just wants to put you in a hospital bed so you can write her checks," my father urged him. But according to my grandfather's own wishes and his obvious medical needs, Dr. Burchard admitted him for two weeks. He was discharged feeling much better.

However, when my grandfather suffered a fall on an MBTA public bus, leaving him bruised but otherwise healthy, my father took him against his wishes to Jewish Memorial Hospital, where my grandfather's local family doctor, Zachary Reznik, admitted patients. I heard my father tell the doctor, "Keep him here forever. We'll sue, and MBTA will pay for *everything*." My father did the same when my grandfather suffered a minor fall getting out of a friend's car to attend a ballroom dance. Over my grandfather's protest and shame, my father insisted that he sue the friend's insurance company. My father dragged him to multiple medical and physiotherapy appointments to hike up the expenses. But I was still naive to the depths of my father's iniquity, which would become apparent by and by.

Despite my father's claims, the only money my grandfather gave me was reimbursement for what he asked me to buy him from the grocery store, with two exceptions. Years before, my mother had brought my older brother Richard to my grandfather to ask for a contribution to a down payment on a house for him. My grandfather had given him $5,000. He said to me then, "Mirileh, I gave your brother $5,000, and I've got $5,000 for you, too. You just tell me when you need it."

My grandfather's ethics were as old-fashioned as Mount Sinai. He only wanted to be fair. He wasn't offering me one cent more than he gave my brother even though my brother had no relationship with him, and I would never have asked for it. As it was, I was reluctant to ask for the pledge. I didn't want my grandfather ever to entertain the thought that money played any part in my attachment to him.

But as the tension escalated with my father over my grandfather's care, I knew I had better ask for the gift before it was too late. I would never receive anything from my own father after my grandfather was gone. So when I enrolled in my next college course, I asked my grandfather for the money to buy a personal computer and printer, a new and still pricey technology then.

After my second consultation with a social worker over my father's tampering with my grandfather's medication, my father retaliated against me. "You can forget about your $5,000. Pop-Pop's never going to give it to you," he gloated. Yet my grandfather insisted that my father give me the check from his bank account. A computer, a $200 check for the cost of a Judaism class that my grandfather spontaneously offered me one evening, and a twenty-dollar bill on my birthdays were the only gifts I ever received from my grandfather. Money was irrelevant to our relationship. What I got from and gave to my grandfather was love.

His best friend Alvin told me he had never witnessed a relationship that was born from more pure, unadulterated love than ours. Once when my grandfather and Alvin walked me to the subway after a visit, as I boarded in haste, Alvin said to me, "You forgot to give him a kiss on the cheek," with a wistful, almost jealous acknowledgement of the warmth that marked our bond. Neighbors were witness to the unusual connection that grew between this Russian grandfather and his lonely American granddaughter.

I had a single, Italian friend named Anita, a fellow secretary at the hospital, and sometimes I brought her with me to visit my grandfather. She was a Catholic with European parents, who understood the meaning of tradition and respect for one's elders. My grandfather burbled with delight as he served us both his tender roast chicken. I was so proud of my grandfather's character: his kindness, honesty, humility, and good humor. He might have been dressed in ancient, stained garments, and he might not know any Freud, Erikson, or Piaget, but he was as faithful, reliable, and trustworthy as the dawn.

Eventually, on the computer he bought me, I critiqued European Jewish Enlightenment treatises that would impress my future husband when we were dating. In addition to the strings I know my grandfather pulled for me in Heaven after his death, his gift fostered my lasting happiness.

When his health was stable, my grandfather got his monthly heart prescriptions from Zachary Reznik, his family doctor. Dr. Burchard, the cardiologist, managed his acute episodes of heart failure. While I took my grandfather to his cardiac checkups and maintained his medications as best as I could, I didn't live with him; therefore I couldn't personally give him his medication each day. After I confided in my boss, an uncommonly kind chief of a hospital department named Trevor Carlson, MD, about the family intrigue that ensnared my grandfather, he informed Dr. Burchard, a colleague, of the sensitive dynamics of the case. Dr. Burchard took the wise step of ordering visiting nurses from an agency called Olsten Quality Care to come to my grandfather's home to supervise his medication.

Yet at the age of eighty-nine, after his third hospitalization to drain his lungs, my grandfather acknowledged he felt too vulnerable and frightened to live alone anymore. He declared himself ready to move to Golda Meir House—a Jewish seniors' home where many of his friends lived out their sunset years.

He asked me to help with the transition, so again I called the Jewish Family & Children's Agency and conveyed my grandfather's wishes to an intake coordinator, who assigned a third social worker to my grandfather's case. We made an appointment for her to come to the house in a few days' time to explain to my grandfather the process of gaining admission to

Golda Meir House. I called my father to inform him of the meeting. Marjorie, the social worker, came to my grandfather's house that day to explain to us what was involved, leaving him the paperwork to review and sign. My father hadn't turned up in the end. But I felt gratified to be helping my grandfather take a brave step that would lead to more security and peace of mind for him.

Barely a minute passed by after the social worker left before I heard the screen door squeak. The front door flew open and my father thrust himself into the room, his red face bursting with rage, followed by his sister, my aunt Faigy.

Alarmed by his appearance, my grandfather gasped, "Moisheleh, what's wrong?!"

"She's what's wrong, that's what," he shouted. "How dare you meddle in his affairs! Pop, it'll cost you $75,000 just to get into that place. You'll go into that home a prince and you'll come out a pigeon without a dime. Is that what you want? Don't you see, Pop, she just wants to put you in a home so she can steal your money?"

"Dad, that's what he wants; it wasn't my idea," I put in.

"You shut up, you little [expletive]! If you dare to meddle in his affairs from now on, I'll get a restraining order and you'll never see your grandfather again, you stinkin' [expletive]. She had me investigated like a common criminal, that little [expletive]. I had to answer to the ethics board at St. Elizabeth's Medical Center. You'll never see Dr. Burchard again, Pop, and she'll rot in hell, this little [expletive]. Your doctor is Dr. Reznik from now on, and he doesn't want to hear from *you*," he said, turning to me. "So you'd better stay out of it, or I'll call the police."

My father sneered, "Pop, you think she cares so much about you. You think she loves you so much. I tried to get her on the phone today and she didn't answer 'cause she was too busy [I have too much dignity to record the absolutely vulgar sexual act of which my father accused his own daughter in front of her European grandfather]. She's a dragon in pussycat's clothes. She's just like her mother. All she's after is your money!"

My aunt Faigy shouted, "Pop, if you go into that home, the nurse will give you a needle so long you'll never wake up! They'll tie you to the bed and starve you. All they'll do is take your money. And you'll be eaten by the rats running all over the floor in that place."

"But that's where he wants to go," I urged.

"You shut up, you little [expletive]," my father yelled. "You better get the hell out of here before I slam you against the wall!"

My grandfather ambled, bewildered, between my father and me, trying to protect me and calm my father down. My father was pushing hard against his father and wildly flailing his arms. I thought he would knock him down and assault us both.

I stayed in my grandfather's living room as long as I could, defending his right to live where he wanted. But my father's rage overwhelmed me. It was beyond my capability to level any accusations back at my father. I was a traumatized child who had lost her voice. Although I had the will to stay for my grandfather's sake, I couldn't let my father see me break down.

When I felt myself unravel, I cried, "Pop-Pop, I'm sorry. I can't stay. I love you," as the tears spilled down my cheeks, flushed with shock and shame.

"You go and don't come back, you little whore. Don't you dare meddle in his affairs again, or I'll get a restraining order and you won't come within ten feet of this house! You'll never see him again, you little [expletive]," were my father's parting threats.

I was broadsided by the assault. I didn't see it coming. I stumbled to the subway, shaking. I had been so foolish. *I had invited my father to this meeting.* Why hadn't I realized what his agenda had been all along?

Devastated by my grandfather's dismissal by the third Jewish Family & Children's Agency social worker—who refused to proceed with our family at this point—I decided to seek counsel with Simon's rabbi.

Chapter 6

Rabbi Glen Shuster presided for almost thirty years over one of the largest Conservative synagogues in Boston, the Harbor Fellowship Synagogue. I had long admired Rabbi Shuster for being an articulate proponent of the liberal philosophy of *tikkun olam* (repairing the world). He peppered his sermons with lots of big words that sounded erudite, so I hoped that he would apply his religious insight and experience to a real live domestic crisis. Abiding Simon's reserve, I did not have a warm personal relationship with Rabbi Shuster, yet the rabbi had seen me in the auditorium many, many Friday nights with Simon, who was a member.

When I arrived for my scheduled appointment with the rabbi, I was ushered upstairs to his study by his secretary. I sat on the other side of his desk and proceeded to detail all the painful interactions between my father and me over my grandfather's care, including the fruitless help I had already sought. Because Rabbi Shuster said absolutely nothing, I kept talking. Feeling ashamed disclosing the sordid melodrama that was my family, I took Rabbi Shuster's silence for patience and a willingness to allow me to unburden myself of the heavy weight I carried.

Once I'd covered absolutely everything, I said to him, "I've come to ask your advice. What should I do now? How can I protect my grandfather?" Rabbi Shuster continued to say nothing. He silently stared at me with a blank, expressionless face reminiscent of an owl—motionless but for blinking its enormous eyes and occasionally turning its head at the neck. He stared. I waited. He stared some more. When a buzzer on his desk broke the silence, I startled in my seat. His secretary spoke to him by intercom, and he announced to me that he had to go.

"Could you come back tomorrow evening at 7 p.m. to continue our consultation?" he asked me.

"Yes, of course," I said, still hoping for a breakthrough.

The next night I arrived at 6:55 p.m., but the synagogue was locked and dark. I waited outside in the cold for half an hour before leaving a message with my name and phone number on Rabbi Shuster's personal extension of the synagogue's answering service. I never heard from Rabbi Shuster again. Looking back, I find his behavior as a congregational rabbi appalling. But at the time, this was just one more indignity I suffered among many, and I hardly took notice.

Tragically for my grandfather, from this moment on, my father took calculated steps to isolate his father and put his life at risk. For several years, my grandfather had paid for an emergency medic alert system for his home called "Care Call," operated by a private businessman, Leonard Hoberman. When my grandfather pressed the button on his bedside unit, an EMT technician arrived at the house, and three people were notified according to Pop-Pop's directive: his son, his best friend Alvin, a pharmacist who lived nearby, and me. A few days later, my grandfather told me he pressed the button early in the morning, feeling ill and afraid, yet no one responded. I had no idea. Mr. Hoberman told me my father had insisted on changing the instructions so that only he was informed if my grandfather called for help.

After my grandmother's death years before, my grandfather had begun taking a hot lunch during the week at the neighborhood Frankel Senior Center, a Jewish Federation outfit that served the needs of the remaining Jewish elders in Roxbury, Dorchester, and Mattapan. The center had a cheerful air aided by a kind staff who put on the schmaltz to please their clientele. On the Jewish holidays, when they arranged a party, I sometimes met my grandfather there to sit with him at lunch, to hear him joyfully serenade his peers, and to escort him home. Known by the staff, I was never anything but courteous, but that didn't help me at all at this point. Following what must have been my father's libelous ravings, the Frankel Senior Center refused to admit me, and the social workers there wouldn't send my grandfather to the phone when I called. I had become the villain in this dance of deception.

I was truly frightened that my father would make good on his threats. I couldn't allow him to separate me from my grandfather, who was simply too vital to me. In truth, I had no one else in the world. Yet I also feared for my grandfather's life. I was becoming unable to cope myself with the grave responsibility of being the only one protecting my grandfather while a net of isolation and danger closed around him. Beside myself with anguish and worry, I couldn't function at work.

I decided I had no choice but to put my grandfather's medical needs exclusively in Zachary Reznik's hands, since he provided my grandfather's prescriptions. I asked his neighbor Olga, a Russian widow who adored my grandfather, to keep an eye on his daily pills. I continued to visit him once a week. My grandfather complained to me that his daughter Faigy had threatened never to speak to him again if he moved to Golda Meir House, the seniors' home.

Watching my grandfather deteriorate, I sent Dr. Reznik two letters, two weeks apart in November 1995, detailing my grandfather's worsening symptoms and intimating my father's negligence and irresponsibility toward his own father. I urged

Dr. Reznik to insist on seeing my grandfather in his office instead of treating him from afar and to communicate with Dr. Burchard, the cardiologist, and me about his care. I begged him to send visiting nurses to supervise his medication. I sent copies of my letters to the Jewish Family & Children's Agency and the Frankel Senior Center. I left phone messages, which Dr. Reznik didn't return. I never heard from the doctor even once.

Toward the end of December, my grandfather was ailing terribly. One evening when I visited, I could see he was hallucinating. He believed there were children clustering around his feet for whom he was making potato latkes for Chanukah. The fluid collecting around his heart and filling his lungs was cutting off the oxygen to his brain. His condition was chilling. I knew I could no longer be a spectator, watching him die.

"Pop-Pop, I'm taking you to the doctor tomorrow. I'll be here at eight o'clock."

I planned to take my grandfather to St. Elizabeth's emergency room, which would restore Dr. Burchard's involvement in his care. I intended to call Dr. Burchard in the morning to announce our arrival.

Unfortunately, I never got the chance. My grandfather's neighbor Olga became alarmed when my grandfather didn't answer the phone at seven in the morning. Rushing over, she found my grandfather unconscious at the bottom of the tall steps from the second floor, dressed respectably for visiting the doctor with me. He was rushed by ambulance to Jewish Memorial, the closest hospital.

As soon as I heard from Olga what had happened, I took the step I had feared to take. I called the Boston District Attorney's office and reported the elder abuse my grandfather was suffering. A DA staff social worker, Mrs. Vietz, was dispatched, who told me she confronted my father at the hospital, saying, "Are you going to release this man's money, or do we have to prosecute?" My father agreed to cooperate. But my grandfather was in awful shape. He'd suffered another heart attack. Though he regained consciousness, he was unable to speak.

Simon brought me to Jewish Memorial Hospital, where I found my aunt and my father in hostile silence in my grandfather's room. I went straight to my grandfather's side, clutched his hand, and looked into his eyes. I thought I saw him relax—I thought I saw his fear subside. I stood by him for many hours, gazing into his eyes, murmuring reassurance. I held his hand and stroked his arm and his cheek. For the entire day, I practically never let go. I didn't know, but these would be my last hours with my grandfather.

My father and my aunt ignored me, talking about me bitterly as if I weren't there. In the early evening, my grandfather's vital signs began failing, and he slipped into a coma. Simon came to support me, and he was there for the cynical denouement.

As my grandfather lay dying, my father and my aunt rallied to demand that I drop the charges against them through the district attorney's office. "Surely that's the way Pop-Pop would have wanted it," my father and his sister insisted. "I'm not dropping the charges," I said flatly. I was simply not absolving them. That's when the room erupted. My father punched my boyfriend and ripped the buttons off his jacket. Simon hit him back. My father yelled, "Police, Police! He hit me! He assaulted me! I want a report! I've been assaulted!" he shouted.

Security guards came, but they did not file charges. My father's outburst did not impress anyone. Yet sadly, my grandfather died before the theatrics of his children. When my grandfather died, I believed I'd done all I could, and Simon took me home. I didn't yet know that one should never leave a deceased person unattended. I didn't know that my grandfather's soul was hovering nearby. I only wish I had known.

Cinder-*oy*-la!

The day my grandfather died, just shy of his ninetieth birthday, a blizzard like those in his Russian boyhood fell upon Boston. The whole city was deadlocked by days of silent snowfall. I didn't know what would be done for my grandfather's funeral, and I wasn't informed. My grandfather's friend Alvin later called it disgraceful that a man who brought a smile, good cheer, and mellifluous prayers to so many was buried like a common derelict in a graveside ceremony without so much as a minyan to say Kaddish. And the one who loved him most in the world wasn't even invited.

Despite the inclement weather, I feared that my father lay in wait for my boyfriend and me. I knew we hadn't seen the end of his treachery. But my father had the negligence of others to hide behind. When I contacted Mrs. Vietz after the city had dug itself out from under the snow, she told me that Dr. Zachary Reznik had signed my grandfather's death certificate, declaring that he had died of natural causes. Guilty of neglect, he also stood to lose if my father's behavior was investigated. The district attorney lacked proof of foul play, given Dr. Reznik's testimony. Without a victim to protect, the district attorney closed the case. Whatever we had suffered was mine to carry alone.

Aside from a close friend or two, the only condolences I received were from Claude, the African American janitor who came every other week to tidy my grandfather's house. His card, a spontaneous gesture of compassion, touched me deeply and stood out amidst the callousness of so many members of my own tribe. Claude had witnessed how I cared for my grandfather and he knew how much my heart ached.

About a month after my grandfather died, I wrote a scathing letter to Dr. Reznik. I never sent the letter, and my bitterness festered. The hospital where I worked had recently hired a female rabbi as a chaplain, and I sought her support. She listened to my story about the various rejections by the Jewish Family &

Children's Agency, Rabbi Shuster, the Frankel Senior Center, Dr. Reznik, and my own family. She maintained that if I didn't take steps to work through my grief, I might become disillusioned with the entire Jewish community. We talked about my taking on a ritual to help me remember my grandfather. She taught me what she believed were the rudiments of prayer. To console myself and convey my gratitude, I wrote the following tribute to my grandfather.

I never admired people idly. Although I longed to love and be loved by family, as I grew up, fatal differences forced me to renounce what would have been a passionate attachment to my forebears, pulling a sapling from her roots. What grew between my grandfather and me was a gift I enjoyed as an adult when my breach with my parents freed me to see him independently. While his essence always beckoned me as a child, I was too afraid to come close to it—too afraid to lose another person I'd come to love. God must have played a part in the mysterious reckoning by granting me a grandfather whose life bore many lessons and whose love I knew, though his crusty Eastern European roots kept him from ever speaking the words. His deeds will inspire me and my children to honor his memory in the living chain of tradition.

Abraham Portnoy, my grandfather, was the son of a tailor born in a rural village outside Kiev, Russia. He attended Orthodox *cheder* until he was six years old, when his classroom study was interrupted by family misfortune. After the tragic, early death of his mother, he had to learn a trade to help support himself and his ten siblings. My grandfather told harrowing tales about hiding in barns from Russian soldiers and being harshly treated by various townspeople for whom he labored. As an apprentice to a saddlemaker, he was saved a beating serendipitously when the first saddle he made measured too small—since the town constable needed a saddle for his son's pony.

Abe: A Russian soldier came upon a man carrying two bundles when rationing strictly prohibited the possession of even food staples. "What's that you're carrying, old man?"

"I have here a pound of sugar and a pound of flour."

The soldier took out his club: "Well here's a lump for your coffee and a lump for your tea."

The religious persecution in Russia compelled my grandfather to seek freedom. Despite his tender age of eleven, he trekked with his older brother Moishe on foot across the Ukraine to reach the Black Sea, where he set sail for America through the Dardanelles Strait. Another brother, Hymie, who had started a small fishing farm in Provincetown, Massachusetts, promised to vouch for them at Ellis Island in New York. Abe lost two things on that journey: his brother-protector Moishe and his own right eye, put out by the butt of a Russian soldier's gun.

Abe: Fidel Castro's commander rounded up three anticommunist fighters: an Italian, a Polish man, and a Jew.

Communist Commander: "You have each been charged with obstructing the Revolution, and you will receive a hundred lashes apiece. But because I am a kind man, I will grant you one request."

To the Italian, he asked, "What would you like us to put on your back before you receive your lashes?"

"Me? I'd 'a like'a you to rub'a my back'a with some gooood I-talian olive oh-yel."

To the Pole, he asked, "You, what would you like us to put on your back before you receive your lashes?"

The Polish prisoner answered, "You can't hurt me. I'm as strong as a Polack. I don't need naa-ting on my back. You can give me as many lashes as you please."

To the Jew, he asked, "You, Finkelstein, what would you like on your back before you get your lashes?"

"Pardon me, sir, but I wouldn't mind if you'd put that Polack on my back."

My grandfather's spirit is captured best by the story of his arrival in America as a twelve-year-old boy, with no knowledge of English and no means of self-support.

Hymie Portnoy, married with small children, brought his younger brother Avraham home to his Provincetown fishing farm. In the middle of the second night of his stay, my grandfather heard his brother and sister-in-law quarreling bitterly: "We don't have enough to feed our own children, and you have to go and bring us another mouth to feed?" his sister-in-law shouted.

The next morning my grandfather requested a dime from his brother for the ferryboat to Boston.

"What will you do? You don't know anyone. You don't know the language. How will you survive?" asked his brother.

My grandfather thanked his brother Hymie for his concern yet persisted in his request: "Please, just give me a dime for the ferry. I can take care of myself."

Hymie acquiesced, and my grandfather left with his meager belongings. Abe set about finding work in the thriving marketplace of Boston before the Depression.

Going door to door among the Jewish merchants on Blue Hill Avenue, he found a suitable position with a fishmonger. My grandfather wrote the names of each fish in Yiddish and placed them behind the corresponding items in the counter display. When the owner would translate the customer's request into Yiddish, my grandfather would fill the order. After one week's work, he was paid a few dollars, with the promise of an increase if he stayed on. The first thing my grandfather did with his earnings was to buy groceries— fresh chickens, fish, vegetables, challah—two huge grocery bags full of food. He took the ferryboat back to Provincetown before the Sabbath to present them to his brother Hymie and his wife and children.

But my grandfather's lifelong aesthetic inclination would not tolerate the smell of fish brine for long. Without experience, he applied for a job as a paperhanger's partner. The skeptical employer gave him a nearly impossible test: a row house, paper, paste, scissors, and one day. If the house was papered by morning, he had the job. My grandfather prevailed.

Abe was not above plying his trade for secondary gains. He was offered a job papering Miss Kitty's Dance Studio in Boston's South End. My grandfather found himself hypnotized by the melodies and sinuous movements of the dancers. He struck a deal with Miss Kitty: "Teach me to dance, and I'll paper your studio for free." After hours, Miss Kitty gave him private lessons in the merengue, the cha cha, the rhumba, and the jitterbug. My grandfather's lifelong passion nettled my grandmother Miriam, who refused to take part in her husband's hobby.

My brother, Richard: *"Pop-Pop, why don't you like to dance with women your own age?"*
Abe: *"Because I'd rather smell cologne than Sloan's Liniment."*

Following the Depression in the 1930s, when no one could afford to paper their houses, my grandfather unloaded ships at the Charlestown Navy Yard. Though just a laborer, he was invited to all the captains' parties to dance with their wives while the officers played cards and got drunk. In time, he worked his way up to become chief acquisition officer of the US Naval Supply Depot.

Abe: Wiseguy: *"Hey, Mister, you want to buy a horse? He's strong, but he doesn't look so good."*
Buyer: *"That's okay, I don't need a beauty. I need a worker."*
Sometime later... Buyer: *"What do you mean, buddy? You sold me a blind horse!"*
Wiseguy: *"I told you, Mister, the horse doesn't look so good."*

My grandfather was a mix of contradictory ingredients: fierce independence, stubborn pride, and pastoral investment in the earth's creatures worthy of a biblical shepherd. For instance, the Navy Yard teemed with stray cats that my grandmother wouldn't let Abe bring home. He had two favorite mama cats, Minnie and Rachel, whose progeny—overpopulating the Boston Navy dock—he fed from his own pocket. His heart would break every year when he returned from his annual vacation to find cats dead from starvation.

An inadvertent protégé of B. F. Skinner, Abe built an ingenious device that would enable the hungry cats to feed themselves when he was away from work. He taught the cats to pull a chain to release a portion of Friskies cat chow, while the remainder remained safe from rats and other predators. A buddy of his sent a picture of the contraption to Purina, Inc., whose public relations department generously rewarded Minnie, Rachel, and their entire brood with a case of Friskies.

One of my grandfather's favorite pastimes in his later years was feeding the squirrels in Horatio Harris Park, a few blocks from his home. I often accompanied him on these journeys and witnessed a rare harmony between man, man, and nature. Inside a park in a tough, urban neighborhood at bracing hours of the morning, my grandfather was tolerated blowing furiously on a carved peach pit—the flute he used to summon the squirrels. I had to stifle my urge to bury the pit in the ground, while the neighbors and park dwellers politely indulged the racket my grandfather created. "Here, squirrelie, squirrelie! Here, squirrelie, squirrelie!" he would yelp, in between whistles. Mesmerized squirrels would spill down from the treetops, venturing from city blocks away.

However, my grandfather had a rule. He refused to toss the peanuts to the squirrels from afar. They had to pay him homage. He trained them to come up onto the park bench next to him and stand on their hind legs so he could see the expressions of gratitude on their little faces. If they were too afraid to come near, he would leave them hungry. One little *ganef* got wise and came so close he stole the whole bag of peanuts from Pop-Pop's jacket pocket.

My grandfather never stopped evolving. Aging was as optional as dieting to him. In his late seventies, long after his retirement, he heard a cantor deliver a High Holiday service at Ohr Yisrael Synagogue. Moved by the melodies of his childhood, he approached the cantor afterwards and asked, "Do you think you could teach me to sing like you do?" The cantor asked him to repeat a tune. With mutual admiration flowing, he accepted Abe as a pupil. When he was ready, my grandfather—with a rich baritone seasoned by a lifetime of simple living and honest labor—revived Congregation Shevet Achim, in a longed-for return to his roots. Shevet Achim—the oldest Orthodox synagogue in Roxbury—had been shuttered previously from neglect. Abe led their weekday and Sabbath services until he died.

With no formal education, my grandfather spoke three languages and enjoyed the pursuits of the aristocracy—dancing, music, gardening, and prayer. Amidst urban squalor, he cultivated an oasis behind his Roxbury row house. His garden—its border carefully decorated with handpicked Revere Beach seashells—bloomed with pink and yellow roses, coleus, and marigolds every year until the last two before his death.

A man of great thrift, my Pop-Pop begat curious invention with his frugality. One year on my birthday, I visited him with a friend. With no cake in the house, he melted and fused twenty-four candles to the back of a plastic dinner plate and cut the prettiest pink roses off the bush for a table centerpiece. After dinner, he enthused, "Guess what I have for you? Those big black grapes that you like!"

I enjoyed my grandfather's cooking immensely—not only because he knew how to make exquisite pea soup or roast chicken like a *bubbe*. It was through his cooking and feeding me that I most keenly felt his love. His voice teemed with tender mercy when he prepared food for me: "Eat a little salad...it's good for you. Have some soup; it's getting cold. Have another piece of chicken, Mirileh. You don't eat like this every day." His prodding could be maddening, but to me it was priceless. I felt adored at his table as I had never before. Imbibing his creations for years beyond when he was safe to be in the kitchen, I swallowed Borax with a smile to uphold his dignity.

A gal with an overactive superego, I found abundant reasons to feel guilty. This tendency frustrated my ability to deliver a white lie with aplomb. Yet my grandfather inspired a breakthrough. For his birthday one year, I searched for a special gift he could wear with pride. I found an antique gold tie clip decorated with a musical G clef. I thought his love of music, dancing, and cantorial singing made it a perfect choice. I imagined him announcing proudly—when he received the anticipated compliments—"My *granddaughter* bought it for me." But my grandfather was not formally schooled in music, and the clef symbol was unfamiliar to him. Being a man of personal discernment—and habit—he rarely wore it.

Sometime later, he presented me with a ring he had found on the sidewalk. He was giddy with excitement over its sparkling blue stone, ringed in gold. In his near-blindness, he did not realize that it had come from a bubble gum machine. I oohed and aahed on cue and put the ring in my jewelry box, where it still lies.

One evening, when I was visiting him before he left to go ballroom dancing, I asked him why he wasn't wearing the tie clip I got him, as he came downstairs in his sharpest suit. He answered, "I don't know. How come you're not wearing the ring I gave you?"

"It's too beautiful to wear on the street, Pop-Pop. I'm afraid it might get stolen," I responded with consummate finesse.

Once I came to a decision that I was excited to share with my grandfather. Although I concluded as an adolescent that clinical psychology suited my introspective, analytical temperament, in college, my subconscious stalled me for reasons I didn't yet understand. In an elective course in classical Judaism, I tasted the sublime for the first time, reading and analyzing the Torah. Changing course, I decided to become a rabbi.

My grandfather was not a chauvinist, but he was practical. He disapproved of my plans, but not because he didn't think women should become rabbis. "You won't find a job. My friend's son is a rabbi, and he can't find work. So-and-so's daughter is a cantor, and she had to move to Europe to find a good job. No one cares about Judaism anymore. You have a good job now—why would you want to leave it?"

I illustrated for my grandfather the flexibility in a rabbinical degree: "I can work as a hospital chaplain. I can work in a social service agency or on a college campus. I can write and teach," which I most wanted to do. I explained that I wasn't interested in making a lot of money; I just wanted to feel challenged and fulfilled.

Although my grandfather could not be persuaded, I let him know that I would pursue my ambition even without his blessing.

A few months later, my grandfather asked me to come over on a Wednesday evening after work. I agreed, but told him I would have to leave in time for my evening continuing education class at Hebrew College, a rabbinical school in Newton Centre. His voice burbled with excitement as he begged me for details about my studies. When I got to his house, he forgot why he had asked me to come. "Mirileh, how much did it cost, your class?" "Two hundred dollars," I told him. Before I left, he pressed a check into my hand, saying, "Mirileh, tell me when you're ready to quit your job."

Some years after she passed away, I asked my grandfather if he had loved his wife Miriam, and if he missed her. He gave me an answer reminiscent of Tevye, the milkman: "Love, what is love? I took care of her. She was my wife." When I prodded him to elaborate, he revealed a refreshingly modern attitude: "She was a good talker. Since she was blind, she'd listen to the radio. When I'd come home at the end of the day, she'd tell me all about the news. She knew everyone's birthday in the neighborhood." I smiled hearing that, of a marriage that began in the 1920s, he didn't reminisce about her cooking or the way she kept the house—he appreciated her mind and her companionship.

Miriam Portnoy was an excitable, high-tempered woman with a sharp mind and a playful imagination. As a teenager, I had asked my grandmother how she met her husband. She launched into a gripping tale of her near-death experience at Revere Beach. Miriam had foolishly dived into the waves on a day when a sudden squall turned the water turbulent. She was carried out by the undertow and bobbed above the surf far from the beach. Yet she wasn't a good swimmer. Losing strength, she struggled to stay afloat. Each wave carried her further from the shore. As my grandfather pushed his way through a crowd of people gawking on the beach, he saw lifeguards in a rubber boat wrestling with the pounding waves. My grandfather jumped into the Atlantic Ocean himself and swam out to rescue her. Reaching her before the lifeguards, he swam back to shore carrying his *yiddishe* mermaid in his arms. He stood over her while paramedics resuscitated her. She would marry this fearless man who saved her life.

After my grandmother passed away, my grandfather clarified the story. He had engaged a matchmaker who gave him three names. My grandmother was bachelorette number three, whom he found pretty and engaging. Miriam Kalischer and Abe Portnoy went out on two dates. On their second date, after a picture show, they agreed to marry in one year. Because my grandmother was poor, my grandfather paid for the dress, the catered hall, and a honeymoon at Niagara Falls. On one occasion when this had come up, my grandmother interjected—from her chair where she perched in the corner of the living room, listening and piping in to every conversation—"Ahh, Niagara Falls, Shmiagra Falls! All I saw was the ceiling."

My grandmother had always resented her greenhorn husband. Born in the United States, with an ancestor of high rank in the Prussian army, she dreamed of marrying a wealthy, educated American who would raise her above her station. My grandfather was twenty-two when they married in 1928. My grandmother was a few years older and perilously close to becoming an old maid. Her parents and brothers pressured her to marry my grandfather, a lone suitor, lest she remain a burden to her family. She was blessed to be cared for by him much of her life.

My grandfather died on Shabbat, the fourteenth of Tevet, January 5, 1996, just before his ninetieth birthday. Amid a colossal Nor'easter blizzard—weather that must have resembled his boyhood Russia—he was buried without funeral or eulogy. May he dance forever among the angels.

Slowly, slowly, I got over the sorrow and the pain. The last time I ever saw or heard from my father was in his father's hospital room as Pop-Pop lay dying. Several months later, I heard from Alvin, my grandfather's friend, with a twinge of Schadenfreude, that my aunt was suing my father for her half of my grandfather's estate.

Coping with my father's threatening Pop-Pop's life left me no time to contemplate what my grandfather and I had built in our bond. We were on the brink of an emergency for three years. But after he was gone, I thought about the orphan embarking on a journey across the world, having to prove himself as a child in a new country and survive by his own mettle. He had become fiercely independent and had been reluctant to relinquish the role of giver. I believe he was afraid to acknowledge his needs and find that no one cared to meet them. That my grandfather grew to trust me and reached out to me for help was one of my most cherished accomplishments. In his simple love and dutiful care for me, he restored a foundation for me to care for a family of my own one day. In our short but dramatic relationship, we healed each other's wounds.

Chapter 7

With my beloved grandfather gone, I was forced to turn my attention back to the muddle of my own life, which every good codependent is loath to do. Between my job, Simon, and caring for my grandfather, I hadn't had the time or energy for a college course in over a year. I couldn't bear the thought of remaining a hospital secretary, yet obtaining my degree part-time was taking forever. At the age of thirty-one, I applied again for financial aid to Latham University as an independent student. Eureka! The college agreed to waive the requirement for my parents to submit their tax returns. My financial independence for more than thirteen years was finally recognized. I was offered a package of loans and grants that would enable me to finish my bachelor's degree in just one year of full-time study.

Meanwhile, Simon was occupied with applying to various MBA programs, for which he liberally relied on me. A crisis erupted in Simon's own family, which we faced together after my grandfather's death. Simon's father, Sidney, was diagnosed with stomach cancer. Within seven weeks, he was dead. As he lay dying, Sid told me that he wanted his son to marry me, but in order for Simon to recover his desire, he urged me to stop pressuring him. Sid's death exposed dynamics in Simon's family that I wished I'd never glimpsed. His mother spoke angrily at the funeral before her deceased husband's casket, as though condemning him for abandoning her. Shortly afterward, her younger longtime business partner was wearing Sid's clothes, sitting awfully close to Simon's mother in their living room, and had practically moved in to the family's home.

After Simon and I lost close relatives, we were both moved to take stock and advance our own lives, but of course, only I was bent on getting married and building a family. Although Simon had promised me the previous winter to propose by the spring, he was living the same Peter Pan lifestyle, when he wasn't in Cambridge taking all my time. Now, business school interviews also drew him to the West Coast.

The previous summer, while my grandfather had been hospitalized for congestive heart failure for the third time, and Simon was traveling in Israel, my family suffered another blow. My older brother Richard was hospitalized for a psychotic breakdown that would permanently mar his mental health. He heard voices commanding him to meet the messiah in a remote Western state. The police found him driving erratically not far from his home and brought him to a psychiatric ward. When I heard, I begged my father to visit him in the hospital, but he refused. I was feeling too overwhelmed with my grandfather's care to come to my brother's aid. In my anxiety and sadness, I urged Simon to formalize our relationship, which seemed to contain some kindness, love, and nurture amidst the degradation.

I believe my brother's psychosis was the price he paid for remaining in relationship with our abusive mother. Though I pitied him, I also feared him. He learned at her knee to be as selfish, exploitative, and vengeful as she was. It is tangential to this story to describe what my brother did to me while he was still sane. But his chronic mistreatment finally disabused me by my late twenties of my lifelong vocation of caretaking and rescue.

Simon had agreed to act by the spring, which had arrived. Yet he was becoming more preoccupied, dismissive, and remote, as he jostled between visits to his New York agent and business school interviews. I was feeling ever more as though I was receiving only the dregs of his attention and care.

Although I had prepared his application, Simon didn't tell me that he had been admitted to Latham Business School's prestigious MBA program. At a dinner with his mother, brother, and me a month *after* he had received the good word, he coquettishly undressed at dessert to reveal a T-shirt emblazoned with an oversized Latham logo, leaving us to guess his glad news. He gave me neither any credit nor thanks for rehabilitating his life and putting him on a path to success that only a grand blunder of his could jeopardize.

I admit the sunk cost effect played a part in my reluctance to leave Simon. With Rabbi Hayley, who counseled me after my grandfather's passing, I identified my core values and dreams for my marriage and family life. She reassured me that my wish for a relationship founded on honesty, trust, respect, and mutual giving was entirely consonant with the Jewish idea of marriage. And my longing for us to take an active part in a Jewish community, hosting others for Shabbat dinners and performing social service, were conventional features of Jewish life.

Even though we had been attending synagogue together for years, we formed no friendships with other couples, because Simon seemed bent on avoiding identifying as a couple. After months of complaint, Simon introduced me to one couple with whom he was friendly with a brittle "This is Miri," leaving them to wonder, was I his sister? His chiropractor? Perhaps only his groupie? Only in retrospect did I realize that Simon attended synagogue only to recite his favorite prayer, "Dear Lord, may You frustrate the plans of those who would plot against me"— hoping he would get further in life with God on his team. He had a competitive rather than cooperative attitude toward others. Although I still didn't realize it, I was merely a tool for his advancement.

In the spring we had what I hoped would be a frank talk about the dynamics of our relationship. We had what Simon represented to be a monogamous relationship that would culminate in marriage, yet I wanted to understand how he conceived of his marital obligations. Would he work if needed to provide for us? Could I depend on him while I was bearing our children?

When I asked how it could be that he could afford such an indulgent lifestyle when he wasn't even working, he provided a dubious cover. He claimed his grandfather had loaned him money to buy his condominium, which he had bought for much less than the amount of the loan, granting him a substantial surplus with which to enjoy himself. Although he was preoccupied with the stock market, he would never tell me why.

I argued that the mystery promoted mistrust and suspicion between us. Simon knew what I had and where it came from. He hadn't worked a conventional job since the day I met him, yet he lived like a bon vivant. He agreed to come clean but evidently, lied; thereafter, we continued to split things fifty-fifty and do together only what I could afford. He kept up his conspicuous consumption, while I carried on my budget-minded, modest living. Eventually, with Simon still dragging his feet instead of proposing, I concluded I had given enough and waited long enough. I had to admit that Simon did not share my wish for a future.

Leaving Simon put a cap on the years of anguish wrought by both him and my father. I hoped for a fresh start. In early summer, I gave notice at my job and prepared to embark on a final year of undergraduate study assisted by college loans and grants, allowing me to dedicate myself to learning for the first time. I bid my kind boss, Trevor Carlson, MD, goodbye over a farewell lunch, grateful that his employ had been a safe port in a family storm.

I chose to take one summer course as a warm-up to the fall academic year. I was fortified in coping by aphorisms from a self-help group called Recovery, International, which I had been attending for a few years. Recovery, Intl. is an ingenious mental health self-support system with chapters in many North American cities. Dr. Abraham Low—a European Jewish psychiatrist with personal roots in observant Judaism—developed the system in the 1930s in counterpoint to the expensive Freudian analysis in vogue in his day. Some credit him to be the true father of cognitive behavioral psychology—pioneering no-nonsense self-help strategies that reduce patients' need for psychiatric medications and therapy.

I took aim against my perfectionism and concomitant performance anxiety with Recovery slogans such as "I only have to write an *average* paper," "We seek to be exceptional because we fear we are not even average," and "Lower your standards so your performance can rise." I suffered gastrointestinal meltdowns while composing essays, and the affirmation "These sensations are distressing but they are not dangerous—I can endure the discomfort until comfort will come" helped me survive. I chanted these mantras as I wrote my first papers in several years with the sweat pouring down my face and my stomach turning over like a rabbit on a rotisserie spit.

Meanwhile, Simon sent me letters pleading with me to come back to him. He claimed his father's death had taught him how much he loved me and couldn't live without me. He even started therapy and prevailed upon me to join him; although I found his therapist was unwilling to confront Simon for his outright selfishness. He would interrupt her to give long soliloquies about his vision of the perfect relationship, which he complained ours didn't quite meet, yet. Simon and I jockeyed for her favor, while she seemed too charmed to call him on his self-absorption. At first, I was so delighted we were even in therapy, I was afraid to rock the boat. But I could not accept the expectation that I would continue to try to build this idyll with him, while he continued to dedicate himself to his own pleasure. I couldn't breathe anymore listening to his childishness. After a handful of sessions together, I felt surer than ever that I was making the right decision to move on.

I invested all my unfulfilled yearning for security in my summer college course. My ethics professor earnestly accused me of plagiarism in my amateur analysis of Hobbes' *ethical egoism*. Persuaded of my innocence, he gave me an A+ on my second paper. Yet investing all my strength in one course still camouflaged the problem that would erupt with a full-time academic schedule in the fall. Then I learned the truth of the adage "Be careful what you wish for—it might come true."

At the end of the summer, Simon told me he was seeing a new psychologist, who informed him that Simon suffered from narcissistic personality disorder (like my mother and father). He claimed to be determined to reform and to win my hand in marriage, if only I would give him a little more time. Thrilled to be vindicated, I nevertheless remained guarded and refused to resume our physical relationship. Simon did his best to prove his commitment by politely abiding my reserve for a couple of months until I surrendered. I am ashamed to admit that I eventually acquiesced in the hope that this man would become my lifetime mate and husband.

I had always been old for my age, with too many cares on my back. As a full-time undergraduate for the first time at thirty-one, I was forced to face all the ways in which I was immature. I had never mastered the time management skills necessary to juggle multiple courses. My voice shook when I tried to express my opinion in class discussions. I felt somewhat pathetic walking around campus alone lugging books in a backpack, whereas everyone else my age had graduated to briefcases.

The one redeeming feature of this semester was my professor, Gaby Rakover, with whom I was studying modern Judaism. Gaby and I had kept in touch a bit over the years while I had taken time to finish my final paper for his first class. Now, he noted my attendance and asked after me by email when I failed to come to class on the days I was frantically writing papers. I shared with him my embarrassment being an older undergraduate who did not feel the equal of my confident, privileged fellow students. He reassured me, providing crucial support. He told me he had taught only a handful of undergraduates who could analyze a text and write about it as movingly as I could.

My strategy for survival—borrowed from Recovery, Intl.— was to turn in "average" papers, but to turn them in on time. I was determined to avoid my penchant for unfinished business. "Average" was Recovery's word for mediocre, good *enough*. The logic ran: if I were only striving for *mediocre*, which was fairly easy to reach, I would feel a lot less tension, and paradoxically be freed to do my best work. The strategy worked like a charm, and I turned in seven straight-A papers, one after another.

Simon was an appreciative bystander as I completed my assignments, eating, drinking, and sleeping Recovery slogans. He was pleased to be riding a winning horse. I received romantic cards even more ingratiating than usual. It seemed we could look forward to a future with each of us fulfilling our personal dreams. He was looking forward to business school and I dreamed of enrolling in the local rabbinical college after graduation—this time for real, not just an evening class.

While I lacked the poise and charisma to be a pulpit rabbi, I imagined enhancing my interest in psychology with the fortification of Torah knowledge to become a pastoral counselor. As a rabbi, I hoped to find a vehicle for my spiritually oriented writing. Gaby assured me that Boston's Hebrew College was a nurturing seminary where I could escape the cutthroat competition of graduate school and immerse myself in religious Jewish texts. I felt too old and far too insecure to compete in the world of academia. Simon and I agreed that the following September, we would begin living together with our formal engagement. Simon would start Latham Business School, with our wedding shortly thereafter.

Trembling and quivering, I was meeting my academic deadlines for the first time in my life. One exception was a course called Philosophy of Mind, which required reading assignments and exams instead of papers. (By now, I had switched my major to philosophy, allowing me to take electives in Judaism and Jewish philosophy.) Each time I opened one of the books, I could barely get beyond the first sentence. The concepts were so remote and incomprehensible, they might as well have been written in cuneiform. I had no choice but to ignore the course, while I kept cranking out analytical essays for my other classes.

The night before the Philosophy of Mind midterm exam, I was saved by a miracle. I opened the very same books that had previously been Greek to me and read every single reading assignment given over half a semester—from midnight until morning. I understood all of them easily and received a B+ on the midterm.

Why did the very same gibberish suddenly become clear? This was one of many questions and mysteries I brought to Carrie Pressburg, a gentle Quaker obtaining her doctorate in education, who worked at the university's Tutoring and Learning Resource Center. I referred myself to this clinic feeling as if I was dancing on the head of a pin. Class assignments were getting longer in the second half of the semester, and I could feel myself beginning to totter. Carrie gave me intake questionnaires to fill out and return for her to examine before we met for the first time.

In our first meeting, Carrie asked me if I'd ever been evaluated for attention deficit disorder. The diagnosis had exploded in the 1980s but was still regarded skeptically by many, myself included. She asked me to dig up report cards from childhood and look for early signs of ADD. I had always regarded my tendency to procrastinate and self-sabotage in school to be a vestige of the war I couldn't stop waging with my mother. Yet it didn't make sense. Was I still punishing my mother when we were so long out of contact? Had that ever really been my motivation? Why would I allow myself to excel in an assignment of fewer than ten pages but seek failure in longer papers?

Looking at my pattern of answers to her questionnaires, Carrie explained, "It's not your choice. That's the way your brain works. The reason you can function in a crisis, staying up thirty-six hours to compose a short paper or memorizing all the facts for an exam, is because adrenaline kicks into circulation the neurochemicals that enable attention." I had all the telltale signs: a messy house, chronic lateness with paperwork and bills, a houseful of secondhand books on organization and time management that had failed to bring me deliverance. I had even been featured anonymously on a segment of Boston's *People Are Talking* as a before-and-after client of professional organizers. When the expert organizer came to inspect my apartment for use as a prospective set for the television shoot, she craned her neck around 360 degrees at the surfaces piled with paper and exclaimed, "This is *perfect!*"

I had a history of setting out each day with grand dreams for accomplishment and ending the day wondering exactly where the time went and why I had so little to show for it. Yet I was convinced that it was my entire fault, that I lacked self-discipline—that I only sought censure in a helpless Freudian repetition compulsion. The idea that I had something neurologically awry was utterly new. I didn't know whether to feel ashamed or relieved.

Carrie urged that ADD explained why I was more likely to fall asleep over my books when no exam loomed to compel me to focus, and why material that was unintelligible would become lucid right before an exam. My lifelong procrastination was intuitive self-medication rather than sheer irresponsibility.

She explained that people without ADD circulate the neurochemicals fostering attention *without* a crisis. They can perform consistently, despite the boring daily round. Anything routine and dry, like paperwork, is especially hard for those with ADD because our brains are under-stimulated. No wonder we put off these things! The time warps I would suffer—four hours lost in a bookstore—were a result of my chasing a neurotransmitter high. Those with ADD show a paradoxical ability to get deeply absorbed in something they find interesting, a phenomenon called *hyperfocus*, to the neglect of the banal duties of living. In fact, experts regard ADD to be an attention inconsistency or instability, rather than a mere deficit.

I had to admit her hypothesis explained quite a lot, but it was still just a theory.

I found some documentary evidence in the comments of my grade school teachers in the early 1970s, before ADD emerged as a diagnosis: "When Miranda pays attention, she is an excellent student. But sometimes she seems so lackadaisical and has trouble completing her work." Subjects such as math that required mastering and applying cumulative concepts—as boring to me as census reports from Lisbon—I began to struggle with in grade school. My interest in the humanities and social sciences propelled me through subjects with words and ideals to tangle with.

Carrie explained that ADD was not just a handicap but often brought creativity and originality—drawing people to novelty, innovation, and pioneering. She wrote a letter introducing me to Paula Ferguson, coordinator of the Program for People with Disabilities in the university's Office of Affirmative Action, recommending me for evaluation for learning disabilities. If I indeed had ADD—a legal disability—I could receive academic accommodations that would undoubtedly help me to graduate.

Meanwhile, I was facing a four-car collision. Three of my four classes required long, complex final papers, and everything was due at the same time. I couldn't dance that fast. I didn't know how to organize a large paper, and I couldn't keep more than a few ideas in my mind at once before I'd become confused and overwhelmed. Carrie felt sure that she and a learning instructor could teach me how to adapt techniques of writing short papers to longer papers. But we would need more time.

Paula Ferguson admitted to me that, having ADD herself, her heart went out to silent sufferers. She looked at my college transcript speckled with incompletes, Carrie's letter, and my anguished face. She couldn't see my racing heartbeat. She approved my testing for learning disabilities at the Hospital of Latham University at the earliest opportunity. Meanwhile, I froze like a deer in headlights, failing to write a single final paper. My semester of promise ended with a horrifying thud.

Paula and Carrie insisted that I find a way to stay in school despite crashing at high speed with four new incompletes. The support services of the university and the medical insurance to fund ADD treatment were conditional upon my remaining a student. After a scathing rebuke, a college guidance counselor agreed to allow me to continue if I reduced my schedule by half in the spring, in order to finish my fall courses. Yet I didn't know just how rocky this next semester was going to be.

The formal, comprehensive testing six weeks after the start of the next semester made sense of my most mystifying experiences. I had never understood why my closest friends were now doctors, lawyers, and social workers, while I was still knocking my head against the ceiling of a bachelor's degree. Why did my teachers regularly praise my insight and intellect, though I found many of the pedestrian tasks of living so difficult? Was I gifted or was I retarded?

According to my test results, I had impaired executive functions, and a clear attention deficit, but very superior verbal and analytic skills. Because of my shortfall in practical intelligence—which is acquired, incidentally, through *attention*— my overall functioning was reduced to average. Yet I had areas of exceptionality. The psychologists explained that most "bright" people test well across the board and can proceed swiftly toward achievement. But my weaknesses were sabotaging my strengths. I had long ago dubbed myself "functionally handicapped," and this was not so far from the truth. Inside me, however, lurked a brave and visionary soul who had not yet found her muse.

Since I performed in the "impaired" range on every test with a specific attentional component, the five-hour state-of-the-art Hospital of Latham University psychological testing confirmed unequivocally that I had attention deficit disorder. The evaluation also resolved concerns about my character, as I was cleared of any psychopathology save for chronic subclinical depression, anxiety, and feelings of guilt and inadequacy. The entire single-spaced, five-page report yielded one sentence that gave me pride: "Miranda has good ego strength for coping with life stressors." Had that not been true, I would have joined my brother's unfortunate club years before.

The diagnosis of my disability at age thirty-two delivered a shock—inducing a kind of disorientation. While this disability might explain my addled past, what would it mean for my future? Was this discovery something to celebrate or to mourn? The investigators gave me the business card of Craig Cohen, PhD, director of cognitive therapy at the Methodist Medical Center of Latham University, who specialized in treating students with ADD and learning disabilities. He was my next port of call.

Chapter 8

I entered Dr. Craig Cohen's office with the hope of a new recruit. I clutched my diagnosis of ADD like a banner—this defect would explain all the unfulfilled promise, all the frustrated ambition, all the aborted glory. Someone had given my anguish a name and thereby saved me from surrender. I was eager to master basic training and earn my wings.

I was lucky that Craig's enthusiasm and dedication to helping students overcome their disabilities matched my own determination. Craig's methods were only slightly unorthodox. He introduced a technique that would prove life transforming: he invited me to choose three goals for each day and report them on his answering machine in the morning, following up with a nightly telephone message revealing my success or failure in meeting the goals.

Since few therapists welcome contact outside the formal appointment, Craig impressed me with his investment in my recovery. This simple technique of self-monitoring became the most effective strategy I have ever discovered for staying focused. After a few months of troubleshooting, for the first time in my life, I was following through on my intentions instead of getting distracted by my thoughts, feelings, or the countless unsolicited diversions visiting everyone who walks the earth.

However, our hardest task was extinguishing my most pernicious and pervasive habit of constantly kicking myself. At any moment, I was most likely to be thinking, "I'm a bum. I'm going to fail. I'll never graduate." Unfortunately, I had plenty of evidence for my doubts. I was, despite pockets of triumph, more than likely to finish semesters with irritated professors shaking their heads. Reviling myself, I was unconvinced I could overcome my bad habits. Craig taught me to change my attributions for failure from matters *internal*, *global*, and *permanent* to matters *external*, *specific*, and *temporary*. Thus, "I'm a failure" became "I failed to do *such and such* in this instance, but with awareness and effort, I can do better the next time."

Craig explained that my tendency to anticipate failure and condemn myself—ostensibly to motivate myself to work harder—only interfered with my concentration, increased my anxiety, and led me to give up in despair. Yet this was my lifelong pattern. Replacing it felt like a battle against nature.

Although I shared with Craig the familial roots of this self-excoriation in my mother's abuse, neither of us wanted to waste time trying to change ancient history. I was only too happy to keep my focus on the present, which I could hope to influence. Nevertheless, learning I had ADD inspired a curious spike of compassion for my mother. Since ADD is a heritable condition, I wondered if undiagnosed and untreated ADHD might have contributed to her frustration and aggression. The tendency I had to accumulate paper everywhere was a feature of my childhood home, as my mother forever claimed to be in the middle of organizational projects that she never seemed to conclude. I even called her to express my understanding and pity, but shrank back again when her emotional pathology made it unbearable for me to stay in contact.

Craig and I began to examine exactly how and where my plans for productivity broke down, feeding the discoveries back into my schedule for improved daily planning. He drew my awareness to patterns of delaying activities highly demanding of my attention in favor of less taxing ones, so that I could intervene and choose to stay the course. I experimented with taking short, timed breaks after sprints of intense focus. Craig took a decidedly objective approach to behavior management: each week I had to complete four self-assessment tests—among them the Beck Depression and Anxiety Inventories—enabling us to gauge my improvement.

While I was working with Craig, Carrie encouraged me to become active in Helping Educate about Learning Powers (HELP), a Latham undergraduate organization representing the needs of the learning disabled, to reduce my isolation. In HELP, I met students of all stripes who were striving to keep parity despite their handicaps. Though I was the most recently diagnosed undergraduate, I was everyone's senior by at least a decade.

Carrie assigned me a learning instructor named Erica O'Donnell, who became an unparalleled support and confidante. With Erica, I worked on reading and paper-writing strategies that would begin to yield improvement. Yet sometimes I got lost in emails to Erica rather than composing my papers. She found the confessions in my emails so revealing about the inner world of a person with ADD that she included excerpts in her master's thesis.

The semester of my diagnosis became an experiential tutorial in the behavioral management of ADD. But I was foolish to think I could simultaneously keep up with two senior seminars in political philosophy and the philosophy of religion. Once again, I wrote excellent shorter papers and aced my oral presentations, yet faltered in completing the long final papers. My performance was further compromised by the rocky road to drug treatment.

Robin Levine, MD, the campus psychiatrist who supplied my monthly antidepressant prescription, was now authorized to treat my newly diagnosed ADD. According to my friends from

HELP, medication was the key to successful coping. We began trials of different drugs, which yielded more complications and side effects than benefits. On Dexedrine, I stopped sleeping at night and pulled muscles in my back and shoulders. On Ritalin, I got headaches and an irregular heartbeat. It wasn't easy to find a medication that didn't upset my fragile ecology.

Paula Ferguson had assured me that the official university letters informing my professors both past and present of my disability—providing them with the list of legally mandated accommodations—would go out immediately. Yet I was aghast to discover at the end of the following semester that none of my professors had ever been informed. I felt sheepish enough asking them for extra time for a condition that some maintained was simply an excuse for laziness. I was even more embarrassed that, without official documentation, it must have appeared to them as if I *was* malingering. It was a difficult time trying to get this new suit of clothes fitted properly, with no embarrassing plunging necklines or splits in the seat of my pants.

Adele Chertoff, the director of Tutoring and Learning Resources, heard about my experiences from Carrie and suggested that I speak at an upcoming symposium for students and staff about my experiences as a learning-disabled Ivy League student. I was gratified that I moved a few students and faculty to tears with my speech, one claiming I had "unmasked her private pain." Paula Ferguson—whose performance I subtly criticized—nevertheless asked for a copy of my speech. And some of my suggestions for policy change were incorporated into a guide for learning-disabled students that Carrie compiled. In presentations by HELP all over campus, I was winning some prestige I never had as an ordinary student. Given my humiliating tendency to end successful mid-semesters in defeat, I had formerly carted around shame at Latham for a decade.

Cinder-*oy*-la!

In the midst of the rockiest semester in my college career, I suffered another loss. The daily student newspaper reported that my cherished Judaic studies professor, Gaby Rakover, was leaving Latham University. After ten years, he was rejected for tenure, but given the annual Provost's Award for distinguished teaching. I arrived at my weekly therapy session embarrassed to be in tears. Dr. Cohen persuaded me that my feelings of loss were entirely healthy and not to be discouraged: "How impoverished we would be as humans if we couldn't form attachments," he said.

Together we filled out an "automatic thought record," a cognitive therapy tool, about my fears of asking Gaby whether we could keep in touch. Craig was teaching me to do daily mood logs and cross-examine my thoughts whenever I felt an abrupt change in mood, giving me the tools to manage my own emotions. Craig urged me both to express my wish to Gaby and to share with Craig the outcome. Along with being a skills-oriented behaviorist, Craig genuinely cared about me. We were a fruitful team.

I told Craig about the *People Are Talking* TV segment on professional organizers, which captured on video the special loyalty I felt for Gaby. When Tom Bergeron, the host, asked me at the end of the show what I'd grab from all my clutter if my house were on fire, I said, "My cats!" When he pressed me for a more revealing answer, I said, "The papers I wrote for college," meaning those very analyses of Torah, which had so stirred my soul. Gaby had been a catalyst for my best work and restored some hope I'd had for myself as a child. I wrote Gaby a thank-you note expressing my appreciation and posing my request. He wrote me a letter absolutely insisting we keep in touch, vowing to kill me if I didn't invite him to my wedding. It was a satisfying outcome to a small risk.

As I struggled to apply my new time-management skills to completing my assignments, Craig and Robin Levine, my campus psychiatrist, both urged me not to relinquish the need for recreation, irrespective of how much I accomplished. Features of my condition conspired with my family history to keep me in a state of perpetual self-denial. Like all those with ADD, I sorely underestimated the amount of time tasks would take. Because I never finished what I set out to do, I rarely felt entitled to take a break and reward myself. This tendency to promise myself a reward and then withdraw it in punishment was, also, another way I replicated my mother's abuse.

With Craig, I learned to pare down my daily goals to make them more realistic and to pad my schedule with extra time to keep ahead of my ambitions. I used the feature of tracking and accountability provided by the daily telephone reporting to compel myself to follow through. In three months, I had whittled down my depression and anxiety scores to only one-third of what they had been before I started treatment. In Craig's care, I was beginning to accumulate something entirely new: a reservoir of self-respect. Ending each day with my missions accomplished gave me a feeling of personal efficacy for the first time in my life.

Unfortunately, these seeds of self-esteem had a peculiar effect on my romantic relationship. At first, the change seemed positive. I began to make claims upon Simon—that he would accompany me to a concert or film after a week of assiduous study. I objected to the asymmetry in our relationship: that he did all his socializing by himself or with others but turned to me for emotional support and satisfaction of his physical needs. He responded in a particularly devious way, by insisting that I accompany him for long getaways, which he knew I couldn't, struggling as I was to complete my coursework. He complained vehemently when we spent one evening out together, and I formerly would have felt guilty for imposing on him. But something had shifted in me and I was no longer feeling so undeserving.

Initially, I used my newfound knowledge of ADD to rationalize Simon's bad behavior. I learned from Sari Solden's book *Women with Attention Deficit Disorder* that those with ADD lose our fragile short-term memory when we are flooded by emotion. I wondered if this was why I was so disappointed with my beloved despite his small acts of caring, such as picking me up late at night at school or helping me grocery shop with his car on occasion. Searching the past, I speculated that this ADHD-inspired short-term memory lapse is what led to my mother's accusations of selfishness—so painful to me growing up— immediately in the face of my gestures of caring. So as not to be guilty of the same, I decided to keep a list of the kindnesses Simon performed. I was still so afraid of asking for my due that I turned my new self-awareness into demands of myself, instead of Simon.

I was reluctant to broach the topic of my relationship with Simon in therapy, fearing that Craig would reject me once he witnessed yet another dysfunctional side of my life. But when Craig reassured me, "I'm in it for the long-term; I know that ADD involves ups and downs," I relaxed and truly trusted him. We began to discuss some of Simon's communication patterns, which, according to Craig, smacked of a kind of "gaslighting." Craig guessed this manipulation and obfuscation of the truth was designed to keep me in a weaker position.

Craig explained how dissociation from trauma could induce a kind of emotional anesthesia. A person subjected to enough abuse in childhood would turn off her sensory equipment in self-defense, in a quest to avoid pain. She would thereafter not even register slights that would disturb a healthy person. Early on in my relationship with Simon, he attacked me one night with egregious rage. I slept on the couch that night. In the morning, I told him if he ever screamed at me like that again, our relationship was over. To his credit, it was years before he again lost his temper to such a degree. But insults and cutting slights mixed with sweet nothings were routine elements of his communication.

I observed with growing concern that Simon was leaving to me the task of finding us a place to live for September. My lease ended at the end of August, and we had plans to find an apartment closer to campus, simultaneous with our engagement and Simon's beginning business school. Simon had agreed to rent out his waterfront condo and pay our rent with the income for the first six months, while I finished my courses.

Over many weeks, I reported on the assets and drawbacks of each apartment I viewed, yet Simon was dragging his feet about seeing most of them. I began to call Simon on his mixed messages and his intentions. Whereas he claimed to be too busy to see apartments, he had plenty of time for racquetball and art gallery openings.

At a coffee shop, I brought up the subject again. Simon burst out with, "If you bring this up again, I promise you, I'll drop you off on the sidewalk and you'll never see me again!" He got up to leave. I remembered being four or five years old in a restaurant. My parents were fighting loudly. Customers were turning their heads. My father stormed out and left us there; it happened too often. Other times my father would force my mother out of the car on the highway, and I would get out too—scared for my mother to be abandoned in the dark.

The next time I brought up the topic, Simon shouted at me, "If we have one more argument like this, so help me God, I'll spend the rest of the year in a hotel! I'll do the most trivial, insignificant, petty paperwork for business school before I'll do the most important thing for our relationship." Simon's threats, so much like my father's, were awakening primal memories and buried pain.

After six weeks of stonewalling, finally he told me: Simon intended to live by himself in an apartment in a building his mother and her partner bought and renovated near campus. I was livid. We argued through the night until we came to the following agreement: Simon would take his mother's place — too small for the two of us — for six months and cover my rent for six months, while I stayed where I was. In March, we would move together to someplace we both chose. I told Simon I would speak to him only in Craig's office, for the time being.

A few days later, before our first session with Craig, Simon called to say he had something to tell me he was sure I'd be happy about: he had signed a lease on a different property for the both of us. I was apoplectic. I couldn't believe that he would take a step so fundamental to my security without even asking me.

I told him I wanted to stay where I was, and I expected him to honor our agreement. He accused me of being strictly out to drain his wallet. He was furious with me for not being grateful. I was mortified that he was making decisions about my life and welfare without even consulting me. He claimed his decision was irrevocable and the only way he could get out of it would be to pay the owner many months of rent. And he would not pay my rent as well.

The next morning, with a bitter pill caught in my throat, I called Simon and thanked him for doing something, however disappointing, that he thought would please me. I got up, got dressed, and walked all the way to the address of the property that was to become my next home. I felt sick to my stomach. I was angry and disgusted that I was involved with a man who believed it was his right to play fast and loose with my welfare. I suddenly also wondered whether he was telling me the truth. I copied down the name and telephone number of the real estate broker on the "For Rent" sign and hurried home. Claiming to be somebody else, I called and discovered Simon had lied to me. No one had signed a lease on that property. It was still available.

I don't remember what Simon said in Craig's office. It is too painful to recall. It was something full of projection such as, "I don't owe you anything. I never promised you anything. You just want me to get cancer like my father keeping up with your spending habits." I finally realized that he had never intended to keep his word about getting married.

Grasping what the terms really were all along, and how stupid and blind I'd been, the spontaneous cry "You *whored* me, you *whored* me" shot from my innards like bile. I exploded in a paroxysm of tears. A geyser of emotion erupted from my depths that had been held at bay by a great hoax, a conspiracy of deceit.

Gallingly, however, Simon claimed, then and there, that he didn't want to break up—he wanted everything to stay the same. It was then that I confronted Simon with his lie. I told Simon that I knew he had never signed a lease on that second property. And that's when he uttered the fateful words that vaporized three and a half years of self-sacrifice and investment: "*I* didn't lie. You were *snooping*," he said. I finally realized I was involved with a budding sociopath: "I didn't *lie*. *You* were snooping." Three and a half years of compulsion ceased with a shocked inhale. Simon was a man who would not only lie to protect his interests, but would blame those who demanded ethics of him.

There was a terrible case in the news at the same time. The Delaware Valley's Craig Rabinowitz had murdered his wife and attempted to conceal it, when she was on the verge of discovering the thousands of dollars he had spent on a stripper. With a man who would portray his victim as a perpetrator, I realized I could be a victim too. I was filled with determination to get as far away from Simon as possible.

With my gangrenous wound cauterized, I never again dwelled on my rendezvous with Simon. My conviction was never keener. I have never looked him up on Facebook. His memory, rarely summoned, conjures only shame. I consider having gotten out of that relationship alive a great mercy of my Master.

I was alone with the wreckage of a year of calamity. I had no family or security to fall back on. The student loans I was living on would soon be due for repayment, and I would not be graduating this year, with six final courses to finish. Extricating myself from Simon's lies was the reward of building up my self-esteem through my work with Craig. My only wish was that I would have time and opportunity to complete my recovery. I still had hope that I could master the organizational techniques I was acquiring with my learning instructor and would fulfill the requirements for graduation, but I needed more time. That's when I decided to ask for help.

Part Three

On My Knees

And it shall come to pass on that day, that I will make Jerusalem a stone of burden for all the peoples...and all the nations of the earth shall be gathered together against it.

—Zechariah 12:3

Chapter 9

I didn't know what I was going to do. In a matter of seconds, my future had turned into a mirage. I had no doubts about the wisdom of leaving Simon. I knew my very safety was at stake. I wasn't yet able to make sense of how I'd gotten involved with him to begin with, let alone dedicated three and a half long years to him. The only thing that mattered to me now was finding a way to stay in school. Returning to full-time work—which my economic circumstances would now require—would mean saying goodbye to my bachelor's degree forever.

My performance that year at Latham continued to tantalize me with a sense of academic promise. Although I had failed to finish the semester because of the ADD, my grades surpassed those of many of my peers who nevertheless managed to finish. I was still in the midst of learning to remediate my disability. Months of working with Craig, Carrie, and Erica, my learning instructor, had yielded breakthroughs. I no longer felt like a bit of driftwood in a storm. Understanding where my limitations came from, I had reformed many habits. Yet the new belief in myself drove me to challenge Simon's deceit, undoing our "love." I was on the crest of a great redemption, if I could only keep going. I didn't know whether help could be found, but I was determined to look for it.

I made an appointment with Adele Chertoff, the director of the learning resource clinic, to ask her advice. Adele knew I had been working to master all I'd been taught by her staff, and she had witnessed my leadership role in HELP. Privately, I shared with her what I had endured with my father for my grandfather's sake, and the terrible mistake I had made getting involved with Simon. She glimpsed the fear and shame I felt over a future with no college diploma. Adele listened with compassion and summed up her assessment this way: "Miranda, you've helped a lot of people in your life. Maybe now someone can help *you*." She telephoned Linda Brewer, the associate vice provost, who recommended a meeting with Nina Musconi, head of the Latham University Women's Center. Nina assisted female students in crisis who did not have the support or resources to help themselves. Adele offered to telephone Nina to introduce me.

Nina Musconi and I met the following week in her Latham Women's Center office. It was a spacious office furnished in dark wood with arched, beveled windows overlooking the main pedestrian thoroughfare of Hamilton Lane. Two Victorian couches with quilted, velvet green upholstery faced each other, one abutting the edge of her massive desk. Nina's appearance didn't exactly fit the Victorian décor. She was a tall woman whose body resembled the shape of a spinning top—narrow at the face and ankles, yet portly in the middle. She wore slate-colored jeans with a black leather belt and brown hiking boots. Her hair was cut in a butch style reminiscent of a pencil eraser, with a longish blonde cornrow down the back of her neck offering a multicultural accent.

Nina took a yellow pad and pencil and settled into one of the couches, offering me the other one. "Now tell me why you've come," she said with a reassuring smile. Not knowing where to begin, I hesitated. She urged, "Really, Miranda, you can tell me everything that's happened to you. I have all afternoon to spend with you." Encouraged by her warmth, I bared the key betrayals in my life: father, brother, Simon, my grandfather's death at the hands of his own son. Although for once my mother's cruelty was not the key to my pain, Nina heard that my mother had been a devastating figure in my life. She understood that I was before her because I had nowhere else to turn.

It seemed as if Nina had had a premonition of my visit, as though I had come to her in a dream and confessed my life story once before. She seemed to understand everything I had been through better than I did myself. It did not surprise her at all that my father had managed to cast aspersions on me for the crime that he committed or that I had fallen for a man like Simon. She claimed my relationship with Simon was the natural culmination of a history of childhood neglect and exploitation. She explained that I chose a romantic partner who would re-evoke all the victimization of my childhood, and that this was to be *expected*: "That is how survivors of childhood trauma behave when they grow up," she said. "It is only natural that if safety, security, trust, and dignity were absent in your upbringing, you would allow those needs to be compromised again. We unconsciously gravitate to the same sorts of relationships as adults," she explained.

Evidently, I went through life with a deformed Fisher Price shape sorter, determined to grant clearance to the romantic partner who would hurt me exactly as my parents did. The *only* man who could unlock my heart had to be as selfish and abusive as they had been. Nina insisted that I was in this predicament because of the conditioning of my upbringing, not through any fault of my own. What impressed her was the bravery I had displayed in challenging the elder abuse that took the life of my grandfather. She commended me for waking up to Simon's manipulation and having the will and courage to walk away— for taking the first steps to free myself from a dangerous legacy.

"You must not think of yourself as a victim anymore," Nina said. "You are a survivor."

"But what do I do now?" I wondered weakly. Without the finances to finish my degree, I anticipated a lifetime of defeat. To pay back my student loans without even a bachelor's degree, I would have to work again as a secretary. How could I live with myself as a secretary? (*What self-respecting Jewish man would marry a secretary*, I thought to myself. *I was already thirty-two. If I didn't marry soon, I would never have a family.*) The shame of being a secretary wasn't mere vanity—it was my conscience whispering to me that I was capable of more. Yet I saw no way to pull myself out of debt and forge a future if I didn't graduate. Were I no longer enrolled in Latham, I would be ineligible for the coaching and therapy that were so crucial to overcoming my handicap.

Nina seemed energized by the challenge I faced. She explained that experiences of victimization such as I suffered leave survivors feeling helpless. In her view, putting me back in charge of my own destiny would foster my rehabilitation, while she offered to become my sponsor. "As Latham Women's Center director, I have the authority to pull together a package of university resources and support that will assist you to graduate—provided *you* fulfill your academic obligations," she said with a smile and a conspiratorial wink.

She told me to make up a list of the types of support I believed I would need in order to finish my final classes and to compile an estimated expense budget. She urged me to be frivolous and include anything that my heart ached for, and my wishes would be considered. She instructed me to identify which college personnel I would like on my support team. In September, she would invite the providers to a case conference committee meeting—which I could also attend if I chose—where duties would be assigned to the members, and the program would be approved for the next academic year.

While I would be completing my assignments, the rest of the support—educational, psychological, and medical—would come from those on the committee. Nina would manage the group and provide moral support. With the approval of the associate vice provost, she could even offer me free emergency housing in a dormitory room for the next academic year. She suggested I make up what she called my "wish list" and prospective budget before we met again in a few days.

With touching solidarity, Nina also offered to accompany me to Dr. Reznik and the Jewish Family & Children's Agency so that I could voice my disappointment over their abandonment of my grandfather. She believed that by doing so, I would regain my morale, bring closure to this tragic episode, and begin to heal. Feeling pity for how Simon had disparaged my clothing, she told me that the Women's Center had a small discretionary fund from which she could help me buy some new clothes, so that I wouldn't feel quite so conspicuously poor on the privileged, wealthy campus.

It was an extraordinary meeting that lasted more than four hours. I felt as if I had been debriefed and re-briefed: gone was my shame. Nina was committed to helping me restore my dignity and independence. Understanding that I had protected someone else at the very same time that I myself was being violated on two fronts, she was moved by my heroism, and I was moved by her faith in me. How could I have become so fortunate! She assured me that she had helped many students in positions such as mine, and that the university had a mechanism and funds earmarked for supporting students like me. "The Women's Center operates on a case-by-case basis, though, so I encourage you to keep our plans confidential," she said.

I left Nina's office elated that I been shepherded to an oasis. I knew that my wish list would be simple. Besides continuing to work with my learning instructor, campus psychiatrist, and keeping the student health insurance that would help subsidize Craig's fees, I asked for one "frivolous" item: to eat lunch at the

Latham Hillel House cafeteria. Working alone on my incompletes would be isolating. I felt self-conscious and lonely already being an older undergraduate without a natural peer group on campus. I believed that the campus Hillel might be a place to forge connections. Longing to draw closer to an observant Jewish life, I hoped that sitting next to students who kept kosher might allow their piety to rub off. And every penny I could save during what would need to be a time of austerity would relieve some pressure.

In my second meeting with Nina two days later, we were sharing the delight of a growing pact. I was overjoyed to be granted help by someone who believed in me. She was excited to be fostering the recovery of a grateful student. We reviewed my wish list, and Nina made notes of which personnel would provide the support and whom to invite to the case conference in September. She assured me that everything I asked for was relevant and appropriate. Examining my expense budget, Nina also suggested that I could use the Women's Center facilities for printing my academic assignments and photocopying library research. If the college would allow me to move me to a dormitory, she would store some belongings, as well as try to locate someone to adopt my two cats.

Nina informed me that she was going on vacation for a month. In the meantime, she directed me to meet with Victoria Russo from the financial aid department to assess the university's ability to help, and she gave me the forms to document my income, expenses, and debts. She told me to obtain two letters of recommendation from Latham faculty and to deliver them to Victoria with my application. She bid me farewell with a wink and a hug: "Miranda, don't worry. You're going to graduate. We're going to do this together." Nina instructed me to schedule a meeting with her in August for the week she returned.

Chapter 10

Unfortunately, as the adrenaline peaked and subsided along with the shock of my unexpected breakup, panic took its place. In the uncertain days following Nina's departure, my anxiety skyrocketed. None of her prospective plans to help me was set in stone, and my future felt utterly tenuous.

The terror of finding myself so betrayed by the person I had believed was my beloved and so vulnerable with no money, no degree, and no family to turn to for support erupted in my brain like a siren. Day by day, my body was breaking down. The gums of my teeth throbbed. My back and shoulders ached. My private parts were sore. I couldn't sit down without an ache in my womb and a keen discomfort in my pelvic region. I didn't know this at the time, but the perverse pain had to do with a sense of sexual betrayal. I had been lying with a man who had used me like a Kleenex, and I had been so blind to it. It was simply too much for my soul to bear. I was beyond panic: my prospects for survival seemed so dim that I saw no choice before me but to jump off the Tobin Bridge. Given my luck, I would survive that fall and be wheelchair-bound.

Despite myself, I had accepted my mother's calculus for self-worth: become a professional or my life had no value. What was I to do with thousands of dollars of Ivy League tuition debt and a forest of incompletes? My yearning to marry and build a family with the one man fate would declare irresistible had been so overpowering that I had mortgaged my soul. The simultaneous loss of my prospects for marriage and graduation brought down the house of cards. Yet I wasn't the type to hurt myself or even the type to threaten to. But I was frightened. Between panic attacks and a crush of somatic symptoms, I felt my body was imploding. I couldn't trust this vessel to carry me any longer. I didn't yet realize that history played a part in my terror. The pain of these circumstances and the strength of my reaction to them were profoundly magnified because the triggering incident closely mimicked something from the past about which I clearly had repressed pain: my father had tricked me in childhood in precisely the same way Simon had.

During the second of my parents' legal separations in my childhood, as a young girl of eleven, I was given the choice of which parent to live with. I chose to live with my father, who was neglectful but at least not abusive. While my memories of that year are vague, I recall being adopted by our Roman Catholic next-door neighbors. Since she was cooking for six children anyway, Mrs. Carmellini welcomed me to their table without paying me much mind. I spent many hours with Maria Carmellini, my age mate, and ate a lot of spaghetti. Sometimes my father didn't come home at night. I was too naive to realize that he was involved with women whom he at least had the decency not to bring home. I also didn't understand at that age that he had rented this house and then abandoned me to escape paying court-ordered child support.

After one lonely year, he announced that we'd have to move to a smaller apartment, as the lease was up for renewal and the house was just too expensive. I remember joining my father for several trips to inspect rental apartments, just as I had with Simon. I still remember the apartment we chose: a rustic flat with hardwood floors that had an unusual living room door opening into a winding staircase up to the second floor. I was my father's chattel, and I was prepared to be schlepped along.

My father told me I would have to go back to live with my mother for two weeks because of a gap between the end of the lease on the house and the beginning of the lease on the apartment. I didn't contemplate that he also needed somewhere to live during that gap.

My father promised to pick me up on Saturday in two weeks' time to move in. Leaving my belongings in boxes at my mother's, I spent as much time as I could at the homes of my friends Penny and Linda.

When I finally realized he wasn't coming for me at all that Saturday, I retched into the toilet at my friend Linda's house. My father just vanished. Nearly a year later, I learned that he had moved to a bachelor's apartment at the exclusive Waterside Place along the Mystic River. When he finally called me, through choking tears I cried, "Daddy, why did you trick me? Why didn't you come back for me?"

"Miranda, you never cooked and you never cleaned. How could you expect me to want to live with you?"

Returning to my mother's emotional menace was an even less desirable fate.

Back to the future: the mysterious venereal pain mixed with the panic I felt led me to schedule an appointment with the campus gynecologist, Dr. Madeline Fishbane. Dr. Fishbane, director of Latham Women's Health, was a compassionate Jewish woman who chose to work at a university precisely for the opportunity to treat a population in need of moral guidance as well as medical care. Lying back on her exam table, I was shaking. I did not know why I had pelvic pain or the other strange ailments I felt. When she asked me what brought me to her, my story tumbled out amid tears. After hearing about Simon, she asked about my family. When I told her of my mother's compulsive clothes shopping while she refused us money for food, she said, succinctly, definitively, "That's abuse." This was still surprising to me, as I had always thought abuse was what landed a child in an emergency room.

I must have looked like a textbook case to her: child abuse survivor grows up to be abused in adulthood. She told me the exam revealed no organic cause for my acute, constant pelvic throbbing, but she believed the pain represented a feeling of emotional injury of the most intimate kind. She told me about a program called Refuge at Bournewood Hospital that had been designed to treat adult survivors of childhood abuse, and she offered to recommend my admission to Amy Seidenfeld, director of Latham's student counseling service. Dr. Fishbane had done research with the founder of Refuge, Regina Folk, MD, and she believed the program would help me regain my equilibrium. Although I didn't yet know what was in store, I knew I needed help and I was prepared to go.

With Dr. Fishbane's recommendation, Amy Seidenfeld promised to facilitate my admission to Refuge, but she kept failing to follow through, necessitating call after call to beg her to do so. Without explanation, Amy forbade me to inform Robin Levine—my campus psychiatrist on her own staff—about plans for my hospital admission; therefore I felt particularly isolated by, beholden to, and dependent on Amy.

To bear the extreme insecurity and be able to complete the paperwork Victoria Russo, the college financial administrator, required from me, I took the vital step of hiring myself a daytime babysitter. Lisa was a friend and fellow philosophy major. For minimum wage, she agreed to spend her summer days with me in an improvised day hospital in my living room. I spent my nights migrating from couch to couch among friends. When I was alone, I fell into full-blown, hyperventilating panic attacks for the first time in my life.

I shared with Carrie, my Quaker learning instructor, the sudden wreckage of my life. "I must have been a horrible person in a past life," I wagered, shaking my head in disbelief.

She responded, "Miranda, I think now is the time you must start to pray."

I did a double take. "What, me, little Miri, talk to God? But I'm not even sure He exists. And even if He does, how could He possibly concern Himself with me and my troubles? And how do I address Him—with my slang, my stuttering, my *um*s and *y'knows*?"

"Miri," she reassured me, "just open your mouth and speak to God from your heart. He'll understand you." When another friend from my HELP advocacy team suggested I pray, a middle-aged African American Baptist who had raised herself from rural poverty to study nursing at an Ivy League university, I finally took note. (Ironically, prayer was simply not on the menu of my Jewish friends.) I couldn't deny being intrigued, however intimidating an idea it sounded. So I tried addressing God the way Carrie urged me to: I just asked for His help.

Thinking of God made me think of Samantha Chadry, the only professional astrologer I knew. Searching for answers to metaphysical questions of "Why me?" had led me to astrology's doorstep. I longed to understand why my family and I had endured so much and how to escape what seemed to be my blighted fate. I observed that the universe had order and that the movements of the heavenly bodies influenced events on earth. What lay behind them must be the guiding hand of a Higher Intelligence. Yet I was estranged from the Master, Who seemed to have singled me out for suffering. So I telephoned Samantha, the astrologer, with a plaintive cry, "What's *happening*?"

Samantha received my call warmly and offered to check for unusual transits affecting my life—that is, to see if the present movements of the planets were making any unusual contacts with the positions of the planets at my birth. After a few moments, she clucked her tongue knowingly and let out a long, musical sigh: "Yup, Miranda, you've got the transiting planet Pluto conjoining your natal moon in the second house, which squares practically every other planet in your chart. I'm sorry to say you're in for a very dramatic ride as Pluto travels back and forth over your moon for the next two years. The moon represents safety, nurture, the influence of our mothers. Your moon is deeply wounded as it is. The second house has to do with material resources and security. The moon in Sagittarius brings in higher education and spirituality. You will be forced to find alternative sources of material and spiritual nurture, as the well you've been drinking from is dry. We're talking about fundamental death and rebirth here. Accept any help you're offered, as it will be painful, but you'll come out of this passage stronger."

Vickie Russo, to whom Nina had referred me, accepted my application for financial aid. Meanwhile, she urged me to meet with Paula Ferguson, the Affirmative Action coordinator, to ask whether I might qualify for a scholarship given annually to a needy, learning-disabled student. Hearing my woeful tale, Paula explained gently why I was ineligible for the scholarship because of my age. But she took pity on me and invited me to join her and her daughter for a weekend at Nantasket Beach. I gratefully agreed with Samantha's message in my ears: "Accept any help you're offered." For a blissful two days, I escaped my anxiety as we rode aboard a fringe-topped surrey along the Nantasket boardwalk. We ate pancakes and French fries at a café, and I soaked up the warmth and humanity Paula offered.

Yet more than two weeks after Amy Seidenfeld had promised to arrange my admission to Refuge, I was still on the outside trembling with fear, and she was still dragging her feet. Day after day, she claimed that she just hadn't had the time to make the call, but she would "do it this very day." I felt tempted to thrust my hand through a window in order to demonstrate how badly I needed help. In bitter irony, I felt punished for coping. It was one of many surreal scenarios I would face in the months to come.

Chapter 11

I don't recommend admitting yourself to a psychiatric hospital unless you are very tough and very desperate. I was only the latter. When I finally got the green light, my friend Jacob dropped me off at Bournewood Hospital in Brookline, armed with a duffel bag of clothes and a spiral notebook I hoped would contain the instructions for navigating the rest of my life by the time I was discharged. Jacob Eisen was an old boyfriend eight years my senior, who had played a benevolent and protective role in my life since our romance ended. Without father, brother, or any other, I sometimes called on him for help. In his goodwill and caring, he always came to my aid. Unfortunately, I was still much too tormented to find someone as nice as Jacob a suitable object of long-term love and commitment.

When I first arrived at the Refuge Unit, I was ushered to an art therapy group led by a kindly older woman named Freda. Freda offered us crayons, white paper, and an invitation to express ourselves. I reached for the green crayon and, scribbling furiously, covered every square inch of the page. Next, I covered the entire page with black, utterly obscuring the green underneath. I thought the consummate pointlessness of my use of two colors might communicate the futility and despair that I felt. However, Freda opened the fascinating world of art therapy to me with a simple, wise interpretation: "Something's happened to you to make your world go black, but look at the life and health that's underneath, at the green that's at your core." I looked at her with grateful eyes, clinging to her message of hope.

Refuge was a two-week psychological boot camp for survivors of childhood trauma. Through immersion in a combination of expressive therapies and didactic classes, Refuge attempted to inoculate us survivors from mindlessly setting ourselves up for victimization again and again as adults. Throwing us together with other survivors would force us to practice the assertiveness we would need to keep ourselves safe on the outside. Other patients' life stories, mitigating our shame, would coax us to share and explore our own. I feverishly copied the words of every lecture promising to offer some logic to the madness I felt—from which I had not yet fully awoken.

Refuge was a misnomer for the place I spent those two weeks: I would more likely call it *reckoning*. With relentless confrontation, Refuge bombarded us with our complicity in the traumas we suffered: We were asleep. We didn't protect ourselves. We failed to say no. We longed for rescue and pinned our hopes on princes who turned out to be wolves looking suspiciously like our abusive parents when they alighted from their steeds. We were all caught in what I learned to call the "trauma triangle," a classic triad of perpetrator, victim, and rescuer that trapped survivors in its tortured cul-de-sac. New concepts such as "traumatic reenactment" (unconscious adult repetition of traumatic childhood events) entered my vocabulary and captured the eerie way Simon's deception over our moving in together had resembled my father's, decades before. The program was bracing and painful, yet vital to my recovery.

I felt a mixture of shame and relief learning that my behavior as an abuse survivor was stereotypical. My new peers were not privileged Ivy League pre-professionals but rather mostly working-class women, raped by their stepbrothers, molested by their fathers, and given vodka in their sippy cups by alcoholic, strung-out parents. I didn't mind. I tried hard to fit in, even searching in vain for the vaguest memory of molestation to burnish my image. I wondered, again, was my suffering genuine if I had not experienced the unspeakable?

Carrie, my Quaker learning coach, called the patients' pay phone one evening. Sharing my relief that I had found safe harbor, she averred, "Getting you to a safe place, Miri, is part of God's work in your life."

Every Refuge patient was treated to movie night during her stay: a double feature of Regina Folk's documentary about the physiological effects of domestic violence and Marilyn Von Derbur Atler's tale of recovery from the trauma of incest. Regina Folk's film filled me with aching sadness. Something that had always disturbed me was my difficulty remembering much of my childhood. I recalled being reared in a river of pain, yet the contours of my life were washed away by the rushing current. My foggy memories troubled me. They caused me to doubt my own convictions—given that my parents hotly denied my recollections of violence, abuse, and neglect.

Regina Folk's documentary explained why repression and memory loss were standard for a trauma survivor. According to Dr. Folk, experiences of abuse are stored in the brain and body without language—in pictures and sensations—which is why survivors often have nightmares and somatic pains. The brain's center for language processing shuts down in times of panic and trauma. This explained why Marcie, the psychodramatist, sent my emotions reeling every time she entered the unit, as the clack-clack-clack-clack-clack of her spiked heels on the linoleum viscerally evoked my mother's manic march. It also made sense of the decade of perpetual nightmares I suffered after ceasing any contact with my mother, nightmares that regularly climaxed with my mother choking me.

I knew that the childhood violence I witnessed between my parents had been searing. In my home, violence erupted whenever my mother's verbal and physical taunts broke the threshold of my father's indifference. She would hit him with my brother's baseball bat or throw frozen steaks at him as he lay on the couch with a newspaper over his face. As her insults built to their predictable crescendo, he would eventually get up to chase her—bloodying her nose or pummeling her while she screamed. Terrified, I would jump in, trying to pull my father off my mother.

How a borderline speaks to her intimates is simply corrosive. She will spout the most manipulative, humiliating vitriol designed to put you in a straitjacket from which you cannot emerge whole. But, if you're the victim and you're *not* a borderline, you cannot recall the words because you have blotted them out: unfair slurs such as "you *never*" and "you *always*," the most egregious guilt mongering, unjustified accusations of phantom sins, morbid threats, and foul-mouthed obscenities. A borderline's attack is a cruel stomp through the most unguarded underbelly of your soul.

When I was growing up, I cast my father as the victim. I pitied him, as he seemed wounded, weak, and vulnerable—the innocent target of my mother's ferocious assaults. (My brother and I took our turns before or after him on the sadistic carousel.) But it was dawning on me that he and she were a team. A man who abandons his children, murders his father while blaming his daughter, and batters successive wives is no saint. According to M. Scott Peck's seminal treatise on human evil, *People of the Lie*—a psychiatric examination of families in which children were abused—evil travels in pairs. Mothers and fathers each play an unholy role when children are sacrificed.

In one of the most memorable sessions at Refuge, I was invited to group therapy to create "trauma art." Carol, the therapist, instructed us to take five sheets of paper and to choose a particular traumatic incident from our lives. We were to begin by drawing a safe point before the trauma began, followed by a picture of the transition moments into the trauma, with a third, central picture depicting the traumatic incident itself. Then we were to draw the transition out of the trauma and conclude by illustrating the safe point after the trauma. This exercise would produce a kind of tragicomic strip.

I was determined to cooperate, yet I was paralyzed by the directions, which demanded from me what I couldn't provide. I kept telling Carol, "I can't remember a safe point. I can't remember a safe point!" She kept asserting there was one. I insisted there wasn't. We were stalemated, and I felt myself coming undone. I was panicked at the prospect of disappointing my would-be saviors—failing them felt like risking abandonment and courting death.

Eventually I thought of a way to remain faithful to my experience while fulfilling at least a part of her instructions. I drew only three pictures. The first showed my mother pregnant with me. She towered on stiletto heels, dragging on a cigarette clenched between fingers tapered with her signature false fingernails. I drew her face in profile as she refused eye contact, shooting a dragon's plume of smoke from her mouth.

The second picture was rather gruesome. My mother, rendered as an octopus, faced the viewer; and a small child—that would be me—was smothered defenselessly against her belly. Four of her tentacles were squeezing the life and breath out of me, and four of her tentacles sported razor blades that were flaying my bloody skin in a medieval torture. *Breathe, Miranda…* My final picture, "after the trauma," depicted me as a college sophomore, standing next to Charlotte Brenner, the psychologist who had met with my mother and identified the borderline, narcissistic, and histrionic personality disorders provoking her behavior. She was the first person to urge me to sever my relationship with my mother for my own survival. In this final picture, my belly—the site from which I'd wrenched my freedom—was an open cavity, and my bloody innards lay strewn across the floor. *Breathe some more, Miranda...* Creating these pictures was agony, but I only realized the toll it took on me the following day.

Every morning in a community meeting, we patients sat in a big circle and followed the following formula: "*Good morning, my name is Kelly, and I feel real bad today. My goal for the day is to try not to cut myself...*" As I sat there waiting my turn, I saw a strange, silver, wiggly creature that looked like a centipede in my right eye's field of vision. I kept shaking my head to chase it away, but it refused to go.

As we broke for our first group therapy of the day, I began to feel the sensation of an ice pick plunging into my left temple. I stumbled my way to the group therapy session and sat hunched over, feeling assaulted by the ice pick and unable to open my eyes. I was ordered to open them and participate. I begged to go to my room. The therapist began to berate me: "Miranda, you had better cooperate, or we'll be shipping you home. We don't fall for this crap." Eventually, to be rid of my moaning, she gave me permission to leave the group.

I lay on my bed writhing in pain. I called for the nurse and pleaded for a painkiller. She refused, telling me I had better shape up and get to group. I wailed, but she told me there was no use faking it. No one was buying it: "We've seen every kind of performance before, and you aren't winning an Emmy. *Get to group!*" she commanded.

I remained in my room thrashing about on my bed for hours. I couldn't open my eyes without a blinding discomfort, and I didn't know why. With the change of shift in the afternoon, a new head nurse came to investigate. I was still moaning softly in my bed, asking for some medication. She told me to sit up and open my eyes. I managed to sit up, but as I did so, everything in my belly shot forcefully out of me, decorating the wall, the carpet, and the head nurse with whatever was left in my stomach from breakfast. It was at that point that the staff realized I wasn't acting. The nurse gave me an injection of Demerol for pain, and I fell mercifully asleep until the morning.

The next day, I met with my doctor, Kendra Lamont, who told me I'd had a particularly bad migraine. "What's a migraine?" I asked. She believed the episode had to do with the pictures I had drawn the day before. "Miranda, your biggest *reenactment* has to do with rescue. That's why your safe point showed you with your therapist. You should have been rescued from what you were suffering in your childhood, but you weren't. No one is going to rescue you anymore. You have to rescue yourself."

According to Dr. Lamont, I had many of trauma's hallmarks: I had poor boundaries. I failed to protect myself. In a typical example, a male patient became preoccupied with me, coming uncomfortably close to stare at me while I talked to female patients. The women started to tease me about him. Yet instead of telling him to leave me alone, I endured the discomfort, tried to ignore him, and hoped that he would give up for lack of encouragement. Instead, he became emboldened by my passivity.

Sometimes I would listen to others' tales of childhood abuse and become overwhelmed when my own memories and feelings started to emerge.

"Miranda, you can't live your life in flashbacks," chided Dr. Lamont.

"You mean I shouldn't listen?"

"Your first duty is to yourself. You can't allow yourself to be flooded with other people's pain all the time."

She introduced me to the novelty of checking with myself and then excusing myself with "I'm sorry, I can't listen right now," when I felt my equilibrium undermined by others' confessions.

"You will be worried a lot about hurting other people's feelings, Miranda, but you must endure this discomfort while you learn how to protect yourself," she said.

According to Dr. Lamont, I tended to rescue others, starting with my own parents and brother, progressing to friends, my grandfather, Simon... I was always repairing or taking care of others, both the eager and the reluctant, hoping that in the process of civilizing my family or consoling friends, I might receive the succor and the expiation from misplaced guilt that I craved. I attempted to meet my needs through meeting the needs of others—which left me wide open to exploitation. Simon provided the precise elixir for my soul: union with a man of the character of my parents, who pretended to seek reform and redemption through a relationship with me.

According to Dr. Lamont, I was also a great intellectualizer: I used my powers of analysis to escape feelings of anger and sadness. Child of a vengeful, violent mother, I had swallowed my temper for thirty years, becoming numb to my own feelings. Now that the cork had finally popped, my feelings poured forth so furiously that I feared my own aggression for the first time in my life. The anger swallowed for three decades was coursing through my veins like wildfire.

I had been in denial about Simon's anger, too. Like many abuse survivors, I refused to accept the evidence of his hostility. Threatened by his rage, I had persuaded myself that he really felt insecure and his anger was just a front. I imagined Simon was like me and felt fear when he did not: he just felt rage. Under my loving tutelage, Simon would learn to lay down his guard, I had thought. Intoxicated by the opportunity to humanize a man so much like my parents, I took Simon's tenderness and solicitation as signs of his transformation, rather than a veneer Simon flaunted to keep me hooked and giving. I had deluded myself about Simon to forestall my greater fear of loneliness—although I hadn't the courage to admit it. After three and a half years of symbiosis, I couldn't allow myself to conjure his memory. I was simply too shocked and too ashamed.

Part of the purpose of the creative therapy groups at Refuge was to evoke our feelings in a safe, controlled way, so that we could experience them without losing ourselves. Toward the end of my stay, I sampled the power of psychodrama to get to the root of a person's wound. Whereas I thought my present panic came from the worry that I'd never graduate college if I couldn't stay in school to complete my degree—and that would spell *d-e-a-t-h*—the psychodrama arranged for my benefit elicited a surprising acknowledgement from deep within my soul. Marcie, the psychodramatist, cast other patients as my father and a skeptical social worker. She threw a blanket over a third patient to represent my beloved grandfather. At the height of my wailing over my grandfather's death, *"YOU KILLED HIM, YOU KILLED HIM,"* amidst a fountain of cathartic tears, Marcie had the audacity to shout, "But what about your incompletes?"

"You have a hole inside of you so big the state of Texas couldn't fill it, and it doesn't matter if you ever finish your incompletes!" came the bellowing cry from my innards.

Refuge staff tried to warn me that it might be unwise to insist on finishing my degree right now, after a hospitalization and the rupture of a dam holding back a sea of repressed memories and pain. I had just begun to acknowledge the shambles of my soul. Perhaps I ought to postpone finishing my courses until I was farther along the road to healing, they suggested.

Yet I was too shattered to entertain a change in plans. In my mind, obtaining my degree was my sole stake in a normal future.

Everything else had been reduced to rubble. A middle-aged Jewish woman without a college diploma, never mind a career, was barely a prospect for stocking the shelves at Kmart, let alone social respectability and marriage. I felt devoid of any value without a career. If I didn't finish my classes now while the material was still fresh and I had supportive connections at the university, I feared I never would.

One morning, a Refuge nurse remarked innocently, "You look so bright today, like you're ready to go home."

"I'm just beginning to enjoy it; I'm not going anywhere," I snapped. "Besides, I have no place to go."

"Enjoy it?" she asked skeptically.

"Well," I hedged, "I'm just starting to feel comfortable…to feel…safe."

Her comments jarred me. I realized I would not be spending my life in a fishbowl indefinitely contemplating the repercussions of the past. Soon, I'd be back to navigating the dangers of the present.

Dr. Lamont informed me it was time to plan for my discharge. She warned me that everything in my body would scream, "I'm not ready," but she urged me to plan my aftercare while I was still on the inside, where staff could support me.

Dr. Lamont chided, "You are still living in your trauma art. You torment yourself the way your mother used to. Everything about how you live today is perpetuating your pain: the self-deprivation, the self-denial, the fear of rocking the boat and honoring your wants and needs. You must send yourself a strong message deep down that you are not in your childhood home anymore. Show yourself through deeds that you have survived. The best thing you could do for yourself is to rebuild your life: find a job, find money for school, find people to live with. Convince yourself through your actions that you are not helpless.

You have strength and resources to protect and care for yourself."

One proposal fraught with the dangers of traumatic reenactment was an offer by Paula Ferguson to board with her and her teenage daughter, Jennifer, for the year while I completed my academic work for Latham.

"I think they take in strays," I confided to Dr. Lamont.

Dr. Lamont cautioned me against adopting the identity of a stray. Although she heard my wistful wish to convalesce in the bosom of *someone's* family, she warned me that Paula could never provide the mothering I truly needed. Both of us were wary of this apparent godsend. I would find out soon enough how sober my instincts were.

After my discharge, Paula invited me to join her and Jennifer for dinner at their home. During the meal, her daughter took offense at something her mother said. Jennifer lunged across the table and with a sweep of her arm knocked three bowls full of hot soup onto the floor. Paula sat there helplessly looking to me for protection. After her daughter stormed out of the dining room, Paula confided to me that her own alcoholic former boyfriend had carried on a secret sexual liaison with Jennifer for months. Everything in their lives was a mess. I was still too dissociated to be able to feel anything in the face of her daughter's aggression, but at least I had the self-preservation to smell a rotten deal when I was offered one. However well-intentioned Paula was, she ultimately proved to be feeble in her role as an advocate for Latham's learning-disabled students. I could only imagine how she would have fared as a housemate in a home so lacking in boundaries.

With the staff's encouragement, I began making phone calls to reconnect with my contacts from Latham University—to knit some net of support beneath me. I hoped Craig Cohen would play a crucial role. His wisdom and encouragement had already catalyzed such a healthy revolution in my life. Yet my panic and need for hospitalization had shocked both of us. Although I never hid my family history from Craig, neither of us understood how deeply I'd been scarred, until I lived through a traumatic reenactment with Simon. Whereas Craig had signed on to help me with my ADD, he hadn't necessarily opted to be my lifeline while recovering from a crisis. I asked Craig tremulously over the phone whether he would continue to treat me after discharge.

"Well, of course I will, Miranda! But why would you doubt it?" he exclaimed in surprise—the warmth in his voice conveying all the reassurance I needed. I heaved a huge sigh of relief, knowing that at least I had an excellent therapist who believed in me in my corner.

Next, I placed two calls to Nina Musconi. Both times her secretary asked me to wait on the line, yet came back to tell me that Nina was unavailable. I left my phone number at Refuge, asking her to call me back, to no avail.

Vickie Russo reassured me over the phone that she was simply waiting for Nina to call the case conference to authorize the additional student loans the college was willing to provide, to enable me to remain a Latham student. I was deeply grateful and hopeful that I might yet pull this SOS plan together.

Refuge staff gave me the phone numbers of agencies that could provide support after discharge, such as Women About Change and Women Organized Against Abuse. They told me that Women About Change provided a two-year-long series of classes designed to teach the habits needed for healthy self-reliance to survivors of childhood abuse. I was eager to sign up. I wore my badge as a member of this benighted club with a mixture of shame and exhilaration: at least I belonged somewhere.

I checked into Refuge in shock. I left chastened but sober. Despite appearing the princess in the beginning—falling apart because my boyfriend had jilted me—I had the begrudging respect of the staff by my discharge. I heard their warning. I understood the dangers of my past, and I was determined to free myself from its clutches. Barely able to contemplate the mistakes I'd made with Simon for all the shame that welled up inside me, I threw myself into the quest for survival.

Chapter 12

My campaign to keep myself afloat and finish college began with admitting that I could no longer afford the one-bedroom apartment I had rented for four years with my two cats. The one item Nina Musconi didn't promise me was dormitory housing at the university. I couldn't bear the uncertainty over where I would live and stay calm. I immediately sent a letter to my landlady informing her I would be terminating my lease and set about finding cheaper quarters. The hunt for a decent but affordable apartment focused my rattled nerves. I lived in a part of the city with property dating back to the 1700s, and in happier times, I had enjoyed exploring the interiors of the vast array of romantic colonial architecture.

I had a stroke of good fortune when I stumbled upon Timothy Creadle's gabled brownstone building on a lovely street off Latham Square. The apartment available in the basement was tiny: one small, square room with a coat closet and a short corridor leading to a bathroom. Yet the apartment was functional and had lots of charm: a private gated entrance, two large domed windows, built-in shelves in the walls, sliding door storage along the corridor, and glamorous vanity light bulbs surrounding the bathroom mirror. The tenant even had the use of the laundry facilities in the basement. It was cozier than any studio I'd seen and, at more than a hundred dollars a month cheaper, an incredible bargain.

The only sticking points were my cats. Timothy insisted, "No pets." To say I begged is an understatement. I pleaded. I even stooped to bribery. With a deposit, Timothy agreed to let me keep one of my cats. Faced with "Sophie's choice," I did the unthinkable: I gave Ivory back to my ex. We had rescued Ivory from the double yellow lines of a highway during a bike trip, and he got his name from the dishwashing liquid we used to cleanse him of motor oil from his brush with becoming roadkill and his pristine fur once he was washed clean.

When Simon came to pick up Ivory, a poignant slapstick ensued: I came down the steps to deliver Ivory to Simon, weeping tears of self-pity, indignation, and shame. However, Ivory leaped from my arms and bounded back up the stairs into my apartment. Simon had on occasion been cruel to Ivory, and the cat was no sucker. After the third fruitless trip down the stairs with the cat—still refusing to make eye contact with Simon—I remembered to close the door behind me first, trapping Ivory on the outside. Giving up Ivory was hard, but I had adopted Honey from an animal shelter with forethought and intention. I had pledged to give Honey a home for life, and I was truly attached to her.

My earlier attempts to find emergency resources for Jews in Boston had proven Kafkaesque. The Jewish Family Service of Boston featured a twenty-four-hour crisis intervention hotline, connected to an answering machine. Neither of my attempts to contact them fetched a human response. A few days after leaving my third or fourth anguished message, I finally received a call from a social worker. After listening to my story over the phone, she concluded, "You sound too resourceful" and told me I would be ineligible for help. My desperate efforts to hold myself together were being turned against me to justify denying me any help. *Would I have to commit an unthinkable act of violence against myself or someone else to have my troubles taken seriously*, I had wondered at the time.

Despite this exasperating rejection, I summoned the courage to call the Jewish Crisis Line again after my hospital discharge. This time the same social worker approved a grant of my first month's rent of $410.

Following Nina's guidance, I had consulted with Vickie Russo about the university's willingness to help me financially, supported by character references written by Craig Cohen and Gaby Rakover, my Judaic studies professor. In a meeting with Vickie after my discharge, she proposed a plan to maintain my Latham student status by retroactively withdrawing me from two classes from the previous fall and reregistering me for those same classes for the upcoming academic year, a plan requiring the approval of my college dean. In the meantime, she advanced me a loan of a few thousand dollars I had unknowingly left in my student account by living frugally during the past year. If approved, her plan would require me to accept nearly ten thousand additional dollars in student loans, but allow me to remain enrolled at Latham for the next year, preserving all of the associated benefits. Some of these, such as free treatment by my campus psychiatrist, were crucial to my well-being. I accepted the extra financial burden with the expectation that the rest of the support Nina Musconi had offered would follow.

During the time I waited for Vickie to get back to me with the dean's answer, I did everything I possibly could to provide for myself. After signing a lease on the studio, I placed ads in the *Boston Herald* to sell all my belongings except my kitchen table, my bed, and my computer. I sold the fruits of almost two decades of economic self-support: furniture, stereo, appliances, jewelry, guitar, artwork, clothing, records, and books. In two nine-hour street sales in front of my building, assisted by Jacob Eisen and a friend from Refuge, I netted more than $1600 in cash. If I could come up with the funds to live on while I finished my incompletes, I could finally conclude the undergraduate chapter of my life at age thirty-three and move on.

Although I had never turned to friends for financial help before, now seemed to be the time and place. I felt myself in a struggle for survival, and I hoped my closest friends could be called upon to help. Yet when I asked my two closest friends for loans, I observed something surprising, which I attributed at the time to *tribal* loyalty. Neither of my two closest friends was Jewish. Allyson Picker was a physician whom I began working for at Boston Children's Hospital in 1984. We became the closest of friends, and I spent many hours supporting her through romances, as well as professional and family crises, over the years. I traveled across town at my own expense to take care of her cats whenever she left town for medical conferences, helped her move several times, and had taken care of her infant son for negligible pay. I had been a loyal friend for thirteen years. She had since moved to Nashville with her husband and son, and we kept in regular touch. It never occurred to me that she would refuse to loan me money, but she did. And I never heard from her again.

My best friend Phoebe from Latham was a non-Jewish housewife of a Jewish investment banker, now living in a big home outside Los Angeles. I'd given her hours and hours of support and encouragement, some during a protracted sexual harassment case she had brought against a supervisor at the workplace where we met. Our years of friendship included lots of practical support: flying across the country to be her maid of honor and schlepping to rural Maine alone by train to accompany her to the funeral of her estranged father. My devotion, I felt sure, would earn Phoebe's help in my time of need. Though she lived in what I thought was luxury, Phoebe offered me $500 and hung up the phone when I protested that wasn't enough. In the end, she sent nothing, and five months passed before she even called me again.

However, my two longtime but casual Jewish friends volunteered to help. I would never have dreamed of asking them for loans, because I hadn't done nearly as much for them. Barbara was an unmarried environmental educator with a low-salaried public service job in DC, and she sent me $1000 of her hard-earned savings. Jacob also came through with a couple thousand dollars. Even my professor, Gaby, and his wife offered to pay my rent until I got back on my feet, though I was too ashamed to accept their kindness. The whole experience gave me my first taste of the sweetness of the Jewish soul.

What gave me the chutzpah to pursue (almost) every possible avenue for financial aid? Nina Musconi had reassured me that I could count on her and the other Latham University personnel to provide a safety net of academic and psychological support as I finished my incompletes, while Dr. Lamont at Refuge had convinced me that I would recover from this setback only through my own efforts. I was determined to set the stage for finishing my degree.

Yet when I got out of the hospital, that's when the earth really began to crumble beneath my feet.

Chapter 13

E vidently, "One whom God loves, He crushes with suffering" (Babylonian Talmud, *Berachot* 5a).

I was apparently a sinking vessel—only I myself didn't yet know it—therefore, my entire crew scrambled to jump ship. Without warning or giving me any time to adjust, Robin Levine, MD, terminated my campus psychiatric supervision at our first meeting after my hospital discharge. Robin had been my student counseling service psychiatrist since well before my diagnosis with ADD six months before. She was caring and competent, and we had a good working relationship. Robin had seen me through the waves of disorientation following my diagnosis and the jittery, discomforting trials of Ritalin. She prescribed my monthly antidepressants, and because I was enrolled at Latham, her care was free.

Although Amy Seidenfeld, the director of the counseling service, knew that plans were underway to preserve my Latham enrollment, nevertheless, she instructed Robin to terminate my treatment. Robin herself had warned me about the danger of leaving a critical situation to go to a hospital, only to return to the same crisis afterwards. But she hadn't told me that I was liable to be bereft of all the support I had come to depend on.

Next to forsake me was Craig Cohen, my faithful cognitive-behavioral therapist with whom I had forged such a warm and therapeutically effective bond—the very person who had written the Latham financial aid department an earnest letter of reference praising my motivation, discipline, and character only four weeks before.

Although he had reassured my Refuge discharge coordinator and me that he would be happy to continue treating me, in our first appointment, a day after my hospital discharge, Craig insisted that I was not seeking cognitive-behavioral therapy anymore. He claimed he was unable to provide the services I needed and made vague references to "character issues" that sounded ominous. I countered that I *was* seeking cognitive behavioral therapy: our hard work cultivating my self-discipline had raised my self-esteem—giving me the will to end a humiliating relationship with Simon, beyond the gains we had made in mitigating the effects of my ADD. Craig's services were exactly what I needed because they had proven so effective.

When I tried to explain to Craig the precise events in my family history that had erupted in the traumatic reenactment with Simon, Craig refused to let me speak. He barked at me: "Cognitive-behavioral therapy DOES NOT ADDRESS THE PAST!" I was gobsmacked. Craig's body language and demeanor telegraphed a sudden, unprecedented contempt for me. Yet he denied his change in attitude, insisting that he was just looking out for my interests.

We remained at this inexplicable impasse for ten sessions strung out over three months. In these sessions, Craig insisted that I would not benefit from cognitive-behavioral therapy—I insisted that I already had. I accused Craig of having contrived a false and sinister hypothesis about me. Craig denied anything of the kind. Every time I tried to explain the circumstances of my hospitalization, Craig wouldn't allow me to talk about it.

Why did I stick around and submit to ten sessions of persecution and obfuscation? I wanted justice. I wanted to be acquitted of whatever phantom crime Craig was punishing me for, and I was not willing to slink away in shame that was not mine. I was also motivated by self-interest and appreciation. I was supremely grateful to Craig for providing me his formula of the three goals on the answering machine. He had revolutionized my self-esteem with this uncommon sacrifice of his privacy beyond the fifty-minute hour. Our work together had restored order to a life torn by ADD and trauma. Together we had witnessed rapid gains in my well-being, and I knew we were a powerful team. I wasn't willing to be deprived of his help so fast.

But I was suffering profoundly from his double-talk: renouncing his commitment to treat me after my discharge, yet denying my allegations that his demeanor toward me had fundamentally changed. Craig was doing everything possible to get me to quit treatment—including repeatedly canceling our sessions on the day of my appointment, refusing to reschedule, and communicating in every facial expression and gesture his downright disdain for me.

Finally, after three months, Craig consented to hear me out about why I had needed hospitalization. He threatened to discontinue my treatment immediately if my explanation didn't meet with his satisfaction. This "trial" was utterly humiliating, but I was driven to be vindicated. When I told Craig just a few of the details of my family background that had foreshadowed the incident with Simon, he murmured remorsefully while shaking his head, "I didn't know. I didn't know. I guess in retrospect you have been trying to tell me." And then he disclosed the kind of assumption that I suspected lay behind his unspoken rebuke: "I assumed you had fabricated the trauma and hospitalized yourself to manipulate the university and your friends for money to take care of you, since it was clear Simon wasn't going to."

At this point he explained to me, by way of contrition, that—having mulled over the trepidation in my voice with which I had asked him just before my discharge from Refuge whether he would continue to treat me—he had concluded that evidence of character pathology must have been uncovered at Refuge: otherwise, why would I have been worried? He never thought to check his outrageous and foolish assumption with the staff at Refuge.

While it was undeniably satisfying to have my belief confirmed about Craig's change in attitude, this didn't undo the damage. I had fallen into a grave depression from the pain of the rejection I had suffered since my discharge from Refuge. In the few sessions following my "trial," Craig's demeanor toward me softened. Yet he seemed unable to appreciate the toll his betrayal had taken on me. He was unsympathetic to my difficulty in pulling myself out of bed in the morning. Sleeping had become my anesthetic against sadness, fear, anger, and loneliness— though it only increased my isolation. With no support and the pain of mistreatment, I had lost the will to fight.

Craig never said the words I longed to hear that might have begun to restore the trust between us, such as "I'm sorry." He offered nothing in compensation, though I had now used more than half of my twenty annual insurance-subsidized therapy sessions protesting his undeserved incrimination. Our therapy couldn't begin again until that false guilt had been wiped away. When Craig callously canceled once again on the day of my treatment, I concluded I had to find a new therapist for the few sessions I had left.

While I was livid with Craig, my anger concealed a broken heart. In the months before my personal life unraveled, Craig and I had touched each other on a human level. He had seen me as a student utterly determined to overcome her handicaps, and I had blossomed with his wise and skilled care. I could not have been a more devoted and disciplined client, who gave her therapist those rarest of rewards: immediate improvement and a heap of gratitude. And yet, he'd betrayed me. He allowed baseless suspicions to poison his regard for me. And I was deeply, deeply hurt.

The mockery his behavior made of the principles of cognitive therapy was not lost on me.

I wrote him a very angry letter when I said goodbye. I accused him of committing many of the cognitive errors he taught me to avoid, such as "jumping to conclusions," "ignoring the evidence," "blaming," and "shouldisms." I urged him to examine his sense of invincibility, accountability, and the appropriate use of the power vested in him when he is contracted by a patient in pursuit of her mental health. When he read the letter, he was stunned, but he still didn't say, "I'm sorry." In fact, he refused to say anything, insisting, "Since the therapeutic trust has been irrevocably broken between us, there is no point in my saying anything at all."

"I think that's disgusting," I spat, as he sat impassively, unwilling to express a shred of remorse for his behavior. I walked out of his office into a void far lonelier.

But the most ironic and astonishing turn came from Nina Musconi, the self-appointed savior of trauma victims on the Latham University campus. I had called Nina twice from Refuge and twice since I had come home, and sent emails. I received a dull, dead silence. On September 5, two weeks after my hospital discharge, I entered Nina's office for an appointment secured through her secretary. With breath as cold as the gust from an opened meat locker, Nina began the meeting with a faux naive "What brings you here?" as though we had never met before.

I responded, astonished, "I want to continue where we left off!"

She asked cautiously, "What does that mean?"

I reminded her of her plan to lead a case conference to establish support for me in my quest to finish my bachelor's degree, the Women's Center resources she had volunteered to contribute, and her offer of moral support to help me express my grievance over the abandonment of my grandfather. But she retracted every offer of advocacy.

Nina asked about my hospitalization in a suspicious tone and furrowed her brow at my answers, chiding me, "I never heard that from *other* students we referred to Refuge." She started to speak about me in the third person, beginning a sentence, "People who have been sexually abused..." While I had neither suffered nor alleged sexual abuse by anybody *ever*, I did not speak up at this point to say so. Frankly, I didn't think she would believe me, and I didn't trust her with any more personal confessions, since her attitude toward me had so clearly changed. I felt shocked, unsafe, and on trial—for what, I did not know.

Nina was evasive about convening a case conference on my behalf. She refused to consult the wish list or budget she had asked for, which we had reviewed in our previous meeting. She wouldn't accompany me to the doctor and social workers who had failed my grandfather so that I could achieve a healing "closure"—in her own words. She denied that she had offered me the help of the Latham Women's Center with clothing or copying or storage of my belongings, if the college would grant me housing. She claimed I never asked to eat lunch at the campus Hillel, although the item was on my wish list in black and white, flanked by her corroborating handwriting. I left her office reeling and disoriented. What had I done wrong?

When I learned that Nina had canceled a follow-up meeting I had scheduled with her for the following week, I complained to Sophia Sanchez, the associate director of the Latham Women's Center. "I can't help you because I'm not privy to what Nina offered you, but I'll convey your concerns to Nina," Sophia said.

Persevering, I met with Nina a second time in mid-September. I told her that Paula Ferguson from Affirmative Action had offered to call a case conference on my behalf, if Nina was unwilling to. Nina was angered by my persistence. When I asked her to refer me to someone else at the university who could provide victim support and empowerment counseling, she said, "I am the only person charged with that mission at Latham."

By the end of the meeting, Nina agreed to call a case conference, but she insisted she had no idea when it would occur. She claimed it was very difficult to get such a group of people together and warned me it could be a month or two before the conference would take place.

I reminded her that back in July, she had encouraged me to select the attendees, submit requests, and attend the meeting myself, in order to restore the sense of self-control that she insisted was robbed by my victimization. Since I had come up with financial resources of my own after our first meetings—by moving to a studio, selling my property, and borrowing money from both friends and the university—I asked for her permission to submit a new budget and the names of those I wished to attend. I wanted new facts reflecting my self-improved circumstances to be the basis for the meeting. Nina agreed to wait for my materials and to inform me of the meeting's date so that I could be present. She insisted we had nothing to talk about until after the case conference met and dismissed me with barely disguised hostility.

Before leaving, I asked Nina to tell me why her attitude toward me had changed so completely and why she had retracted her promises of assistance. She answered, "You went to a hospital." Flabbergasted, I asked, "What has that got to do with anything?!" She paused for a moment and said, "I sensed you would have expectations of me that I couldn't fulfill." I said, "I only expected you to do what you said you would do."

Less than three business days later—while I was in the middle of composing a personal statement to distribute at the meeting—Nina called and left a message informing me that the case conference had already taken place, and she wanted to inform me of the results. As I listened to the message, some of the somatic symptoms that distressed me before my hospitalization returned, including the mysterious pelvic pain. My body registered the threat Nina posed to my well-being; my heart was filled with misgivings.

Receiving me icily in her office a few days later, Nina informed me that I had been granted four main benefits at the Latham University case conference. Amy Seidenfeld had designated a counseling service psychiatrist to take the place of Robin Levine, MD, who would supervise me once a month— Phillip Yeager, MD. Paula Ferguson agreed to arrange a Hillel House lunch plan; Nina told me that university funds had already been allocated for it. Involved as she was servicing the needs of the learning-disabled at Latham, Paula was tasked with providing emotional support to me during the year. Knowing that the unstructured time without formal classes posed a particular challenge to a student newly diagnosed with ADD, Adele Chertoff, director of Tutoring and Learning Resources, volunteered to supervise my work with a new learning instructor to help me stay on schedule and finish my coursework. Finally, Rabbi Benjamin Farber, the executive director of the campus Hillel, had offered $300 from an anonymous student charity fund to help me buy some clothes for going back to school.

I was so moved by Rabbi Farber's kindness that I wept. Nina responded with surprise, "What, this *touches* you?" as though she had concluded that I wasn't truly needy, but only grasping, and wouldn't be capable of feelings of gratitude. Nina told me that she was the manager to whom everyone reported; it was her job to make sure that I received the support pledged by each of the case conference members.

Chapter 14

I cannot convey how ruinously Nina failed in her mission without describing the stonewalling, humiliation, and abandonment in all their excruciating detail. Dr. Yeager, the student counseling service psychiatrist, called to inform me that he would only treat me as long as I did not require any change in my psychiatric medication. What was the use of consulting with a psychiatrist who refused to treat my condition? I complained repeatedly by telephone to Amy Seidenfeld, the clinic's director—the same woman who had unconscionably delayed my Refuge admission. After a month of promises by Amy to straighten things out with Dr. Yeager, and no results, I turned to Nina Musconi, whose job it was to see that I received the benefits I was granted. Nina dismissed me with "I think you ought to solve your own disputes."

Eventually, I wrote to Amy Seidenfeld, protesting that treatment by a psychiatrist who won't adjust or change my medication is hardly better than no treatment at all. Finally, she informed me that Dr. Yeager had agreed to adjust my medication as needed. I met with Dr. Yeager for the first time on October 29, more than two months after my first and only discharge from a psychiatric hospital and the abrupt termination by Robin Levine, MD.

Because the dramas with Nina and Craig had unfolded simultaneously, I was so fearful of confessing one's disposition to the other—for fear of giving either of them the impression of a colleague's rubber stamp—that I suffered both of their rejections with no one to support me at all. Although I was already quite depressed, Dr. Yeager urged me to "grieve my losses" and refused to medicate my condition. During our second and third monthly meetings in November and December, I contended that I was suffering a growing clinical depression and needed an increase or change in my medication. Dr. Yeager advised me to wait at each consultation; he would not change my medication. His neglect compounded the profound stress I was facing, and I grew more critically depressed.

Paula Ferguson caught the same virus as Amy Seidenfeld, whose chief symptom was compulsively false promising, in this case, to arrange the Hillel cafeteria lunches. After six weeks had passed, my stomach and social life were still empty. I complained to Nina Musconi, who again refused to get involved. I emailed Paula one final time in early November. Two days later, she wrote, "Nina Musconi is now arranging the Hillel lunch plan and will be calling you soon."

I waited for Nina's call, which never came.

But the cruelest form of torment Nina reserved for the clothing money donated by Rabbi Farber. First, Nina told me I could pick up the Hillel check for $300 from her secretary any time after September 25. She instructed me to collect receipts as I spent the money and return them to her for her files. When I came to the Women's Center on September 29, there was no check; her secretary knew nothing about the matter.

When Nina—stalling further—changed her mind and told me to pay for the clothing with my own money, claiming she would reimburse me afterwards, I stretched the donation as far as I could by visiting secondhand shops. Two weeks later, I gave Nina receipts for approximately half the money. She promised a reimbursement check would arrive at my home within two weeks and asked me to call her when the check arrived. A month later, I began leaving messages with her secretary to say I had not received the reimbursement check or her expected call about the Hillel lunches.

With no check, no Hillel House lunch vouchers, and negligent psychiatric supervision, in a face-to-face meeting at the end of November, I read Nina a letter outlining my difficulty focusing on my academic studies while I had to run my own crisis intervention program with nothing but neglect by the various providers, reflecting Nina's abdication from the top. Nina again refused to intervene on my behalf. She merely mirrored my feelings pejoratively with a sting in her forked tongue, saying, "I hear that you are impatient with the time it's taking *to get what you want.*" In tears, I told her that I felt deeply betrayed by her. She asked me skeptically, "So how are you coping?" I answered—revealing a latent wish—"With God."

One morning in mid-December, Nina left me a vague, rambling phone message saying, "Have you heard about the kosher meals?" and asked me to call her back. I called three times over the next week. Each time her secretary paused to check before returning to the phone to say Nina was unavailable. The fourth time I called, Nina picked up the phone while I was speaking to her secretary and angrily demanded to know why I was calling. Weeping, I repeated Nina's own request for me to call her—reminding her that Rabbi Farber's clothing check never came and mentioning Paula's email informing me that Nina would now be arranging the Hillel lunch plan. Having to ask for charity had been difficult—being forced to beg was torture.

Nina said in a low voice, "Well, Paula dropped the ball; she gave it back to me to handle...I've just been too swamped to follow up." Nina promised to call me when she returned to campus after the holiday break to arrange Hillel lunches for the spring semester. She never called. I received neither the reimbursement for what I spent on the secondhand clothing nor any part of Rabbi Farber's kind donation, and I never once ate at the campus Hillel. Instead, I had a semester of sheer affliction.

The only dubious benefit I did receive from this travesty was the extra thousands in student loans by the efforts of Vickie Russo, which meant I was in greater hock to the university and now even further away from both economic solvency and graduation. If I had known I would be battling the entire case conference committee to receive what I was pledged, I never would have attempted to complete my degree at this time, completely starved of support and caught in a web of broken promises. I certainly would not have accepted further debt in order to do so.

Paula Ferguson, the hapless advocate for the learning disabled at Latham, fumbled my case completely and didn't even show up for appointments she made with me. Yet I knew the extent of her family problems; she was simply too overburdened to offer me support. Adele Chertoff, the head of the learning resource clinic, a sympathetic ally before my hospitalization, met with me once after the case conference and then backed away from me. I evidently accrued guilt by association: everybody assumed that if his or her colleague had forsaken me—which they heard about from me or saw on my anguished face—I must have done something to deserve it, so each in turn decided to reject me too, before I committed the same unspecified offense against them. No one wanted to be caught bearing responsibility for a parasite, a loser, or even worse, a nudnik. I wasn't just a hot potato at Latham University; I was a pariah.

Parenthetically, I have come to hypothesize and maybe even understand why there is such a powerful temptation to blame a victim. We want to believe that life is just because a just God created us and imbued us with His gift of conscience. The suffering of the innocent offends our God-given sensibilities and expectations. Yet we'd rather assign guilt to the unfortunate than face how negligent each of us may be in bringing about a just and compassionate world—our mission, which is not only achievable but obligated by God.

In the year after my father's premeditated killing of my grandfather, I received a disability diagnosis, woke up to Simon's deceit, and lost my misbegotten dreams of marriage and hopes for graduation. In the next few months, I was abandoned by everyone of significance in my life—everyone upon whom I depended. I was a quaking, shaking shell of my former self. The resolve, guts, and fortitude I displayed after my Refuge discharge were spent in a fruitless quest for my lost dignity. I had lurched from victim to villain, and I still didn't know what I had done wrong.

When I first woke up to Simon's sociopathy—and shuddered from my proximity to it—I began praying for God's rescue. But I felt compelled to conclude, in the ensuing loss of all my former supporters, that God must hate me. I could only read divine punishment into the extraordinary humiliation of the last months of 1997.

With my final ounce of pride, at the end of the year, I sat across from Linda Brewer, Nina Musconi's supervisor, and accused Nina of endangering my health and welfare with her defaulted promises at not one but two crucial junctures in my life: before my hospitalization and after my case conference. When Linda defended Nina—insisting that Nina Musconi would never withhold resources or services from a student "without good reason and careful consideration of her effect upon a student"— I asked to return with evidence to prove my claims. She told me to call for an appointment in January. I left her office quietly seething.

In Craig Cohen's parting act of atonement, he prevailed upon a fellow cognitive-behavioral psychologist, Dr. Patricia Metcalf, to see me as an urgent consult, informing her that I had few remaining visits on my health insurance policy and even fewer resources. My upcoming visit with Dr. Metcalf, scheduled for January 3, was the only thread that kept me tethered to humanity. Except for this appointment, which held some faint promise of rescue, I had no one invested in whether I lived or died.

Part Four

Awakening

And the appearance of the glory of the Lord was like devouring fire on the top of the mount in the eyes of the children of Israel.

—Exodus 24:17

Chapter 15

Christmas brought a hush over the streets as people clustered in their homes in celebration. My loneliness was driving me to desperation. My solitude was so total that I feared disappearing into the void with no one to look for me. A usually reserved person, I spent Christmas afternoon trying to track down someone compassionate who might remember me and offer me some words of comfort.

Searching my past for a figure of warmth, I could come up with only two. One was my mother's old boyfriend Tom, who had graced my adolescence with his kindness and affection. Tom had only sons from his first marriage, and I delighted him as the daughter he always longed for. We were both water signs, and full of fellow feeling. Unfortunately, my mother jilted Tom in the end because his bankbook wasn't big enough. He wrote me in Israel when I was seventeen that he felt compelled to end their relationship, after my mother refused to visit him in the hospital when he suffered a heart attack. While he had wished to stay in touch with me, our relationship foundered after their parting. I was doubtful he was still alive and despaired of finding him now. So that left only one.

She was my first therapist, Elaine Kaminsky, whom I began seeing as a young girl of twelve. We bonded deeply over three years, yet I had to let her go when she retired to take care of a son born with Down syndrome. When we parted, I gave her a sterling silver heart on a chain that I had bought with my own money. I found her name in the phone book in Chestnut Hill. Though I knew it was crazy, I dialed her number, not knowing what I would say if she answered. It had been eighteen years.

A young man answered the phone and sounded startled when I asked to speak to Elaine Kaminsky. In a grave tone, he asked me who I was and why I was looking for her. I explained that she had been my therapist when I was a teenager, and I wanted to say hello to her. He said she was his mother and that she had passed away from breast cancer four years before. I shared with him how kind and loving his mother had been to me and what a difference she had made in my life. We connected in a moment of sorrow and said goodbye.

I still acknowledge myself for having the presence of mind not to call a member of my own family. Never had I felt so vulnerable and alone. But I didn't invite more chaos and pain into my life by turning to the well other people would have—I knew that it held no water and only snakes and scorpions.

On January 1, alone on the first day of the New Year, I finally turned to God. Completely bereft of human comfort, for the first time in my life, I truly sought God, knowing there was no other address for my needs. Wailing like a babe left on a stranger's doorstep, I collapsed in a primal sobbing. I feared I might expel my soul from the intensity of my convulsions.

Purified by a cry from the depths of my being, I suddenly realized that I had been searching in the wrong place for my security. All my fruitless chasing after crumbs from humankind had left me broken and bleeding. Yet here was God, the Source of all succor and sustenance, just waiting to embrace me with His love and shelter. How had I missed His presence all along?

All at once, I understood that I had put duplicitous humans in the place that ought to be occupied by God. Spending my life running after approval to fill up the emptiness inside me left by selfish parents who defaulted on their duty to raise me, I had conducted my life as though various authority figures—stand-ins for my absent parents—had control of my destiny. I had thought pleasing and performing for them would bring me the protection and patronage I needed.

Yet here with me was a limitless Source of blessing. The awareness of how I'd displaced God for the love of feckless human beings hit me with the power and force of a thunderclap. God had been by my side forever, merely waiting for me to turn to Him with a whole heart. I began to pray, speaking to God aloud. Quite unexpectedly, God gave me His seal that my new understanding was true: in a calm, soothing quiet, I witnessed some sort of emanation for the first time, in beautiful yellow light. I silently imbibed what I took to be a sign from God, mesmerized, as orbs of swirling golden fire appeared wherever I cast my gaze. Alone in my tiny apartment, spurned by humankind, I beheld what I felt was a veil of the very Source of creation for the first time.

God's manifestation in the form of light matched the vividness and power of His birth in my awareness. The impact of recognizing God's presence was like throwing a generator switch that instantly infused me with a passionate current of ecstasy and gratitude—for knowing I was no longer alone and forsaken—coupled with remorse at having ignored Him until now. And I believe God responded by sending me a sign—an unmistakable sign—that He was acknowledging me: the ethereal light shimmering wherever I rested my gaze.

While I could not explain the phenomenon I was witnessing, I regarded what I beheld to be divine communication. The power and force of my recognition of God was matched by His response, measure for measure. God was testifying to me with an echo of my own desperate, passionate affirmation. I believe an emanation from God had come to me in a tender manifestation of mercy because I was so profoundly alone—to reassure me, to comfort me, and to help me rebuild on the only secure foundation.

God knew that as long as I had my surrogates—therapists, teachers, friends—I would remain as dependent on them as a small child upon the parents I might have wished for. As vain and erring human beings, they could never match God's love and limitless power. Only when no one and nothing was left to depend on—only when I was betrayed by absolutely everyone—did I realize Who remained. I knew I wasn't guilty of anything; I hadn't driven those who had responsibilities toward me to forsake me.

Now I understood that if I was to return from my island of despair, I needed to know God: God sustained me with every breath. I was filled with regret for denying God's place of honor in my life. And I felt pity for myself and for all of humankind for our mad pursuit of glory by any means except connection to Him—the only Source of eternity.

Although my life was unusually barren without structure during this period between college semesters, I began to make sessions of spiritual contemplation an anchor of my day. One of my favorite places to pray was the bath, as I shed my clothes and with them all connection to a temporal identity. God seemed to be cleansing me of a lifetime of misplaced yearning in all the wrong places, for safety, for approval, and for attachment. The "hole inside me" uncovered by the psychodrama at Refuge was beginning to be filled.

I would sit cross-legged in the bath—the warm water surrounding me and comforting me like amniotic fluid. To an oasis of spiritual calm amidst worldly chaos, I returned nightly for my mystical nurture. As I arranged myself in the bath, I looked ahead at the white tile walls with a mixture of eagerness and release: here I would receive. As I pronounced, unselfconsciously and naturally, the Hebrew name for God I knew from childhood, the shimmering yellow orbs would begin to appear. Wherever I darted my eyes, they emerged, swirling brighter and more brilliantly. I gazed in awe and ineffable joy at the stunning spheres of golden fire, silently turning, expanding, deepening in intensity. My face suffused with wonder, I took in this glorious mystery pageant night after night.

My adopted stray cat, Honey, played a curious part in my sessions of prayer that I only came to understand after I began to study Torah years later. Honey was undeniably a surrogate child to me. When I was at home, either I carried her in my arms or she lay curled in my lap. We were, in contemporary parlance, enmeshed.

Yet Honey instinctively kept a safe distance behind me whenever I began to pray while sitting in my living room. After anywhere from twenty to forty-five minutes of silent contemplation, I would withdraw my attention, and the light would rapidly cease. At the precise instant of my imperceptible break in concentration—while my back was still turned to her— Honey would meow plaintively and sidle into my lap. Bearing witness to something extraordinary, not once did she disturb me for attention in the middle of my sessions of spiritual meditation. Years later, in a women's Torah seminary, I learned that animals can sense *kedushah* (holiness) or the presence of supernatural forces. Honey was intuitively obeying rules that many people spurn, such as not to talk during private prayer in a synagogue.

According to Patricia Metcalf, my new therapist, I was suffering from post-traumatic stress disorder (PTSD) and major depression. In spite of my resilience, which camouflaged my childhood pain, the reenactment I endured with Simon revealed that early family trauma was still influencing me. Yet the abandonment I suffered *after* Refuge provoked new shock—

fresher and even more disorienting. This time, therapy and social work were precisely the domains in which trauma took place.

A hallmark of post-traumatic stress disorder is the drive to avoid circumstances that recall the trauma. Although Patricia patiently encouraged me over the course of many weeks to tell her what had happened to me after my discharge from Refuge, I simply couldn't. I was terrified to describe to her the unanimous rejection I faced after my hospital discharge. I no longer trusted social workers and therapists to act with conscience or responsibility. I could not bear the risk that she would blame me and reject me like everyone else. I was so shaken that I couldn't trust another human soul. However, this is exactly what Providence had in mind.

Although my formal therapy with Patricia couldn't get off the ground, there was serendipity in our acquaintance. She was a deeply believing Christian, ideally suited to bear witness to and validate the burgeoning spirituality inside of me. While I was too shaken to tell her anything about what had happened to me after Refuge, I was prepared to tell her about my visions of light. Mercifully, she did not conclude that I was crazy. In fact, she offered to see me twice a week at no extra charge because she was so titillated by my spiritual epiphanies.

Chapter 16

Whereas my connection with God was blooming, I was still enduring the most perverse treatment by human beings. The physical toll on me began to manifest in a persistent, virulent flu. After my fifth day of unrelenting fever, my friend Alyssa, herself a doctor, recommended that I consult with a colleague and friend of hers, Andrea Stone.

Dr. Stone heard my tale of woe and, on her office scale, confirmed my precipitous weight loss—over fifteen pounds in a couple of months. Dr. Stone and I recognized each other, as we had taken the same course at Hebrew College, and we began to trade anecdotes about our attachment to Judaism. Dr. Stone's eyebrows arched dubiously when I confessed my ecstatic visions in prayer. The incipient feeling of kinship between us forged by our mutual friend Alyssa evaporated, her demeanor chilling considerably. She inquired about any psychiatric medication I might be taking. I told her that my psychiatrist, Dr. Yeager, had refused to increase or change my antidepressant. After taking blood tests, she dismissed me. As fast as she could, she passed my case on to her partner, Dr. Melody Hosfred.

A few days later, Dr. Hosfred called to inform me that my blood tests were abnormal. The most benign interpretation of the results was infectious mononucleosis. She hoped that with remedial care, we would not need to explore other hypotheses. Dr. Hosfred's main prescription for healing was rest, enhanced nutrition, and an urgent course of effective antidepressants. She had heard from Dr. Stone that I was suffering a dangerous depression.

Dr. Hosfred telephoned Amy Seidenfeld, the Latham counseling director, to protest Dr. Yeager's refusal to medicate my depression. Dr. Yeager responded with what he had threatened to do in October if I required a change in medication—recanting under pressure from Amy—only to follow through now that my depression was much more severe, entrenched, and posed a threat to my very life: he dismissed me from treatment. True to form, Amy Seidenfeld offered to find public resources to replace university-funded treatment by Dr. Yeager and then, never called me back.

When Dr. Yeager terminated my treatment, I felt the human family had simply disowned me. I was apparently so unworthy that a doctor charged with guarding my health would simply renounce his obligation to heal. I was unable to explain these events, but they shocked me to my core.

Dr. Hosfred told me that as long as I had fever, I was better off in bed. When the fever subsided, I could resume the simplest of activities. She urged me to eat well, drink lots of liquids, and give myself the tenderest care I could muster. She warned me that mononucleosis, if complicated, could cause damage to the spleen, liver, heart, lungs, and brain. A simple course of illness could last up to three months. When my blood work returned to normal, we could assume I was out of danger.

My fever burned for another two weeks, the days and nights merging into an indistinguishable haze. I felt as if I was gradually expiring, wasting away into nothingness, yet I knew I wasn't ready. I was aware of being at a crossroads, growing more detached from my physical frame every day. My body became the arena of a struggle between death and rebirth.

With my prolonged solitude fostering an ever more intimate congress with God, I spent a couple of hours one night beseeching God to let me live. I watched yellow and orange plumes of fire climb the walls of my apartment, lapping at the ceiling cornices. I could see the air quiver and shimmer in front of the flames as though they truly generated heat. I wasn't afraid of the fire's destruction—I felt sure it was a manifestation from God, not actual fire—but I feared God might be taking my life anyway. I was simply too close to the bridge between this world and the next. I began to beg God, "Please. I'm not ready. I'm not ready. It's not my time. Please God, let me live. Please." When I stopped praying and weeping and pleading with God, my fever was gone. I took my temperature several times to confirm the good news. I felt pretty awful, still, but my fever was gone.

I woke up from this crescendo the next morning feeling like an old woman, arms and legs heavy as sandbags. Rarely without a backpack full of heavy books on my back, I now could barely carry my naked frame across the floor. I felt an exquisite weakness that was utterly unfamiliar. Knowing I was sick and alone, my kind friend Laura arrived with a backpack full of tuna cans, cereal, yogurt, and fruit. She was worried I'd stopped eating. She may have saved my very life.

Instead of improving, my illness seemed to grow stranger and more bewildering by the day. When I moved, I felt the sensation of sharp pebbles shifting uncomfortably inside my limbs. A scaly red rash erupted across my forehead, ran over the bridge of my nose and down both sides of my mouth. I started running a chronic low-grade fever again, hovering around 99 degrees.

When I was a child, I used to feel a throbbing in my legs for hours at a time, which my mother had termed "growing pains." I seemed to be having a growth spurt in my thirties, as I felt a constant ache in my limbs that kept me awake at night. Pain settled like a blanket over my hips and thighs. I regularly scored 49 in the Beck Depression Inventory when a persistent score over 17 indicates a need for treatment.

While I had requested a second meeting with Linda Brewer, Nina Musconi's supervisor, to bring evidence to support my complaint of Nina's negligent treatment of a defenseless student, I was simply too ill, fragile, and frightened to go through with it. Without the relief of communication, I was boiling myself to death in my own anger—rendering myself the sacrificial lamb for others' transgressions. The recently liberated rage of a lifetime of child abuse—coupled with being treated like a leper after my hospitalization—left me incandescent with fury.

But my anger was triggering profound panic and shame. I had always been an obliging people pleaser, an inveterate *nice* girl. My soul hadn't yet enlarged enough to contain the whole gamut of human emotions. Patricia, my new therapist, claimed that all emotions were holy, and that we had no choice but to accept them as a set. All I could see was that my righteous indignation put me beyond the pale. No one cared to hear—let alone validate—the grounds for my anger. I was left to smolder alone.

My next visit with Dr. Hosfred to check my progress and blood work revealed a dangerous deterioration. The doctor informed me I now had the signs and symptoms of lupus, a chronic inflammatory disease in which the body's immune system attacks and destroys its own tissues and organs. And my antinuclear antibody (ANA) test—a main marker for lupus—was positive.

A year or two after this brush with serious illness, I would gain some insight into why I responded to Nina's betrayal with a mixture of emotional fury and physical self-destruction. According to Rabbi Anshel Sokoloff, with whom I eventually studied, children have a deep, essential need to honor their parents. Akin to the laws of nature, God's commandments—of which honoring parents is one—are immutable axioms that sustain humanity within the universe. The need a child has to honor and serve his or her parents as an expression of gratitude for the gift of life—a repayment of the most profound debt—is intrinsic to our nature as spiritual beings.

However, when our parents betray us, the guilt we feel for harboring rage against them—*because* they are our parents—can trigger a lifetime of misunderstood self-sabotage. Nina Musconi's bait and switch, mimicking the chronic seduction and betrayal by my unreliable mother, triggered the fury of needing to hold this tyrannical mother figure accountable at last, and my own mother at the same time, by proxy. Yet the prospect also evoked an unconscionable disloyalty—being a grave violation of one of these essential spiritual laws.

Owing to Simon's betrayal, which so closely resembled my father's, it was finally dawning on me that I didn't have to be everyone's victim anymore. Nina herself had persuaded me that I was following an unconscious script in acquiescing to victimhood that I had to change by my own will. Now I was struggling to hold *her* accountable using her very own coaching.

But changes like this do not happen without exquisite tension. I was redefining my identity as a passive loser. Every particle of me protested: "How dare you!" "Who do you think you are!" "What makes you think you deserve anything?" Along with these aspersions welled up the inchoate terror of a small child who invites her borderline mother's explosive rage with any challenge or resistance.

During this dramatic passage, I had a most remarkable dream one night, unlike any I had before or since. After I recovered from the period of nightmares aroused by my mother, my dreams had been ordinary—filled with the usual strange themes, wacky ideas, nonsense, and chaos. However, this dream was distinguished by simplicity, aesthetic clarity, and lucidity. In the beginning, I found myself alone walking along a rural dirt road lined on either side by trees. The scenery around me was well-defined, without any blending or muddy borders between the enormous blue sky and the brown tree trunks with their vivid green leaves. As I was walking on this dirt road, I heard an unseen speaker saying from above me, "Miranda, look over there." I looked up and saw majestic mountains in the distance. I continued walking. Eventually, from the opposite side of the road, a figure began to approach me. From afar, I could not tell whether this figure walking towards me was male or female. When we met, the creature embraced me, enfolded me in its wings, and whispered in my ear, "There will be peace." And then I woke up, enchanted.

What do I make of this dream? For several reasons, I believe the dream was a gift from Heaven, a message from God sent through the angel who embraced me. My life was filled with shame, isolation, and fear for my sheer survival. I had never before suffered so much rejection and pain in so brief a time. It is implausible to me that I could have fashioned a message of hope and salvation amidst my own anguish. Furthermore, the distinctness of the dream was so unlike any other dream I have ever had; the images remain crystal clear in my mind. Finally, the dream was custom-tailored to reassure me that there would be an end to my suffering, even a redemption. How could I myself foretell such a fate?

The ensuing years have reassured me of the dream's divine origin. I later learned that an image of mountains indicates spiritual growth. At the cost of the human persecution I was suffering, I was achieving priceless insight into the relationship between man and God. Desperate for human acceptance, I had exiled God to the periphery. Realizing my security was negligible without a bond to my Creator, I was doing something about it for the first time—gaining spiritual insight, albeit from the edge of a precipice.

Moreover, I learned that in our Sages' understanding, prophetic communication always involves or occurs in the Land of Israel. Months after I had made Israel my home, I was startled by a needlepoint of the skyline of Jerusalem on the wall of a teacher's apartment, featuring mountains just like those from my dream in Cambridge. I smiled to myself when I first noticed the needlepoint, seeing as I now live surrounded by mountains in Jerusalem, as close as possible to the Author of my dream. I live with new faith in God's love and guiding Providence.

Fast-forward little more than three years: I survived all of the misfortune; and I was blessed, after deep transformation, with marriage to a wonderful man and the gift of a new family. I live the peace that I was promised in that dream. With gratitude and awe—living an observant, joyous Jewish life in Jerusalem—I know peace for the first time. That dream was indeed a prophecy.

Chapter 17

On my way home from another dismal checkup with Dr. Hosfred, barely able to drag myself a city block, I saw a flyer tacked onto a telephone pole advertising a moving sale featuring books on holistic medicine. I was desperate for advice about healing, terrified that my descent into lupus was unstoppable. Jon's studio on a third-floor walk-up was filled with old books, batik wall hangings, and New Age CDs. He was a bit of a cliché—dressed in pale hemp clothing, his hair long, the smell of brown rice and miso soup simmering in the kitchen. Jon was a masseur and a self-taught homeopath who was moving to Hawaii to be a private macrobiotic chef for a wealthy couple. He was friendly and eager to spread the gospel of macrobiotics as a cure for everything from athlete's foot to Alzheimer's. My spirit was broken, and I was willing to try almost anything to regain my health. His warmth and enthusiasm were misty rain in the desert of my days.

While I was skeptical of food fetishes, he urged me to try macrobiotics. I selected five secondhand books on natural medicine and healing, and vowed to attend a lecture by Michio Kushi, the father of macrobiotics, who, serendipitously, happened to be scheduled to conduct a macrobiotic dinner lecture the following Friday night at a Boston natural foods restaurant. The price was enormous—thirty-five dollars—and I was broke, but I felt so ill and desperate I would have applied medieval leeches to feel better.

I gingerly entered the restaurant that Friday evening to find people, many of whom were strangers to one another, sharing square tables for four, adorned with faux silk placemats and brightly painted ceramic dishes. We endured courses of seaweed salad and seitan served by wan, ponytailed beatniks as Michio Kushi crooned and gesticulated to our crowd of lonely hearts.

Even as the evening's obsession with food, chewing, and breathing was a bit repugnant to me, I was spellbound by Michio Kushi's words. He spoke about the role of ego and hubris in the process of disease. He described how the wealthy fly to exotic locales in desperation to dip in miraculously healing waters, springs, and baths. "Then," he related, "They walk seven times around the well, with their anger, their demands, their entitlement, and their vanity. And they get back on their planes completely unchanged and wonder why they are not healed." He spoke about a spiritual world that parallels our physical world, echoing and influencing all our actions on earth. I am sure that he mentioned Kabbalah, ancient Jewish mystical wisdom.

Somehow he succeeded in lifting me from my state of bitterness and dread, infusing me with a bit of hope and wonder. I went home intrigued, though I didn't think the answer lay in spurning raw vegetables or chewing my food one hundred times. It was clear to me, however, that the essence of nurture that food retains in our fast-paced, technological culture does play a part in healing. By feeding themselves so intentionally and tenderly, these lonely people seemed to be trying to taste love.

When I got home, I set up my makeshift mikvah in the bath and stepped into the warm waters. I meditated in the beautiful light and wept. I had a deep epiphany that night which was well worth the thirty-five-dollar admission: "God, if You have given me a disease so that I should finally learn how to love myself and nurture myself, then you have given me a gift and not a curse. OK, God, You are doing this *for my good*. I accept it." I relinquished the fight that very night. I surrendered. And the very next day, I began to recover.

My visit with Dr. Hosfred several weeks later confirmed what I knew to be true. I had been gaining in strength every day. My blood work attested to a vigorous recovery. I no longer had a positive ANA test, and my white blood cell count and platelets were returning to normal. Dr. Hosfred, a sympathetic Christian woman who believed in the power of prayer, marveled knowingly at my recovery.

Riding home from the doctor's office feeling "reborn," I was seized with a wild, visceral impulse. I knew I owed God my life. Words were insufficient to express my joy and gratitude for my recovery. I was overwhelmed by an exultation too great for civil comportment to contain. If I could have sacrificed some part of myself, I might have. But I dared not open up a vein and give God my blood.

For the first time, I could understand why Jews in ancient times could be commanded to slaughter an animal and offer it on an altar in deference to God. Suddenly, this ancient practice didn't seem so utterly barbaric. One of the many explanations behind the offering of an animal sacrifice is that it is intended to connote to the penitent that he or she is alive by the grace of God. The animal's life, which was given in replacement, would have been the penitent's own if God had judged the wrongdoer with strict justice rather than with mercy. The surrogate's death is meant to motivate the sinner's repentance and restore his or her closeness to God. In this case, my healing and God's suspension of my mortal sentence catalyzed a revision of my understanding of God as a Being of vengeance and punishment to perceiving God to be the ultimate Source of love.

For a remarkable few months after my recovery, God continued to gift my power of sight with an added dimension. Every place I rested my gaze swirled with magical light. Golden light shimmered above the stones as I walked over the cobbled streets of Cambridge. My Christian therapist, Patricia—pink light enveloping her face—marveled gleefully as I told her of my gains. I was so joyful in my newfound connection with God that I could see the light brimming from the earth this good God had created. I could see the supernatural sparks in every object of creation. Like a kernel of popcorn blasted open by heat, the inner sacred core of each object of creation was revealed for my eyes to see. The light was a gift I received from my descent to the depths of the earth. I gaped into the void and found the light concealed at its Source.

But this extrasensory perception was a fleeting gift. Strengthened by my recovery, I began to invest ever more effort into building a sanctuary for God in *this* world, relying less and less on solitary spiritual contemplation *(hitbodedut)* for my sustenance. As my tether to the earth grew stronger, the light from the heavens returned to its place.

Yet I know that this emanation of light is what reality truly *is*, although we are not usually privileged to see it. Jewish Sages teach that many people passed by the inimitable burning bush at Mount Sinai, but only Moses took notice of this wondrous sight and recognized the presence of God (*Midrash Rabbah*, Exodus 2:5). Our customary this-world obsessions blind us to the transcendent magic of creation.

As my worldview shifted cataclysmically—owing to my newfound bond with a loving God—I fell into wholesale projection and transference in choosing a topic for a research paper for one of my Latham courses. The Dutch Jewish artist Jozef Israëls (1824–1911) painted in the mid-nineteenth century. When the Enlightenment opened doors to Jewish participation in the wider Christian world, many European Jews fled the ghettos, throwing off what they came to regard as superstitious religious practices in favor of assimilation. Israëls came from a traditional Jewish home, yet his personal and professional life reflected this exodus from ritual observance. Although he occasionally depicted classical Jewish subjects, these paintings were bathed in pathos. His favorite secular theme was the nobility of vulnerable fishermen and their families dueling with the heartless sea.

I hypothesized that Jozef Israëls' dour, melancholic paintings issued from a man who despaired of belief in a transcendent Creator. With no providential Being to bear witness to his suffering or reward his virtue, Israëls rendered on his canvasses a spiritually empty universe at the mercy of an indifferent Nature. I argued that he was wrestling with agnosticism in his work and that his paintings bore the unmistakable imprint of a Jew who had lost his faith in God. Letters by and biographical materials about Israëls supported my theory, and my professor was impressed with my thesis.

I wrote with a passion kindled by my own rebirth, sustained by a gossamer umbilical cord to the limitless Source of light. I now understood and deeply felt the cost of defaulting on my own duty to know and love God. My final paper for Art History 325—concluding one of my six incompletes—became an indictment of myself as a former atheist forged with the passion of a new believer. It is among the few works I am truly proud of from my undergraduate career.

My period of isolation graced with the contemplative prayer of *hitbodedut* came to a natural close in the summer of 1998, as my strength and will to live returned. I began the next stage of my journey, to discover what Judaism could teach me about the mystical.

Chapter 18

The Jewish Sages teach that redemption comes "in the blink of an eye," once the conditions are ripe or salvation is earned. For example, the people of Israel, enslaved in Egypt for 210 years in a seemingly inescapable vise, were *chased out of Egypt by their captors* just hours after they followed God's command to slaughter the Egyptian "deity" and smear the lambs' blood on their doorposts. By this act of courage, they signaled their rejection of Egyptian idolatry and their dedication to the one true God. As soon as I revealed I was ready, God opened doors for me too.

After attending a Conservative Judaism–sponsored talk on "Jewish Mysticism, Astrology, and Divine Providence" at the local Jewish community center, I noticed a flyer at the back of the auditorium advertising lessons in Jewish mysticism from the kabbalistic work the *Tanya*, at the home of the Downtown Boston Chabad rabbi, Mendel Zaritsky. In my first lesson, I became acquainted with Jewish mystical philosophy, which would begin to offer some answers to the riddle of my life. Within the week, I was offered my own key to the Boston Chabad House, with an invitation to stay over every Shabbat.

The Chabad House resembled the type of off-campus house in which I rented a room as a young undergraduate, with several floors cluttered by mismatched secondhand furniture. The house parents were a warm, affable couple in their forties with seven children, two of whom were foster children. Mendel and Leah were returnees to Torah observance themselves. Their lives had been touched by Rabbi Menachem Mendel Schneerson—the Lubavitcher Rebbe—as college students, and they dedicated themselves thereafter to bringing the joys of Judaism to others not yet so fortunate. In every major and many minor American cities, Chabad rabbis and rebbetzins set up shop with the sole mission of teaching Jews about Judaism, for little to no cost and without expectations.

Mendel found ways to sanctify his secular interests, and one of them was to play Chassidic rock and roll with his drums, in the inimitable Hidden Tzaddik Band. Leah—a no-nonsense woman with an irreverent sense of humor—often had her wig perched at a precarious angle as she responded breathlessly to the demands of her many children and guests. Their home was built for hospitality, with an enormous kitchen in the shape of a long tunnel, where twenty-five people sat at five rickety card tables pushed together and united by a roll of plastic tablecloth unfurled the whole length.

Every Shabbat, lively Chabad services with circle dancing in the aisles took place at two nearby synagogues on Friday night and Shabbat morning. Three local Chabad rabbis divvied up the flock after prayers for generous repasts. On Friday night, we were treated to a four-course meal featuring roast chicken that rivaled what my grandfather used to serve, with steaming cholent (meat stew cooked overnight) and kugel on Shabbat day. (When a pugnacious guest once publicly accused the rabbi of exploiting his wife—burdening her with preparing food for so many guests week after week—Mendel revealed that he was the chief cook responsible for the chicken and kugel.)

Chabad life revolves around Shabbat and the Jewish holidays where long meals, graced by singing and words of Torah, create an atmosphere tinged with the future world after the coming of the Messiah, when learning Torah, serving God, and feasting will be our primary endeavors. Jews with various levels of commitment to Orthodox practice, prospective converts, and curious non-Jews were welcomed warmly and indiscriminately to their table. Some, like me and a few new friends I made, had caught the bug of observance and were eager to learn and take on Jewish practice. Others were "cholent Jews," attracted by the warm hospitality with no investment in spiritual growth. In Chabad lore, all Jews form the greater Jewish body; the feet, those far from the religious ideal, are considered no less essential than the head. Every Jew's needs were acknowledged and nourished in fulfillment of the biblical command "Love your fellow as you love yourself" (Leviticus 19:18).

Discovering the Chabad community was like stumbling upon an underground of passionate shtetl life coexisting secretly amid postmodern urban nihilism. Gone were my solitude, my loneliness, and my struggle for significance. I had found a pulsating river of Jewish life from which I was welcomed to satisfy my thirst. My Friday nights were spent with new girlfriends sleeping on foam mattresses covered with old sheets and mismatched blankets, and I greeted each Shabbat morning amid the rabbi's children, eating cereal out of Styrofoam bowls with plastic cutlery. Imbibing mysticism with bites of mozzarella at weeknight pizza fests, I learned Chassidic philosophy as Mendel rendered the Lubavitcher Rebbe's analyses of the weekly Torah portions.

In the poetry of Providence, I was now praying in Ohr Yisrael, the same synagogue where my beloved grandfather had reconnected with his roots twenty-five years earlier. Ohr Yisrael, the synagogue where Pop-Pop found his cantorial teacher, was taken over by Chabad after the Jewish community in Downtown Boston flocked to the suburbs.

Like a sleeping bear that emerges in the spring, I felt ready to encounter a mate again after my long, lonely exile. Yearning for a home, or at least the comfort of someone's arms, yet as fearful of actual acquaintance as the boy in the bubble, I shopped for my companion from the security of my apartment—in the personals.

Sensitive, gentle Jewish troubadour looking for female companion with like-minded interests: music, cooking, spirituality, friendship. With a quivering voice, I invited Ethan Rosenbaum to call me, not realizing how fateful our encounter would be. We chatted about music and his recent cross-country ski trip. After several pleasant phone conversations, Ethan invited me to meet him for the first time at a Balkan folk music concert held at sunset on the plaza in front of Boston's Museum of Fine Arts.

When I first set eyes on my newspaper beau, I liked what I saw. He was compact, lean, and unthreatening, dressed in soft cotton fibers and clunky hiking boots. He had black hair etched with grey at the temples and a trimmed black beard. His upper lip, a perfect bow, hinted at amorous talents within. We smiled at each other shyly. When the accordion player invited the audience to dance, we gingerly took our places among the seasoned couples, determined to illustrate our shared lack of inhibition. With his arm draped loosely around my waist, we stumbled and spun in clumsy imitation of the lead couple's steps. In his dusty white pickup on the way home, I found myself imagining what it would be like to kiss Ethan Rosenbaum, and the thought brought me unmistakable arousal.

On our second date at a kosher Chinese restaurant, Ethan and I faced each other and commenced *the interview.* Fortified by *The Rules*, I sat serenely and shunned premature intimacy, answering questions with a minimum of elaboration and a coy smile. Perhaps relieved that he would not have to share the spotlight, Ethan unraveled before me, confessing between the crunchy noodles and the eggrolls that his wife had divorced him after she came out as a lesbian.

Once a literature major at Reed College, Ethan had dropped out in his junior year, disillusioned or just unable to cope with the pressure. He supported himself modestly doing odd-job repairs and carpentry, still bitter that Jewish mothers would deem him unacceptable as a son-in-law. He found solace in Hinduism, a spiritual practice he claimed brought him peace and transcendence.

Ethan took me next to a concert of Indian music. Swaying along with the hypnotic sitar, I felt almost faint as I lost myself in the fertile rhythms. Woozy from the music and excited from the proximity of Ethan's body, I felt my normal defenses give way; the surging Ganges carried me into Ethan's sinewy arms.

The first time Ethan Rosenbaum and I made love, I wept and wept, shaking in his arms. Cutting to the core of my being, our closeness released all my buried pain. His touch rekindled my humanity, sealing my reemergence into the family of man.

However, Ethan's Jewishness seemed to serve only as a springboard to rebellion. Embracing the Hindu god of Rama— an avatar who sounded suspiciously like a superhero—Ethan had built him a miniature shrine, which occupied a prominent place in his living room. Like a lonely postmodern Adam who denied the progress of history, Ethan boasted of surviving in the woods alone for a month without provisions, not even toilet paper. We found ourselves debating early and often. He was determined to convince me that Judaism was a force for disunity in the world. Meanwhile, he scoffed at the warm reception I had received from Chabad.

Yet Ethan's soul bore a welcome, unmistakably Jewish trademark: he loved to feed me. He was especially fond of making nourishing curried vegetable soups, which I imbibed with the hunger of a stray cat finding a sardine can.

Ethan had turned his back on the upward ladder of mobility, but there was one area of life where he strove to distinguish himself: the bedroom. Ethan had studied the *Kama Sutra* carefully. He had mastered the unusual art of remaining exquisitely still in lovemaking, while evoking the most extraordinary sensations in his lover. It was my luck to meet a Tantric master just when I was trying to forswear the pleasures of the flesh.

My Chabad friends had recommended to me a fantastic book called *The Magic Touch*, which argued that it was wrong to touch the opposite sex before marriage. For an ardent Scorpio like me, such restraint was radical beyond words. Yet I was sold on the message almost instantly. I was determined not to waste any more years of my life wooing a man, in which sexual charms played a strategic role, only to be dumped when commitment time came. Gila Manolson, the author of the book, persuasively argued that the magnetism of touch clouds the clarity needed to determine whether someone is a suitable life partner. Body talk was no substitute for real conversation, but it could fill in the gaps so hypnotically that one might not notice what was missing.

Through Chabad, I was learning of an old-fashioned formula for finding Mr. Right that involved talking, and only talking. Dating in the Orthodox Jewish world was practical: I need only clarify my values, goals, and the kind of home I wanted, and then search for someone who shared my vision. Torah-observant singles met by arrangement—called a *shidduch*—after a matchmaker, family, or friends determined that the man and woman had compatible ideals. Meeting and talking was for exploring attraction, chemistry, and rapport.

I soon found myself leading a double life, seeing Ethan on the weekdays and spending Shabbat with Chabad.

Chapter 19

hrough the study of *Tanya*, the central philosophical text of the Chabad movement, I became acquainted with a spiritual worldview that began to provide comfort, making sense of a life which up until now had seemed an incomprehensible torture. Why was I a victim of the powerful and the cruel so often in life? How could the suffering I was born into be justified, and a good God preside over it? Why did I deserve to be so badly treated?

According to Rabbi Anshel Sokoloff—a close confidant of the Lubavitcher Rebbe—the terms *good* and *bad* are moral categories that can only apply to our free-willed choices. The circumstances of one's life may be bitter, unfortunate, or painful, but can never be "bad." What God brings into our lives is always good, yet often that good is concealed from us. Hidden good is the adversity that forces a person to develop faith, humility, wisdom, and resourcefulness. The Torah (the Hebrew Bible) testifies that undesirable qualities such as greed, complacency, and arrogance often follow on the heels of prosperity, whereas the best of the nation of Israel emerges from trial and tribulation. God gives us hardship when that is the only way to evoke our personal growth.

In fact, mystical sources in Judaism teach that a soul is given a preview of the circumstances of its incarnation, with the hardships and the rewards. Then our souls actually choose whether to descend into the world—for the soul's ultimate benefit or detriment. Could Plato have possibly taken his celebrated *Myth of Er* from the Jewish teachings?

We may never know exactly why we are blessed with fortune ("revealed" good) or misfortune ("concealed" good). Sometimes God brings misfortune to help us atone for sin. Yet sometimes it is to heal us, like a surgeon stitching up a wound. The procedure may be searing, but it is crucial for our restoration.

Suffering is not necessarily a punishment for sin in this lifetime. It may come because of our choices from past lives— previous incarnations of our soul—or it may reflect the consequences of the misdeeds of our ancestors. Yet all apparent suffering arises for our own good. Virtue and blessing may emerge from misfortune when we choose closeness to God in response. Misfortune prompts us to draw God near, granting us the only unquestionable good there is.

Three of the four Jewish matriarchs, Sarah, Rebecca, and Rachel, were each afflicted with an agonizing infertility so that they would pray. The Jewish people, their descendants, needed the closest possible union with God in their collective DNA. Rabbi Sokoloff urged me to beg God to change the circumstances of my life for the better. "Only He can change the rules," he said.

Rabbi Sokoloff explained that suffering was not necessarily a sign of divine displeasure. Sometimes God "tests" people to reveal their enhanced capacity for trust, faith, and divine service. God commanded Abraham to grapple with the limits of his faith in the episode of the binding of Isaac, his son. Abraham's obedience, along with the voluntary self-sacrifice of Isaac (who was an adult at the time), provided unparalleled examples of submission before God, which earned merit for and gave strength to all their descendants. Rabbi Sokoloff encouraged me to conform my life to God's will and let go of understanding "why" until the picture became clearer with time.

In college philosophy classes, I had learned about the difficulty reconciling a scientific, materialist understanding of humankind with the subjective perception of our freedom. If we are only sophisticated, biologically determined machines—just like animals—then what explains our experience of free will? On the other hand, where is the evidence of and what is the source of the soul, which the dualist claims to be the engine of our freedom?

From Chabad, I learned that humans are unique in the animal kingdom. We have not only physical bodies but also divine souls breathed into us by God, which allow us to connect to our Creator. Since Adam and Eve's fall, the two forces in man, the godly and the animal, vie inside us for domination. Undisciplined, our bodies demand unlimited food, sleep, sex, money, power, honor, and prestige and bid us to transgress moral law in order to satisfy our desires.

The sourcebook of Chabad, the *Tanya*, written by Rabbi Schneur Zalman of Liadi in the late 1700s, teaches Jews how to be *benonim*—literally "in betweens"—meaning in between the completely righteous person, who is beyond temptation, and the wicked person. *Benonim*, a truly lofty category, are human beings who feel the pull of temptation coming from the body or the ego yet don't give in. A *benoni* sanctifies herself by refusing to sin, and thereby tames her passions—elevating her godly soul within her body and drawing both closer to her Creator. When channeled and elevated, our desires become the source of holiness.

An observant Jew says a prayer upon awakening each morning to thank God for returning her soul, as sleep is a taste of death. God gives us a perfect part of Himself in our divine souls, which cannot be tainted by our actions. Jews begin each day acknowledging this purity of soul in the prayer *Elokai neshamah*:

> My God, the soul which You have placed within me is pure. You have created it; You have formed it; You have breathed it into me. You preserve it within me; You will take it from me, and restore it to me in the hereafter. So long as the soul is within me, I offer thanks before You, Lord my God and God of my fathers, Master of all creatures, Lord of all souls. Blessed are You, Lord, Who restores souls to the dead.

I yearned to feel such innocence, carrying a lifelong sense of being cursed.

After the destruction of the second Holy Temple in Jerusalem at the beginning of the Common Era in the year 70, the Rabbis enacted that the home replace the Temple as the center of divine service. Seeking to preserve the sense of intimacy with God, which the Jewish people enjoyed while the Temples stood, the Sages commanded us to perform rituals in our homes so that each of us could be a high priest in our own house of God. Our first command of the day is to wash our hands to sanctify them as the priests did so that all our deeds that day should be holy.

I was gratified to discover that the psalms a Jew chants to prepare herself for formal prayer vividly echoed my personal crisis, portraying the feelings of an outlaw:

> Lord, my God, I cried to You and You healed me. Lord, You brought up my soul from the nether-world. You kept me alive that I should not go down to the pit...What profit is there in my blood, when I go down to the pit? Shall the dust praise You? Will it declare Your truth? ...You turned for me my mourning into dancing. You loosened my sackcloth and girded me with gladness. So that my soul may sing praise to you and not be silent, Lord my God, I will give thanks to You forever. (Psalm 30:3-4, 10, 12-13)

> It is better to take refuge in the Lord than to rely on man. It is better to take refuge in the Lord than to trust in princes. (Psalm 118:8–9)

> Do not put your trust in princes, nor in people, in whom there is no help. When his breath goes forth, he returns to his dust, on that day his thoughts perish. Happy is one whose help is the God of Jacob, whose hope is in the Lord God, Who made Heaven and earth, the sea, and all that is in them, Who keeps truth forever... Hashem [God] protects strangers, the orphan and the widow... (Psalm 146:3–6, 9)

> The Lord builds up Jerusalem. He gathers together the dispersed of Israel. He heals the brokenhearted and binds up their wounds. (Psalm 147:2–3)

I learned that King David, the author of most of our psalms, suffered his share of scapegoating, deceit, and civil hypocrisy. David, like many Jewish national heroes, was an underdog with a pall over his pedigree, who rose to prominence through his faith, courage, and integrity.

From *Tanya*, I learned the empowering lesson that each human being waging a personal struggle against her own evil impulses is exactly the mechanism *for purifying the world*. When a *benoni* subdues his or her evil thoughts and inclinations and refuses them expression, a corresponding suppression of evil occurs in the heavenly realm, concomitant with God's joy. My struggle and that of every Jew to choose goodness were the means *for vanquishing evil at large*. The *sitra achra* (the "other side," i.e., the source of evil in the world) is weakened and diminished every time a Jew performs a mitzvah. What is more, when a Jew holds herself back from sinful thoughts, speech, or actions, her self-restraint is as meritorious as the performance of a divine commandment.

But where does the *sitra achra* come from? Who made it? I learned that God withdrew Himself from the world in response to man's rebellion, and in doing so, permitted evil to arise in the vacuum, to test mankind. My amateur thesis from the "Binding of Isaac" paper for Gaby Rakover could be found in the *Zohar*, the mystical work from which Chassidism emerged. When Adam and Eve disobeyed God's sole command and ate from the Tree of Knowledge, they revealed that they took God's gifts for granted, spurning the Giver. Whereas God created the world to give us sublime delight crowned by connection with Him, our wayward behavior demonstrated to Him that being granted *unearned* rewards—"bread of shame," according to the Kabbalah—soured our appreciation and spoiled our reverence.

As a result, God fatefully tempted human beings in order to expel us from the cushy, idyllic Eden. Thereafter, God put the struggle between good and evil inside each one of us, symbolized by our ingestion of the fruit from the forbidden tree. The *Zohar* proclaims that through the temptation and fall, both man and God chose to forge a more genuine relationship amid ambiguity and challenge. If good and evil were obvious and heavenly retribution immediate, no person would ever sin, but humans would be conditioned robots. How could God cherish compulsory faithfulness, the loyalty of automatons? And how could we take pride in our accomplishments as pampered, spoiled children?

In response to our unfaithfulness, God withdrew Himself from the world: He hid His face to give humans the opportunity to return to Him *of our own free will*. Yet God did not abandon us completely. In Genesis 1:26, when God says, "Let *us* make man," one interpretation is that God is talking to the soul of Man himself, inviting him to become a partner in his own creation. To guide us in our quest to purify ourselves, God gave us the Torah, His own words: the Jew's user guide to life on earth. But the

Torah requires study, and its performance is effortful. Careful learning and fulfillment of the Torah's commandments by the Jews imbues the world with holiness and blessing—setting an example for the rest of the nations about humankind's divine purpose and potential.

While blessing comes in this world from following the will of God, it is in the next world where the righteous enjoy the full fruits of their labors. To preserve the ambiguity necessary for freedom—to allow us to earn our rewards—the righteous sometimes suffer in this world and the evil appear to profit. But in the next world, in the *afterlife*—where the soul dwells with God for eternity—the reckoning is measure for measure. A fascinating Gemara tells of Rabbi Yosef, the son of Rabbi Yehoshua, who passed away, entered the next world, yet came back to live in this world again. Asked what he saw, he responded, "I saw an upside-down world...Those who were on top here (in this world) were below there (in the next world); and those who were below here were on top there." His father told him, "You saw a clear world" (Babylonian Talmud, *Bava Batra* 10b; *Pesachim* 50a).

And what is the nature of these commands of the Torah? Passages from the Talmud recited in the daily prayers illustrate the culture the Torah seeks to cultivate:

> These are the things that have no measure: the *peah* [corner of the field that must be given to the poor], the *bikurim* [first-fruits that must be given to the Kohen], the appearance-sacrifice [at the Temple in Jerusalem on Pilgrimage Festivals], acts of kindness, and the study of the Torah. (Mishnah, *Peah* 1:1)

> These are the deeds that yield immediate fruit in This World, while the main reward is reserved for the World to Come: honoring parents; accomplishing acts of loving-kindness; arriving at the house of study early—morning and evening;

> providing hospitality; visiting the sick; helping the needy
> bride; attending to the dead; probing the meaning of prayer;
> making peace between one person and another. And the
> study of Torah outweighs them all. (Babylonian Talmud,
> *Shabbat* 127a)

All of these ideas captivated me. I spent countless hours in my childhood poring over the rules for earning merit badges as a girl scout, yet could never muster the consistency. Though I was compelled by the brutality of my home to fight for the right and the true with nothing but my instincts to guide me, I floundered once my soft sensibility came up against institutional aggression and indifference.

Yet here was a vibrant lifestyle with virtue, kindness, charity, and self-discipline as its core values, and it was Jewish! Here was the original, biblical Judaism — alive — empty of every libelous charge by the liberal camp. Nowhere did I hear about sticking it to the *goyim*, shaming the secular, or compulsory breeding accomplished via a hole in a sheet. This was not what I'd heard religion was about from Habonim, Marx, and Freud!

Talking with Rabbi Sokoloff, I sought relief from the lifelong anguish and guilt I felt over rejecting my parents — violating one of the Ten Commandments — when to do so seemed vital for my own survival. Appeasing my pain, Rabbi Sokoloff urged, "*You* must honor your parents from a distance. Live in a way that reflects well on them. The Torah does not obligate you to become their victim." Judaism was indeed providing solutions to my most agonizing dilemmas.

God knew what I wanted since my first exposure to the Torah in Gaby Rakover's class seven years earlier: I had been instantly and deeply attracted to this. Yet fear of the religious "family" kept me from following my heart. Therefore, God brought me near total desertion by all my former comrades — just the impetus

I needed—to overcome my inhibition. Now I wanted to do whatever God asked of me, and I wanted to do it right away. All I needed was to learn, soaking up knowledge of Torah and Judaism like a sponge. And the response from my Chabad friends was a wholehearted embrace.

But what was I to do about my back-door boy? Ethan Rosenbaum was no disciple of the Rebbe. In fact, the more excited I became about taking on mitzvot, the more skeptical Ethan became. Ethan was not interested. He prized his figurines, his alienation, and his freedom too much to dabble in real spirituality. Our shifting priorities could not have been clearer.

Ethan's apartment was always hot. Between the flies, the swelter, and the Hindu shrine, I was beginning to feel captive in Calcutta. The poles of choice were obvious to me: Ethan wanted to remain an outsider. I wanted to join.

Ethan was my first sacrifice of the flesh. He was good to my body but bad for my soul. Over coconut curried pumpkin soup and steaming naan in his kitchen, I withdrew my affection. A curly strip of gooey flypaper hung from the ceiling fixture above us. A horsefly emitting a full-throated drone zoomed around the room until it landed on the paper, kamikaze style, spending its dying moments writhing about in the muck.

Just after I announced definitively that I was leaving him, that we didn't share any life goals and had no future together, Ethan offered the no-risk pledge: "Miranda, I love you." Determined to suffer, he grasped at a poignancy that was decidedly absent from our parting. My indifference turned to disdain.

Chapter 20

I was like an eager kindergartner at the tables of my new Chabad teachers, but my academic and financial life still lay in tatters. Still aggrieved by my treatment at the hands of so many college administrators, I had managed to complete just one unfinished course out of six. For my essay about the Dutch Jewish artist Jozef Israëls, which gave expression to my own atonement, I was able to quiet the cacophony in my head that otherwise hijacked my ability to focus. Turning my attention to anything else tainted by Latham University, however, I found myself in anguish that I had been treated like such a derelict.

A lawyer friend taken with pity for my plight agreed to accompany me to follow through on my complaint to Nina Musconi's supervisor about Nina's behavior. But the meeting was fruitless; so fearful was I of being indicted by yet another campus administrator that I found myself unable to speak in the supervisor's presence.

With the previous year's plan to finish my undergraduate degree shattered, I now had to resume supporting myself and repaying more student loan debt, accepted during the year I became everyone's football. I saw a half-time job advertised in a Latham University bulletin that seemed well matched with my administrative secretarial experience and would tap my writing skills: managing and copyediting a scholarly journal called *Public Opinion Research*. The journal's editor, Robert Plum, had accepted a faculty post at the Dover School for Communication, a graduate division of Latham.

When I was offered the job, Linda Brewer, Nina's supervisor, proposed to move me to a Latham dormitory free of charge for the coming year so that I could salvage time for my coursework. Gratefully receiving this discretionary resource one year later than expected, I felt Heaven smiling on my new faith and commitment. The gesture was an unspoken admission that someone at the college had defaulted on something, though no apology was forthcoming.

After I moved into this dormitory apartment, which was larger than the closet I had lived in the previous year, I acquired some spare dishes, cutlery, and pots to begin keeping kosher with the help of Chabad. Eating, an activity as essential as breathing, was now regulated by an entirely new set of laws. That was the whole idea: to remind ourselves that we are not from the animal kingdom that eats to survive, but rather, the elite of creation with the opportunity to connect to our divine Source by bringing spirituality into the world with each morsel we eat sanctified by a blessing, acknowledging God as our provider.

In a confirmation of the maxim that "you are what you eat," Judaism prohibits the ingestion of animals of prey, while permitting consumption of certain peaceable creatures, provided they are slaughtered in a way that minimizes their suffering. *Kashrut* is a set of dietary laws designed to promote self-discipline while imparting the sensitivity needed for a nation of priests. Fortunately, Lubavitch provided a round-the-clock free mitzvah service whose access required little more than a phone call. When I dialed the number my rabbi provided, a short, plump boy in sidelocks arrived armed with a blowtorch to *kasher* my oven by rendering any prior contents into ash.

I also picked up a new boyfriend whom I met on a walk with the Mosaic Outdoor Mountain Club, a Jewish hiking society made up of earthy misfits who congregated over sprouts and tofu after walks in local woods. Mark was tall and gangly, with heavily hooded eyes, straight, dark brown hair almost too long for a scientist, and a quaint unconscious habit of chewing on the straggly ends of his moustache. He also drove a burgundy Volvo, dressed well, and happened to be the president of his local Reconstructionist synagogue. I was attracted to his money, and he was attracted to my faith. I was at the peak of my spiritual confidence since enduring my own personal exile and redemption, and I was joyful and exhilarated in my new observance.

To say I was only attracted to his money is selling myself short. Mark was a sweet and sensitive man who took an active role in his community, and unlike Ethan, put Judaism in a central place in his life. But that didn't mean he considered himself obligated by anything. At my core, however, I was wrestling with survival. I had no practical financial safety net, an aging uterus, and bore the scars of too much hardship. I was never going to achieve professionally like my doctor, lawyer, and social worker friends. Finding a home, a refuge, and someone to belong to were keen drives just beneath my rapture.

Mark and I began our courtship with hope and innocence. But my new commitment to an observant Jewish lifestyle put us on tracks with entirely different speed limits. Mark wanted to conduct our relationship according to secular norms, which included premature sex and plenty of time to waffle about commitment. I was looking for a husband and had committed myself to celibacy before marriage, even to obeying the Jewish law called *shemirat negiah* (guarding touch), which prohibits physical contact between members of the opposite gender outside three generations of the nuclear family.

Whereas I was happy with the priority Mark gave Judaism, mitzvot were as optional to him as the items on a Chinese *dim sum* menu. So while I was charmed when he invited me to decorate his backyard sukkah with popcorn strings, I chafed at the pressure he applied to convince me to make love with him afterwards. In truth, I felt for Mark. Though a genuinely good soul, he was devoid of charisma and deeply insecure about his sex appeal. I was to come to learn that he had fulfilled his early longings with prostitutes when unsuccessful in the dating realm. This money-for-sex paradigm with which women were tainted in his imagination made him especially suspicious of my motives. I attempted to navigate this quagmire with what I thought was a reasonable compromise: we petted 1950s style, with our clothes on, with no difficulty on my part feeling genuine ardor.

The very next morning I woke up to an abomination in the mirror: a big red herpes sore on my upper lip. It grimaced at me—jeered at me: "Miranda, what have you done? You were supposed to be chaste. You promised God you'd quit touching men. What are you, some kind of addict? Can't you say *no*?" With horror and shame, I made an appointment with a local physician to diagnose and treat my first-ever sexually transmitted disease. Only the culture came back negative. No herpes virus exuded from my witless sore.

In a few days, the lip sore disappeared, only to reappear like a hangover the morning after our next session of heavy petting. My lust and I wrestled, with my sore a lurid testimony. After each interlude of kissing and fondling with Mark, I found myself writhing alone on my bed in convulsive tears that I hadn't been stronger, that I'd defaulted on my new vows. I knew I was disappointing the God Who'd saved me, but I didn't know how else to convince Mark that I really desired him. We kept our clothes on for my sake, but we succeeded in overheating like an old-fashioned steam engine. I wanted marriage but Mark didn't—at least, not yet. And neither he nor I was prepared to give in.

I seemed to be riding a crest of good fortune powered by my *teshuvah* (religious return). I got a respectable job, a free place to live, a decent Jewish boyfriend, and I was being flown for training in the *Chicago Manual of Style* to the American city where my two spiritual guides resided—my former Judaic studies professor from Latham and my mentor in Chabad, Rebbetzin Adina Blau. I had met Adina during a two-week summer Chabad learning program in Providence, Rhode Island a few months before. She was knowledgeable in both Torah and the ways of the world and had offered much encouragement for my spiritual quest. I planned to divide the free time I had in Chicago between Gaby and Adina.

Hosting overnight guests for Shabbat is routine in the Torah-observant world, and I was thrilled to be invited to spend Shabbat with my professor and his wife. It was indeed the meeting with my professor, or rather, with his wife, that would prove fateful.

Elana, my professor's wife, was a doctor who was good at everything else as well. She was accomplished professionally, she was a talented and efficient gourmet cook, and she was nice. Gaby had once disclosed indiscreetly that Elana kept Jewish law out of her love for him rather than her belief in its sanctity. But to me, Elana—with her covered hair—was Orthodox and a putative Jewish authority. Her word was as good as God's.

While I admit to being less than discreet about my mystical visions, of all the people to whom I believed it was safe to disclose my experiences, my professor and his wife were at the top. He had introduced me to the Torah and its divine Author. Because of the yearning to come close to God our studies had instilled in me, I was riding a wave of heavenly benevolence—his class had set me on this odyssey. Yet I wasn't aware of the stake that different kinds of observant Jews have in their precise understanding of God and His properties.

Over a sumptuous Shabbat morning banquet of bulgur wheat, feta, and arugula, we embarked on a conversation about the reasons for prayer. Elana questioned why we petition God with our prayers if He does not interfere in human affairs but leaves us to exercise our free will and bear the consequences, as my professor evidently believed. I was still naive about the points of theological debate between some Modern Orthodox and Jewish mystics. All I thought was that an emanation from God had appeared to me in my lonely hovel in response to my prayers and was now lavishing blessing on me from behind the scenes, for my running after Him like the hart in the Song of Songs. I was full of the ecstasy of the reborn.

As I effused about the golden light, Elana asked, "Didn't you realize you were having a psychotic depression?"

"*What?*" I stammered.

"Well, you were profoundly depressed and had become delusional."

Oh. So that's what it was, I thought, the color draining from my face.

I boarded the plane back to Boston trembling with unease.

The insult of my teacher's wife hit me like a blow to my solar plexus. With a narcissistic mother with borderline personality disorder and a schizophrenic older brother whose break with reality came at about my age, I was hardly sure I would escape a similar fate. Being crazy was a specter that had haunted me my whole life. Ducking my parents' and brother's distorted projections upon me of their own evil had left me with lifelong confusion about who and what I really was.

After my discharge from Refuge at Bournewood Hospital, those who once formed my support ranks—those whose faith in me confirmed my sanity—deemed me beneath repair. My only refuge had been God. God's revelation had restored me, convincing me that I was not only sane but possessed of crucial lessons about the reasons for my persecution—reasons that were relevant not just to me, but to the legions of men and women who had forgotten God.

Yet here was one of His representatives branding me certifiable. I felt rejected by the only club in which I had found shelter. How could I go on? My willingness to surrender my faith before Elana's aspersions revealed that I had not yet fulfilled the *tikkun*—the repair of my soul—that God was demanding of me: to fear God, not people. It would be years yet before I would achieve it.

When the hand of Divinity set free the enslaved, persecuted Jewish people, weak from backbreaking labor in Egypt, the nation of Amalek promptly attacked them. Without mercy for the freed slaves, Amalek was contemptuous of the fledgling people of God on their way to receive the Torah at Mount Sinai. In need of neither food nor territory, Amalek attacked just to spread doubt—to cause the Jews to question the nearness of God and relinquish their faith. Amalek is the killer of spiritual passion.

Chassidic philosophy teaches that the seed of Amalek, the eternal enemy of the Jewish people, also lives inside of *us* and is roused by doubts about the duty, merit, and value of God's service. Our Sages draw this inference from the identical numerological values of the Hebrew words *Amalek* and *safek* (doubt).

Something perished in me when I came home from Chicago. The burning flame of conviction was dimmed to a pilot light. I allowed myself to be diminished by the skepticism of my hero's wife—sacrificing my newborn faith on the altar of authority once again. How could I put the judgments of people above my love and awe of a God I had come to know so intimately? My spiritual exhilaration was gone, replaced by the vague worry of being an imposter. Within a short time, I was floundering in my relationship with Mark and feeling insecure with my friends from Chabad. If my *religious* surrogate parents didn't love me, but instead, found me suspicious and unstable, how could I love myself? Life once again echoed the core drama of rejection and abandonment, except this time, I was an accomplice.

Meanwhile, I was struggling painfully with how to arrive at a commitment with a man who subscribed to the ways and means of secular culture. In my heart, God knew, I deeply wanted to abide by my new vows of sexual chastity and preserve intimacy for marriage. Although Mark was surprisingly patient, he was unwilling to respect my will. When he confessed that he feared my unwillingness to make love with him was really a smokescreen for my lack of attraction to him, I felt empathetic. Yet I knew that his concern was unfounded. I understood that he was not entirely confident in his physical charms and he was not merely trying to manipulate me.

While we tried to tread a middle ground by embracing without undressing, after each interlude, which was passionate and reassuring, I found myself alone in my apartment on my hands and knees, pleading with God to forgive me my grievous lapse. My tears came from a deep sense of the nearness of God, fully aware of His intimate care for how I conducted myself. I knew I had betrayed God and myself by compromising my commitment to Him in order to "prove" to Mark that I really desired him. Mark wouldn't take me at my word. After each tryst aborted, I developed lip sores. I had never had them before and, thank God, I have never had them since.

One could argue that I was so emotionally distraught at having betrayed a moral code I had adopted that I gave myself psychosomatic herpes. But I view the appearance of the unnatural sores on an exposed part of my body as a supernatural gift from God meant to cause me embarrassment. Our Torah teaches, "God moves people in the direction in which *they* want to go" (Babylonian Talmud, *Makkos* 10b). The unsightly sores were God's way of reminding me that, in the long run, I was not going to be able to build a relationship of holiness with a man who, however decent, hadn't accepted the yoke of Heaven—the demands of a Torah-observant Jewish lifestyle. God was trying to help me along and strengthen my commitment to Him, to myself, and to my new principles. Regretfully, it took me a few more months to have complete clarity about the inviability of our relationship.

Mark and I remained tethered to our respective communities: he to the Reconstructionists, me to Chabad. Although Mark was to deplore the hold of Jewish law upon me, he confessed he submitted his relationship with his newly Orthodox girlfriend to the jurisdiction of his Reconstructionist peers in a board-meeting vote. Attending one such meeting of his synagogue as a spectator, I was appalled and amused at once by the communal preoccupation with fear and loathing of the Orthodox. What seemed to really animate these people was plotting to stop the encroachment of traditional Judaism into the public sphere: preventing the extension of the Boston *eruv* allowing the mitzvah-observant to carry items outside their houses on the Sabbath, sabotaging kosher restaurant certification, and facilitating intermarriage were the most passionately endorsed initiatives.

In their defense, I could remember once thinking and feeling as they did about Orthodox Jews, my condemnation stoked by a liberal media that delights in representing observant Israeli Jews in particular as rabid killers of Arabs. I had been duped along with them watching American television footage of bereaved Israeli parents at the burials of their precious children torn from them by Arab terror attacks—as the voyeuristic cameras close in on the pitiable parents vowing revenge with faces contorted by unimaginable agony.

I too fell for the demonization of Orthodox Israeli "settlers" whose noble lives and resourceful industry "obstructed" the ill-conceived panacea of a Palestinian state. I admit to thinking thoughts such as: *those Jews secretly delight at the murder of their brethren, as they can use these tragedies as pretexts to sate their lust for revenge.* How could I have conjured this garbage? How could I have sunk so low? I now knew the mitzvah-observant from the inside: people of extraordinary kindness, patience, and loyalty—living for God and His Torah, their daily self-sacrifice to care for one another building the most tenacious familial and communal bonds.

Although the relationship with Mark had seemed to show great promise, we reached the same fundamental brick wall as I had in prior relationships. Mark was unable to commit. After six months, I felt we knew enough about each other to forge a common destiny. I saw some of Mark's shortcomings and much of his beauty and nobility. I felt I could cherish the good and accept the ragged edges. To my mind, we shared fundamental values of community, honesty, spiritual growth, and a desire to do kindness for others and each other.

Yet there were signs of deep-seated mistrust rooted in Mark's painful childhood that suggested he would not easily bond. For instance, each time I shared a bit of my vulnerable past with Mark, he jumped to the worst interpretations and conclusions about my motives and behavior. I found myself on the defense against unfounded, far-fetched allegations, which only compounded my shame at confessing something about myself or my family of which I was less than proud.

When I finally met my husband, he distinguished himself in the mitzvah of *dan l'chaf zechut* (giving the benefit of the doubt and judging favorably). I experienced this as a reparation for all the distorted projections I had endured at the hands of disturbed family members, ill-chosen romantic partners, and careless university personnel.

In the end, Mark was unable to overcome his doubts, sacrifice his independence, and accept responsibility for another human being's welfare. He preferred to remain alone, rather than to throw in his lot with another imperfect person willing to cherish him. When it became apparent to me that my only choice was to continue to give to him not knowing if there would ever be a commitment to marry, I broke off our relationship. Although it was extremely painful, and I questioned my decision many times, ultimately, I was relieved that this time I had given only six months rather than several years of my life. Although I was still alone, I regarded myself as closer to achieving my real goal, which was to find a partner who could embrace the opportunity for devotion, security, and spiritual growth in marriage.

Chapter 21

The traditional Jewish worldview teaches that "loving comes from giving," rather than that "giving comes from loving."[1] In the logic of Torah-observant courtship, the feelings that are prerequisites for marital engagement are mutual respect, admiration, physical attraction, ease of communication, and similar values and goals. Love can only prosper in an environment of deep trust and security, taking root where exclusivity and commitment prevail. Love deepens *after* marriage—accruing over years of overcoming one's innate selfishness to care genuinely for a partner's needs. We learn this from the Torah which attests that after Isaac selected Rebecca as a worthy successor to his mother Sarah, "...Isaac brought her into his mother Sarah's tent, and took Rebecca, and she became his wife, and he loved her," in *that* order (Genesis 24:67). What the secular world declares to be "love" is often infatuation—intoxicating but unreliable, and frequently, short-lived.

Jewish law obligates abstinence before marriage, acknowledging the power of sexuality to obscure differences in temperament and values between a man and a woman. It is

---

[1] Rabbi Eliyahu E. Dessler, *Strive for Truth!* trans. Aryeh Carmell (Jerusalem: Feldheim Publishers, 1978), 126–33.

precisely these differences that may preclude a harmonious union. When sexual passion distorts a person's judgment before marriage, objectivity is lost.

Moreover, in secular conduct, a sacred gift that God has given for spouses to bond through the most exquisite physical pleasure—in a sanctified relationship in which God Himself participates—is misappropriated for a tryst meant only to gratify fleeting desire. Judaism teaches that when a husband and wife are intimate in mutual love, the Shechinah—the feminine aspect of God—descends from Heaven and joins them in their joy. Holiness is manifest through the sexual union of husband and wife, whereby parents may merit conceiving a new human being—a gift of God.

There are myriad reasons why casual premarital sexual encounters leave women at a profound disadvantage. These warrant a digression to discuss the biblical story of creation and its vision of ideal male-female relations, in contrast to the sexual politics reigning today.

The creation story tells us of fundamental essences with which God imbued the world. In the biblical story of creation, God initially creates a single, androgynous being with both male and female qualities. However, God declares that autoeroticism *isn't* good, leaving the solitary person both self-satisfied and lonely. God's plan for humankind's elevation—that we emulate God by becoming givers ourselves—is achieved better through two sexes who can give to one another. Therefore, God separates the being into male and female counterparts with equal worth. (This is one reason the sexes yearn to bond, to reunite with the lost "other half.")

In the account of the creation of the first androgynous being, the Torah uses the verb *vayitzer* (and He formed) when God takes earth—simple, visible, and accessible—and forms the composite human. Forming is an easy, straightforward process suggestive of the shaping of clay; this primitive material is subsequently infused with God's breath, with which He endows the newly created person with a soul.

Yet when God separates out the female properties to create a woman, the Torah says that God *built* her—*vayiven*—from a more sophisticated, hidden part of the human body: the rib. Building or *fashioning* is a process involving complexity. Something formed has one dimension—what you see is what you get. A building is notable for the many levels concealed by its facade. A woman's body generates new life within, requiring anatomy and a whole network of hormones for sustaining life both inside and outside the womb. The first woman receives a new name, Chavah (Eve, the mother of all life), in recognition of her unique power.

The verb "to build" reflects women's particular intellectual strength, *binah*, an intelligence marked by perceiving implications and anticipating their consequences. For example, the Jewish foremothers Sarah and Rebecca could foresee the dangers of Ishmael and Esau, respectively, for God's ethical program. Both biblical foremothers were believed to be on higher prophetic planes than their distinguished husbands, Abraham and Isaac, were.

These intrinsic gender differences of masculine simplicity and straightforwardness versus feminine complexity and depth color human behavior. When a man is thinking, "Wow, this feels good," a woman is thinking, "I wonder if he'll make a good father." (Or, at the very least, "Will he still love me tomorrow?")

While birth control has greatly diminished the likelihood of pregnancy, which once forced women to consider consequences in any sexual encounter, a woman's *physiology* remains exquisitely equipped for sustaining and bonding with others. Miriam Grossman, MD, a former UCLA campus psychiatrist, whose account of what transpired at a college health service was so provocative that, initially, it had to be published anonymously, claims there is an "epidemic of depression, cutting, suicidal behavior and eating disorders on our campuses" because the rampant promiscuity in vogue betrays a woman's nature.[2]

This promiscuity—inviting the devastation of heartbreak, sexually transmitted disease, and infertility—goes unchallenged on campus by the ultraliberal psychological and medical establishments unwilling to acknowledge the health risks associated with it.

Dr. Grossman cites a 2003 study of 6,500 adolescents, revealing that sexually active teenage girls are more than three times as likely to be depressed—and nearly three times as likely to have attempted suicide—as girls who are not sexually active.[3] With preternatural perspicacity, Wendy Shalit indicts the campus hook-up culture that has laid waste to women's dignity

---

[2] Miriam Grossman, MD, *Unprotected: A Campus Psychiatrist Reveals How Political Correctness in Her Profession Endangers Every Student* (New York: Penguin, 2006), xxiii.

[3] Robert E. Rector, Kirk A. Johnson, and Lauren R. Noyes, "Sexually Active Teenagers Are More Likely to Be Depressed and to Attempt Suicide," cited in Grossman, *Unprotected*, 4. Grossman also cites the following: K. Joyner and R. Udry, "You Don't Bring Me Anything but Down: Adolescent Romance and Depression," *Journal of Health and Social Behavior* 41, no. 4 (December 2000): 369–91; Deeanna Franklin, "Romantic Stress Tied to Depression in Sensitive Girls," *Clinical Psychiatric News* (April 2005): 31; Denise D. Hallfors, et.al., "Which Comes First in Adolescence: Sex and Drugs or Depression?" *American Journal of Preventative Medicine* 29, no. 3 (2005): 163–70.

and emotional health in 1999's incendiary *A Return to Modesty*, published just after she had graduated Williams College.[4]

Whether you accept neuroendocrinological research on oxytocin[5] or the Bible's account of woman's creation, women are more vulnerable to attachment when they shed their clothes and kiss. The effort to deny this reality and expect ourselves to be as superficial and detached as men (made of *earth*) is risking our mental as well as physical health. (Some might venture that women's physiological propensity for attachment and bonding reveals our Creator's brilliant design to foster love within the family.)

How, then, does Judaism protect women (and men) from sexual exploitation or self-abasement? By a whole fortress of Torah law, the foundation of which requires men and women to be married to make love or even to touch with desire and pleasure. The Torah considers the human being so sacred and sex so holy that it regards sex between unmarried people, *even when no money is exchanged*, to be mutual prostitution.[6] Prohibiting premarital sexual hijinks, Judaism forces men and women to regard one another seriously, even reverently. The Torah restores

---

[4] Wendy Shalit, *A Return to Modesty: Discovering the Lost Virtue* (New York: Simon and Schuster, 1999).

[5] Larry J. Young and Zuoxin Wang, "The Neurobiology of Pair Bonding," *Nature Neuroscience* 7, no. 10 (October 2004): 1048–54; K. M. Kendrick, "Oxytocin, Motherhood and Bonding," *Experimental Physiology* 85 (March 2000): 111S–124S; Michael Kosfeld, et al., "Oxytocin Increases Trust in Humans," *Nature* 435 (June 2005): 673–76; Professor Diane Witt of State University of New York at Binghamton, cited in Susan E. Barker, "Research Links Oxytocin and Socio-sexual Behaviors," www.oxytocin.org; all cited in Grossman, *Unprotected*, 6–8.

[6] Maimonides, *Mishneh Torah*, Ishut 1:4.

the discretionary power to women to compensate for their vulnerability, for they know their deepest desires will be satisfied within relationships of commitment and security.

What else can we learn about the archetypal man and woman from God's words at the outset of creation? When God presented Adam with Eve, crafted from Adam's own body, he euphorically recognized her as his exclusive soulmate (Genesis 2:23). And God declared that the two of them would unite in marriage: "Therefore a man shall leave his father and his mother and cleave to his wife *and they shall be one flesh*" (Genesis 2:24).

Classical Judaism is unabashedly romantic. The Talmud declares: "Forty days before the formation of a child, a heavenly voice proclaims, 'The daughter of so and so will be married to so and so'" (Babylonian Talmud, *Sotah* 2a). "Marriages are made in Heaven" is written at least five times in Midrashic Torah literature, according to Maurice Lamm. He writes enchantingly, "This is not a romantic cliché, but a serious statement of predestination."[7] A little girl's dream that one day she will meet and marry her prince charming—and that she has only one who will cherish her forever—is woven into the fabric of the universe.

Marrying and fathering children are Torah obligations for men so that they may fulfill God's command to "be fruitful and multiply." While women are not obliged to marry, many, even most, want to. The Torah does not compel a person to risk her life—until fairly recently in history, childbirth was a dangerous

---

[7] Maurice Lamm, *The Jewish Way in Love and Marriage* (San Francisco: Harper and Row, 1980), 3.

undertaking, and it remains a woman's prerogative.[8] Yet family life is so central to Judaism that at a circumcision ceremony, we already bless the eight-day-old infant, "Just as he has entered the covenant, so may he enter the Torah, the marital canopy, and deeds of loving-kindness."

One might argue that the degradation of relations between men and women bred by the hook-up culture—and the subsequent erosion of trust between the sexes—accounts for this abysmal finding: the non-Orthodox American Jewish family is becoming extinct. [9] Whereas the Orthodox American Jewish marriage rate is 80–85 percent, [10] a 2017 Jewish People Policy Institute study found that *fewer than a third* of non-Orthodox American Jews under age thirty-five are married, and *two-thirds* under age forty have no children.[11] Without a ketubah (Jewish marital contract) and the security it brings—protecting Jewish women and the Jewish family since the dawn of civilization—

---

[8] Maimonides, *Mishneh Torah,* Issurei Biah 21:26 and Ishut 15:2; *Shulchan Aruch,* Even Ha'ezer 1:13; all cited in Michael Kaufman, *Love, Marriage, and Family in Jewish Law and Tradition* (Northvale: Jacob Aronson, 1992), 9–10.

[9] David P. Goldman, *"Israel's Demographic Miracle,"* Jewish Policy Center, *InFOCUS* 7, no. 1 (spring 2013): 8, available at https://www.jewishpolicycenter.org/2013/02/28/israel-demographic-miracle/.

[10] Nechama Carmel, "The Data on Divorce: Q and A with Dr. Yitzchak Schechter," *Jewish Action* (spring 2017): 46–55, available at https://jewishaction.com/family/marriage/data-divorce-q-dr-yitzchak-schechter/.

[11] Dr. Shlomo Fischer, Sylvia Barack Fishman, and Steven M. Cohen, "Raising Jewish Children: Research and Indications for Intervention," Jewish People Policy Institute, June 5, 2017, http://jppi.org.il/new/en/article/english-raising-jewish-children-research-and-indications-for-intervention/#.Wku8DDeYO1s.

men and women will no longer embark on one of life's greatest joys. While I regret having come late to this conclusion, trading children and grandchildren for sexual liberty now seems to me to be too heavy a price to pay.

Chapter 22

My smooth path to paradise had hit a few bumps in the road. I was shaken by the turbulence with both my professor (my first Orthodox mentor), and Mark. I was experiencing the birth pangs of a new consciousness. While my spiritual life was flourishing, my academic and social lives were not. I was still simmering with temper over the Latham University travesty and feeling helpless to get beyond it and finish my courses. I kept replaying and replaying and replaying the humiliating events over and over in my mind, consumed with fury that I could have been treated as such an outcast—a patent symptom of the post-traumatic stress I was suffering.

Unable to deny my need for support, yet exquisitely fearful of trusting anyone, I sought the help of a new therapist out of sheer desperation. Monica Bornshtein was a plump woman in skirts with a South American accent who proved to be a godsend. I found her through the Association of Clinical Psychologists, a professional guild in Boston whose members were required to treat one financially needy patient annually for a reduced rate. Monica genuinely cared and instinctively trusted my integrity.

Together, we explored the roots of my lifelong self-defeating behavior and traced it to a kind of displaced rage meant for my mother. It was Monica's conviction that my life instinct was bound up in the anger toward my parents I wouldn't allow myself to feel. I spoke about their betrayal with a detached coldness that belied the searing pain I held inside. I acknowledged that my vindictiveness toward myself could be a death wish meant for the spirit of my mother I carried within me.

We began to try to tease apart the fusion of my mother and me as Monica gently sanctioned the anger I felt toward her: "It's your mom who was out to get you," she averred, "not God. God loves you." When I confessed the fear of exploding into an inferno if I gave vent to my rage, she contended, "For *you*, it would be good to lose a little control."

We did some clever and liberating "empty chair" work in which I confronted my parents in absentia. I was shocked by how easy it was to access feelings through this artifice that I had never entertained without it. I couldn't look at my "mother" and felt a keen desire to throw my shoes at her and pull her limb from limb. Monica assured me I could work up to being able to confront my mother eye to eye, even in fantasy.

The empty chair work about my father brought forth some comically obvious dreams conflating Simon and him: Simon coming after me with a shotgun, with my prosecuting Simon for attempted murder. My dad renting a condo for Simon and himself, with my complaining that they should have thought of me too. Meanwhile, I had to coddle the little girl emerging in everyone's shadow. I put myself in the chair and declared my commitment to protecting the child I never was.

Monica, as well as my religious mentors, supported my breakup with Mark. She realized why tolerating long-term uncertainty in a romantic relationship had become intolerable for me, and why the drive to marry had become so strong. She understood that, having been betrayed by both parents, I had never had security and dwelled with an existential threat throughout my life. She maintained the purpose of my dating Mark was to learn that I didn't have to set my sights so low. She termed it "progress" for me to be in touch with a sense of entitlement. "A *little* narcissism is healthy," she said.

Monica was urging me to adopt a new routine of self-care that would foster the confidence of having a good and kind protector in my life: starting my day with prayer, setting small goals and fulfilling them, keeping connected to healthy, spiritual people. Fortunately, my participation in a Jewish community that congregated weekly and over every holiday provided me a new network of caring teachers and peers.

In the summer of 1998, I took a course on the ins and outs of keeping kosher, and this class offered a bridge into a different Orthodox Jewish community, which would become my adopted home. Rabbi Yosef Goodman, our teacher, was a refined British *baal teshuvah* (a Jew who becomes Torah-observant, literally "master of return") who had married a warm and welcoming American girl named Rachel. He was on the staff of a Jewish outreach organization called Derech Emes (Way of Truth) that recruited nonobservant Jews to attend classes and experience Shabbat hospitality in the Boston suburb of Brookline. Instead of the Chassidism of Chabad, the community was oriented around *mussar*, an approach to Jewish ethical self-refinement founded in the nineteenth century by Rabbi Yisrael Salanter. Mussar, with its Lithuanian roots, represented a more sober, less mystical approach to Torah learning, promoting spiritual growth through moral conduct.

I was now blessed to witness from the inside the contemporary examples of Orthodox Jewish movements that I had read about in my second class in modern Judaism with Gaby Rakover. The eighteenth century witnessed a fierce battle for the Jewish soul between devotees of Chassidism—a naive piety that swept the unlettered Jewish communities of Eastern Europe—and the Misnagdim, more learned Talmudists, who were suspicious of the short track to God promised by cleaving to a charismatic holy figure such as the Baal Shem Tov or later dynastic rebbes.

Before I ever knew a *rebbe* from a *rav*, I had once asked my grandfather from which camp we descended. He told me that his parents were from the Lithuanian, Talmudic (*misnagdish*) branch. Despite experiencing my own personal mystical phase, my nature was purely mussar-oriented—relentlessly preoccupied as I was with self-scrutiny, self-control, and self-rebuke. So much so that Rabbi Goodman urged me constantly not to be so hard on myself. The Goodmans took me in for many Sabbaths, during which I was pampered in their sumptuous guest suite and served the most generous and delectable food at Rachel's table.

Being invited for Shabbat—twenty-four hours of feasting, learning, praying, and socializing—provided a welcome relief from my solitude. Something vulnerable in me brought out the tenderest instincts in my new friends to offer shelter and comfort. I couldn't deny I had come far since I spent a desperate weekend at the Nantasket seaside with the dysfunctional Paula Ferguson. I was now a sought-after Shabbat guest whose *teshuvah* formed a dramatic arc in which the kindest and most caring people were invested.

For instance, Maya Landau was an ebullient, wise career Hebrew day school teacher in her sixties whose husband was a retired MIT professor. I was the nudnik always pestering her rabbi with philosophical questions, so she decided she had to befriend me. Sometimes I slept at Maya's house on Shabbat and sometimes at the Goodmans', sharing meals with each of them. When I wasn't in Brookline for Shabbat, I spent it with the Zaritskys or younger Chabad rabbis downtown. Here and there, I made a token financial contribution or paid a small fee for a holiday event. But by and large, I was simply given to by these people without strings, expectations, or guilt. I tried to be as helpful as I could in return, by serving food, washing dishes, and helping with the children.

It must be experienced to be believed, but mitzvah-observant Jews host other Jews for eating and sleeping over the Sabbath, week after week, out of love and kindness, because in giving, one becomes bigger—absorbing a measure of others in whom one has invested oneself, and thereby bonding with the greater Jewish people. Since financial wherewithal comes from God, and God commands Jews to nourish one another, it is an act of faith to trust that God will provide the means.

And we are not talking about boiled hotdogs and a can of baked beans, either. Shabbat meals—three of them in one twenty-four-hour period—are extravagant affairs with many courses: fish, soup, meat and chicken, side dishes, casseroles, gourmet salads, two kinds of desserts. In the Orthodox home, one sees the Jewish love affair with food in its full-blown display. Shabbat meals are the proving ground for the balabosta's reputation. In Rachel Goodman's home, it was like an invitation to Martha Stewart's table week after week.

I cannot describe just how restorative it was for me to be nurtured like this, coming from a home where every penny I cost my parents was resented. This was primal gastric rehabilitation, as good as what my grandfather had bred with his tender roast chicken.

In March of that year, Shabbat immediately followed the first two days of Passover, requiring three days' abstention from work, many festive meals, and the prohibition of just about anything besides eating, praying, talking, reading, making love, or sleeping—along with the fulfillment of two consecutive evening Passover Seders. Rabbi Goodman invited me to join his brother's family in Monsey, New York, for this seventy-two-hour marathon under one roof with three generations of his family. I marveled—during this gentle, loving epic—at the absence of bloodshed, which marred even my shortest-term family gatherings.

Chapter 23

After a couple of months of treatment, Monica saw me still floundering in therapy, mired in self-destructiveness in my private life despite her support. "What percent of you wants to get well and what percent wants to stay the same?" she asked me. "Sixty percent in the direction of stasis," I answered. To her, that ratio sealed my fate.

Seeing how my depression seemed to worsen each time I revealed my parents' shortcomings and released some fury in her office, Monica came to regard my self-defeat as a punishment I levied on myself for harboring rage against them. We also speculated that a whole host of habits, such as kicking myself or promising and then depriving myself of pleasure and rewards, were ways of reviving the presence of parents in my life. The void of absolute solitude was even more threatening.

I had faced the terror of this solitude before—the barrenness of breaking away from truly cancerous parents—unable to make the leap. My survivor guilt condemned me to go down along with them. But what made the leap possible this time was my cultivation of a relationship with God. I had a divine Protector Whose nurture I could feel—though His communication in the form of heavenly light had receded. I could talk to Him, pray to Him, and feel His grace in the slow yet steady repair of my wounded soul.

Monica maintained that loyalty to and love for my parents survived all the pain that I suffered, complicating my efforts to separate from them, even in the sphere of the subconscious. She explained how I could love them and hate them simultaneously, my heart remaining entangled with my tormentors. I felt like a trapped animal—hind leg in a vise—forced to gnaw on my own flesh to set myself free. My mother and I were once one being: how could I abandon her to make a success of my life? Monica urged me to let out the mixed feelings instead of turning them against myself, to see that I could bear and survive them. Only in my mind was I in peril.

My most vivid reenactment was my tango with the alarm clock, which I could dance for a couple of hours on a Sunday morning—the day I ought to have been working on my college assignments. Every nine minutes I relived the ritual of waking up in my mother's house and going back to sleep to escape her tyranny, giving myself a hangover and starting my day with regrets. Refusing to get up, I gave my "mother" grounds for her condemnation, with which I now shamed myself in her absence. I was retraumatizing myself moment by moment in a desperate attempt to escape being an orphan.

I told Monica the hateful things my father had said to me (such as that I had never given him an ounce of pleasure in his entire life), and she grieved with me for the pain I must have felt. Like a *yiddishe* Don Quixote, she insisted on perceiving me benevolently, determined to bear witness to the nobility in my struggle to stay alive and remain good in the face of my parents' cruelty.

In Monica's view, my healing required conquering two tracks simultaneously: grieving over the past in the presence of a compassionate witness and laying down a new foundation in the present—no reenacting, no self-sabotaging, and a steady application of effort to care for myself lovingly and stay faithful to my goals. Only I was not ready. In fact, I was dead set against the whole effort.

At Monica's suggestion, I completed the Beck Depression Inventory (BDI) and the Beck Anxiety Inventory (BAI) just to see where I was holding. I was surprised to find I was laboring with severe depression and anxiety. I had grown so accustomed to extreme pain; I didn't even recognize it anymore. Monica acknowledged me for the superhuman effort it must be taking to get myself to work each day burdened with such gloom.

My job performance at this time was spotty and barely adequate. I was so lucky that Bob, my boss, the communications professor, was loath to confront me. He was a grown-up boy scout—determined to be pleasant, fair, and erring on the side of compassion. It was unlike me to do less than a responsible job at work, but I was simply unable to focus. All my particles were being rearranged on the atomic level. I was being rebirthed, and my struggle to decide whether to go forward or backward took all of my resources. I came to work late most days and stayed late to compensate for my inefficiency—silently shuffling papers and entering bits of data. Bob must have wondered where the self-confident achiever he thought he'd hired had fled to, yet he never said so. To this day, I wonder why such a decent employer got saddled with an employee who was in the midst of a nervous breakdown.

One morning I called Mendel, my Chabad rabbi, in despair, and he urged me to read chapter 33 of the *Tanya*, offering to discuss it with me after work. In it, I read how one can soothe shame by recognizing that one was really a part of God—indistinguishable from Him, for the fact that all creations of God once dwelt within God's mind as pure divine potential. Even in our garments of separation as created beings, we are nothing but emanations of His all-encompassing light, like candles flickering in the daytime. Through devotion to God, one fulfills the human purpose, giving joy to our Creator and finding satisfaction for ourselves in being agents of God's joy—all this while simultaneously conquering the *sitra achra,* the source of evil in the world. I was grateful for Mendel's willingness to struggle with me to find a reason to be happy.

Though I should have been completing my courses, I couldn't endure any more discomfort. Trying to finish academic papers after a year and a half of blitzkrieg required the most acute concentration. Yet I could not nudge my mind off the preoccupation with all my deficiencies, all my weaknesses, and all my mistakes.

Living inside me I had a thousand jeerers all blaming me for not achieving victory: I hadn't protected my grandfather; civilized Simon; redeemed my mother, father, or brother; and I certainly hadn't vindicated Nina and her entourage of hapless Latham University do-gooders who vanquished a helpless student instead of coming to her aid. I was criminal, judge, and jury combined, in the absence of an outlet for my rage. And I knew I'd be a victim forever if I didn't rise up and shout.

It had dawned on me that Nina's bait and switch—with her promise and then denial of aid—was exactly what my unstable mother had perpetrated upon me throughout my childhood: "Come with me to the bank, Miri," she'd purr, "and I'll take you for ice cream." Dare I refuse to apply her frosted mint green eye shadow on my lids on the way out the door? "Get out of my face, you little %@$&%$# (punch!); I'm not taking you for *nothing.*"

Dutifully, I had adopted the bait and switch as an axiom of my own universe: Always promise myself conditional rewards. Always fail to follow through. *Always* deprive myself. For the first time, I was considering challenging the terms.

I had collective forces bearing down on me to rewrite the script of victimhood. I was in the third workshop of four with Women About Change, the two-year workshop series recommended by Refuge staff. We were learning about the need to claim our assertive rights because they would not be freely granted to us. Urged to act "as if" we had high self-esteem, we would compel others to treat us with respect. Only with a change in our own behavior could we hope to elicit a better response from others. *"You have to rescue yourself,"* Dr. Lamont from Refuge intoned. I had the survivor Marilyn Van Derbur Atler's message of *do your work* ringing in my ears. And Monica was urging me to pin my anger on the correct target without fearing I'd become my borderline mother. Solely by feeling my feelings and achieving something positive with my rage would I escape the fires of hell myself.

Monica supported me in the first fateful decision I would make to roll back my persecution—to investigate the prospect of a lawsuit against Nina Musconi, director of the Latham University Women's Center, for discrimination against a learning-disabled student. I couldn't deny I would have sued all of them if I'd had the guts and the resources, including Dr. Zachary Reznik and the Jewish Family & Children's Agency for siding with the perpetrator and failing to protect my grandfather from elder abuse, and Craig Cohen for persecuting a depressed patient who paid him for therapy. I thought of suing my father for libeling me in pursuit of killing his own father, but my stomach and nerves couldn't take it. The university imbroglio was a bit less close to my jugular.

I suspected that Nina's conduct, if not also that of Dr. Yeager—the negligent Latham psychiatrist—violated federal discrimination laws protecting students with disabilities. I believed I had rights and that Nina had transgressed them. The first thing I had to do was to assemble my documentation and detail the events. Hoping to provide a discrimination lawyer with the necessary data, I began to try to write out what I had been through.

Because of my employment at Latham, I was again receiving psychiatric supervision from staff within the college. Frustrated by my inability to discuss what had happened to me after my discharge from Refuge, Patricia Metcalf had passed my case on to an Archie Stall, MD, from whom I received prescriptions for antidepressant and antianxiety medication. Dr. Stall—always official in his coat and tie—proved to be a mensch as well as a good psychiatrist. But he was hard-pressed to make sense of my case. Traumatized, I displayed the classic duality of shock: unable to think of anything else, yet unable to admit and discuss what I had suffered. I was trapped in an inaccessible, impenetrable cul-de-sac of obsession and avoidance that is the hallmark of post-traumatic stress.

Since Dr. Stall was employed by the university, I was terrified to criticize other university personnel, fearing that I would be scapegoated and shunned yet again, so I had refused to speak about it. The decision to document my experiences in writing proved to unlock my muteness. Writing had always been my best medium.

Dr. Stall was the first to grant me the gift of validation. When he read my fourteen-page text detailing my treatment at the hands of Latham staff, he empathized and acknowledged that my pain and torment were legitimate. He could understand how a psychologically well person could become unglued by what I had been through, and he supported my decision to lodge a complaint. He believed that trauma robbed a person of safety, and that self-assertion and communication of my experiences to someone in a position to discipline those responsible could pave the way to recovery. The "narrative," as I came to call it, became my badge of *dis*honor: the chronicle of my degradation at the hands of Nina and friends solved the riddle that I presented as a paranoid, mute mental patient unable to communicate her pain.

Just as Simon's deceit became the trigger for releasing the rage at my father, Nina's betrayal became the key to liberating the rage at my mother. My two-year-long moon-Pluto transit brought with it a tsunami washing away all lying, pretense, and duplicity. I was no longer prepared to accept mistreatment in exchange for approval from narcissistic authority figures. Toward the end of a fundamental psychic restoration initiated by the planet Pluto, indicating death and rebirth, rolling back and forth over my moon, representing my mother, both parents were being replaced in my consciousness with the security of a loving, benevolent God. God was determined to teach me not to rely on human beings. My security didn't lie with them, but it didn't lie with me either. I couldn't have walked forward without God to accompany me.

Jewish time is a circular process, with the annual calendar allowing us to revisit and take nourishment from the energies instilled into the universe at the time of the formative events of our people, on our commemorated holy days. On a personal level too, the planetary rotations guide our lives as they summon forth facets of our souls, which God implants at our birth. As our lives unfold, we are destined to revisit thematic events that will give us the opportunity to achieve *tikkun*, a rectification of our souls. Fulfilling an opportunity for *tikkun* repairs the past in the present, enhancing the future, while the past retains its shadow. Though I wouldn't and couldn't ever fix my mother, I would fix myself in relationship to her through standing up to her proxy, Nina Musconi. And I would propel myself further along the road to my soul's healing.

Only the anxiety about confronting Nina threatened to put me back in the hospital.

Part Five

Phoenix Rising

And there is hope for your future, says the Lord; and your children shall return to their own border.

—Jeremiah 31:16

Chapter 24

While I walked around the earth with an invisible "kick me" sign on my forehead, I was about to remove it. I burned with indignation that a university administrator had arrogated to herself the right to destroy a student's life with such capricious irresponsibility. That Nina was tasked with protecting the rights of victims on the Latham campus was the ultimate travesty.

Writing up the facts, even shorn of their impact, proved to be a gateway to others' sympathy. In a kind of divine embrace, I had many people come forward with support once I decided to step up to the plate. My psychiatrist moved into a pivotal role since he understood the impact of the painful events in light of my family history.

Dr. Stall was an expert in post-traumatic stress disorder (PTSD), the physiological syndrome of panic, avoidance, preoccupation, and hypervigilance that follows trauma. He realized that I was caught in a PTSD time warp because the censure and abandonment by all the Latham personnel echoed the experience of being blamed, scapegoated, and abandoned by my own family. After reading my narrative, he declared compassionately, "You were betrayed not just by one person, but by a whole institution." And the present was uncovering the anguish never healed from the past.

Although I was ashamed to admit it, at the core of my pain over Nina's betrayal lurked the tenderest maternal wound. What is a mother but one who is entrusted with the ultimate vulnerability and helplessness a human being can display? One is never as defenseless as a babe in a mother's arms; however my mother took a pitchfork to my vulnerability.

Nina, in her initial solicitousness, urged me to let down my guard—established through years of self-defense against my own mother—and bare my naked soul. I was awash in shame that I had allowed Simon to mistreat me, yet Nina wrapped me in a shawl of comfort. She urged me to understand that as a victim in my family, when I was too young to prevent it, I had been trained to expect abuse by others, thereby groomed for self-sabotage. When I shared the most humiliating confessions, she affirmed me, restored my dignity, and pledged to help me. It was a healing, almost maternal encounter. Then Nina—my erstwhile savior—turned on me inexplicably, forcing me to grovel for what she and others had promised to provide.

In the summer, fall, and winter of 1997, we vividly reenacted the *trauma triangle* I had learned about at Refuge: from the grandiosity of offering herself as my rescuer, with one swift turn—and the conviction of believing herself sovereign and above reproach—she became my persecutor. Giving me the words to express my pain, she choked me while the words were still in my mouth. Though I myself was just beginning to come to terms with what all of this meant, protecting a victim from retraumatization was the bread and butter of Nina's social work training.

Looking back, I speculate that in between the words that Nina and I exchanged after my hospitalization lurked the conviction with which she tarred me. When Nina rambled about my suffering sexual abuse, which I never claimed and didn't suffer, I believe she suspected that, like my mother, I too must be a borderline personality—a kind of deviant hellcat who wreaks havoc for others to fill insatiable needs left by childhood trauma, which often, evidently, includes sexual abuse. (With the advent of managed health care—limiting inpatient treatment to the most severe cases—borderlines may indeed account for a larger share of compulsory hospitalizations at Refuge, because they are prone to both manipulative self-injury and assault.) Although experts don't fully understand the etiology of borderline personality disorder, it may result from an abuse victim identifying with her abuser and salving her wounds by seeking control over and punishing others.

While I bore grave wounds from my borderline mother, I exclusively chastised myself, choosing a kind of neurotic perfectionism in an effort to eliminate any grounds for reproof. Nina and Craig Cohen both knew that I had a mother with borderline personality disorder. Surprised by my decision to enter a psychiatric hospital, given their impression of my sanity, they must have changed their assessment of me—deciding my actions were those of a manipulative borderline. Thus my hospitalization became part of an effort to frighten people into doing my bidding rather than a sanctuary I sought as my body collapsed from the convergence of past and present traumas. (I didn't understand the reason for my breakdown in a lifetime of responsible coping at the time, but Refuge staff members were able to explain it to me.)

I would guess that the terror of *being* a borderline is universal to her children. I bore an exaggerated fear of my own and others' temper for this very reason. Yet I have finally accepted— persuaded by several professionals—that I suffer from the opposite problem. Rather than exploding, I hold everything in. And rather than hurting others, I tend to attack myself in relentless self-criticism.

Rightly or wrongly, borderlines strike terror into the hearts of many mental health specialists because they are so unpredictable and taxing to treat. Nina and Craig's perverse treatment of me upon my discharge from Refuge was likely an unprofessional example of this, based on an entirely faulty assumption. (Since neither of them accused me to my face of being a borderline, I only understood in retrospect that this was the probable cause of their persecution.)

Needless to say, I was furious with Nina for her condemnation without grounds. Had she asked me directly, looked in my student file, which contained the comprehensive university psychological evaluation that found solely attention deficit disorder, or asked to speak with my psychiatrist in the hospital, she would have discovered that her suspicions were unjustified. Yet I realize that had she given me her support, I never would have turned to God. And my relationship with God would ultimately prove more valuable than any I could forge with a human being.

Dr. Stall reminded me that, though I had been powerless to stop my mother's abuse as a child, I was now an adult who could protect herself. He believed that by communicating my grievance, I would regain my morale and restore the will to prevail over the challenges in my life. "You can't heal from a trauma that no one acknowledges and everyone denies," he said.

To find out whether I had grounds to sue Nina Musconi or the university for discrimination, I consulted an attorney who specialized in protecting the rights of students with disabilities. For 250 precious dollars, Lori McAfee examined my documents and informed me that the courts look favorably upon students who first try to resolve their disputes through internal institutional channels. She encouraged me to take my case to Nina's superiors and to the university ombudsman. Concluding that I most likely had a legal discrimination case according to

Section 504 of the Rehabilitation Act, Title 7, and the Americans with Disabilities Act, she offered to review everything carefully in exchange for even more money.

Whether I chose a lawsuit or an internal grievance, my shameful family history—the context in which Nina offered her support—would be disclosed to more members of the Latham administration. Rather than Nina apologizing, she could be expected to attack—even with false accusations. I would be scrutinized and would have to defend myself. I was hardly feeling ready to stand up to all of this. Yet I believed in the justice of my cause and determined to endure whatever it would take to reclaim my dignity and my reputation.

From the moment I decided to go forward with my complaint against Nina, I was plunged into a state of exquisite tension borne by the audacity of challenging both past and present abusers. By the rules of my lifelong indoctrination, I was not permitted to defend myself, let alone turn the tables, cry foul, and demand compensation. When Dr. Stall saw how anxious I was in the face of this effort, he referred me to a colleague, Gayle Voight, who taught mindfulness meditation to many of his patients. Gayle was one of several angels God sent to escort me through this fearful passage.

In a course lasting a few months, I learned how to bring my attention back to neutral stimuli such as my breathing, so that my anxious thoughts wouldn't become disabling. Gayle was a wiry waif with a gentle voice who circulated among us during the class, coaching us in pace and posture. I don't recall why I chose to tell her about confronting Nina. I think I was so frightened, I couldn't hold it in. But what she said touched me deeply. "When we do these things, it's not just for us; it's another step for man and womankind. It's another step for justice," she said.

After one class, when I explained my circumstances in some detail, Gayle offered some intriguing feedback. She observed that although I sounded articulate and persuasive in my case against Nina, she felt that I was dissociated, cut off from my emotions—speaking with detachment rather than pain and anger about what I had been through. She encouraged me: "Drop your consciousness down into your heart, where the pain lies, before speaking to the Latham administration members. If you're not feeling your pain, others will not feel it either." She didn't know that as the daughter of a borderline, I had to deny my feelings early in life. That was—and is—the way my soul survived.

I also got support from my Women About Change counselors, African American survivors of domestic violence who had personally traveled the journey from victim to victor and were now mentoring others. WAC's clientele were a multiracial swath of economically disadvantaged misfortunates struggling to free themselves from addictions, battering, and family dysfunction. An Ivy League Jew they did not often see. At WAC workshops, I practiced the essential "broken record technique" and took my first baby steps toward assertiveness in crucial role-plays. Taking my final class of four given over the course of two years, I was nearing graduation. In my pursuit of a grievance against Latham University, I had the most authentic stage to exercise my new skills.

Armed with my narrative, I sought someone within the college administration to accompany me to the meetings with Nina's superiors and the ombudsman, to lend me authority. Not knowing whom to ask, I began with those who had shown compassion during my initial breakdown and appeal for help. I turned first to the campus Hillel director, Rabbi Benjamin Farber, who had offered the charitable contribution for clothing that Nina had withheld.

Rabbi Farber was flabbergasted learning that his donation never materialized for me, having forwarded a check to Nina immediately after the case conference. But hearing my story, he was more inclined to regard the breakdown of assistance afterwards to be the result of incompetence rather than malice. Nevertheless, he encouraged me to meet with the campus chaplain, Reverend Dr. Kevin Polsky, to gain an advocate. He felt the chaplain was better connected than he was within the Latham administration and could guide me in how and with whom to file a grievance.

In Reverend Polsky's office, I railed about the injustice of being denied aid Nina Musconi promised me because I chose the life-sustaining measure of two weeks in the Refuge Unit of Bournewood Hospital. I decried that the merit of thirty-two years of responsibility, self-sacrifice, and integrity had evaporated before ungrounded suspicions of mental illness—suspicions belied by my unblemished academic and employment records and my prodigious efforts to help myself after my Refuge discharge. "Why is Nina given the authority to offer and withhold assistance to students in secret, so her personal whims can wreak havoc with students' security?" I demanded.

I described her personal harassment and obstruction of aid that she and others had pledged to provide at my case conference, which she was duty bound as its leader to deliver. I reviewed the multiple incidents of abandonment by Paula Ferguson, by Amy Seidenfeld, by Phillip Yeager, by Adele Chertoff—all facilitated by Nina's resignation. I explained that I was at the most vulnerable point in my life and I was treated like a leper. I deplored the unfairness that I now owed the university student loans with interest, accepted with the promise of support that ultimately was denied me.

I enumerated the medical consequences: the years of severe depression, weight loss; the months with mononucleosis, tottering on the verge of lupus. I explained how the whole experience lodged within me as a chronic case of PTSD that left me so wounded, I couldn't pick up the pieces of my life. Having to take more antidepressant and anti-anxiety medication than ever just to maintain minimal function, I was much more impaired in my ability to trust others—to love, to work, and to finish my degree. I concluded by asking the chaplain whether he would accompany me to the university ombudsman's office to file a grievance against Nina Musconi.

Reverend Polsky expressed a kind of Gomer Pyle incredulity at my story and wished that I had asked for his help earlier as the debacle had unfolded. He kindly told me whom he believed Nina reported to in the chain of command at Latham University now that her previous supervisor, Linda Brewer, had retired. He suggested that I ask for time with Nina's present supervisors, Carla Lopez and Stephanie Wilson-Moore, who themselves reported to the provost. He claimed he would have been happy to accompany me to the ombudsman's office, but he didn't believe he was allowed to according to university policy.

I revealed to the chaplain my concern that in return for my assigning blame for this travesty to Nina, she would try to turn the tables and blame me. Assuaging my fear that I would be tarnished publicly for filing a complaint against Nina, the chaplain assured me that students who suffer negative publicity in going to the ombudsman's office usually seek out the exposure themselves—chasing down *Latham Gazette* newspaper reporters to jump into the fray. Yet he admitted that students sometimes choose this option when they are dissatisfied with the ombudsman's office proceedings.

Still in pursuit of a chaperone, I next met with Madeline Fishbane, the Women's Health director and gynecologist who had referred me to the Refuge Unit almost two years before, when I was coming apart at the seams. Although much time had passed, we easily reestablished a connection, as Dr. Fishbane had never looked upon me as anything other than a good student in pain. Dr. Fishbane was shocked to learn of all I had endured in the two years since we'd met. I explained to her that after two years of suffering, my mental health had improved since I made the decision to pursue a grievance against Nina. Madeline cautioned me that Nina was very powerful, well respected, and well protected within the Latham administration. "I'm afraid you might be hurt even more than you've been hurt already, trying to have her chastised," she said.

Although she questioned whether she could or should step out of her professional role to accompany me to the ombudsman, she offered to do what she could for me, which included trying to find someone who might accompany me, as well as being a listening ear. "I understand that you're seeking to grow from this experience and put this misfortune behind you, and I give you my support," she pledged. She acknowledged that after my discharge from Refuge, I had faced unfair judgments of instability, having been a psychiatric inpatient. "I'll read your narrative and in the meantime, I suggest you meet with Amy Seidenfeld, the director of the student counseling service, for support." I didn't know whether to laugh or cry that kind Dr. Fishbane was unaware what a hopeless broken reed Amy Seidenfeld was.

I must admit that one of the triggers for taking action now was that action was being foisted upon me. I was expected to vacate the college dormitory room at the end of the spring semester, which meant I would have to become entirely self-supporting again. I knew I was in no condition to work full-time, let alone finish my degree at the same time. I was in tremendous despair, and I managed to hold on to my part-time job mainly because I had a kind boss who wasn't scrutinizing my performance as closely as he ought. How was I going to pick up the pieces?

I was still fretting over my future—remaining alone and unable to attract a husband as my childbearing years came to a close, shouldering greater debt without even a bachelor's degree, and suffering poorer health. My sense of foreclosed options and a foreshortened future were classic PTSD symptoms. After the Latham trauma, I was even more disabled, and my anxiety about my survival was genuine. I was utterly alone without a family, but for my newfound relationship with my Creator and my growing connection to many of His acolytes. While I was infinitely stronger in my flourishing spiritual life, God Himself was now a behind-the-scenes-player, providing me with plenty of opportunities to seize my destiny, yet refraining from a cameo or clear stage direction.

In the winter of 1998–1999, I had attended several Sabbath weekends for Torah-observant singles in New York. My mentors were encouraging me to move to an Orthodox population center such as New York or Los Angeles, if I wished to grow further in my Torah learning and find my soulmate. Romping through Crown Heights—a troop of preternaturally hungry women starving for loyal male companionship—we crowded around the feet of Lubavitch luminaries such as Sarah Karmely like mice around the Pied Piper. We drank in her soothing testimony that becoming a wife and mother was as simple as recognizing the heavenly signs that a prospective suitor could be our *bashert* (destined one). In fact, the Torah declares that God has designated for each of us, man and woman, a perfect partner who is fated for us from before our own conception. If this were true, then why couldn't he live nearby and reveal himself already? While I felt too that I was plateauing in my growth as a newly mitzvah-observant Jew in a provincial community like Boston, I didn't know how to restore my economic solvency to be able to move elsewhere, as broken as I was.

Yet again, a confluence of events bespoke the hand of a *guiding Authority*. Prospects for moving to an Orthodox population center were remote. Comparing the choice of moving to Los Angeles or New York, I felt my age. I felt more inclined at a prematurely aged thirty-four to retire to Florida than I did to take up residence in a peripatetic, nonstop New York City. But moving to California seemed as easy as moving to the moon.

Raising these options with my Chabad rabbi, Mendel Zaritsky, he uttered the fateful words, "If you're going to move as far away as Los Angeles, why not move to Israel?" Bingo! Or rather, *shalom aleichem!* The idea felt as nurturing as chicken soup with matzah balls. I had lived in Israel before as an idealistic teenager with Habonim Dror, so Israel wasn't a complete unknown. And the prospect of moving closer to God's domain felt instantly right.

Just then, Mendel, the rabbi with the highest profile and biggest heart in Boston, dropped another bombshell followed by a parachute: he revealed that my mother and brother had approached him for rescue from various crises they had brought upon themselves over the years. "Miri," he said, looking squarely into my eyes, "I *know* your family. Move to Israel and *don't look back.*" Nothing could have dissuaded me from that moment on, and no words could have been more consoling.

The life instinct began to stir in me again when I thought of moving to Israel. I knew the ultimate reason for my breakdown was spiritual rather than material: I had been brought to my knees to correct how I'd banished God from my consciousness. But life in America was powered by dollars and cents. I could do nothing to acquire time for my spiritual incubation in America. Finding a job as a full-time data pusher was the only choice before me, yet I knew I was too smart to spend my life jawing at the coffee station with high school graduates. I began to research options for study in an Israeli women's Torah seminary.

Children raised mitzvah-observant in America often cap their religious education with a year or two of study in Israel before marriage. The 1960s Jewish outreach movement—arising to meet the needs of counterculture Jews stumbling into the sea of spirituality within their (rejected) grandparent's heritage—generated schools for providing a Torah foundation to the uninitiated. I had my choice of many such institutions in Israel, with varying emphases. My religious mentors agreed that Israel was the ideal new address for someone undergoing as accelerated a spiritual evolution as I was.

Yet there were hurdles to navigate, such as finding money for tuition, plane fare, insurance, medication, and storage for whatever belongings I couldn't bring with me. How could I restore myself to wholeness to make this passage possible?

Introducing such a dramatic bend in the road threw into doubt pursuing a lawsuit or grievance against Nina: Should I stay and see this to the end or flee and leave it all behind? What if I got involved in a protracted lawsuit that required my participation stateside? Should I delay a journey that might itself offer the key to my healing? Could a just settlement of a lawsuit provide me with precisely the funds I needed to make moving to Israel possible?

Dr. Stall acknowledged that the sheer number of uncertainties—notwithstanding where I would live and work if I stayed in the United States—was bound to be disabling. According to him, uncertainty was the hardest outcome for people to cope with. He believed that leaving Latham University with so much unresolved pain would prove a stumbling block to moving on with my life. Seeking restitution from Latham would bring closure and be easier to heal from, even if I failed to gain anything. "With failure, you'll feel disappointment, but it will be time limited, like grief. While you can't *expect* to receive compensation, the process of self-assertion is likely to put you back on your feet," he reassured. Ironically, Nina Musconi had once counseled the same when offering to accompany me to speak my piece to my grandfather's negligent family doctor and social workers.

Dr. Stall encouraged me to appear as a person who'd been wronged, demanding respect, rather than a victim seeking pity in my dealings with university personnel. He granted that appearing with legal representation would improve my reception from the outset. And he concurred that moving to Israel, no matter the outcome, could offer me a new beginning— infinitely preferable to lingering in a city that bore so many painful memories.

Dr. Stall advised me, "Those who make complaints and seek restitution are most successful when they come with specific demands. Negotiations over compensation proceed better with a defined agenda." The attorney added that any compensation I received would reduce the scope of a lawsuit, improving its prospects, should it prove necessary. Rather than asking for an apology—since Nina would likely refuse to admit her impropriety—Dr. Stall suggested that I ask myself what would compensate and console *me* for the trouble and pain I'd been through, and ask for that. We were keen that I should not be retraumatized in the process of gaining a hearing.

Thinking over my needs and the extra baggage that had been added to my load, I came up with a short but meaningful list of requests that to me seemed logical and legitimate. Having accepted substantial new student loans in 1997 with promises of support from the case conference members that never materialized, I maintained that this precise year's loan money should be forgiven, while I agreed to remain responsible for all my prior debt to the university. Since I'd been too ill to concentrate on my academic work during the period I lived on the borrowed money, the whole exercise had been doomed by the staff's mistreatment.

My second request was academic: I had earned thirty-four credits over eighteen years at the college and maintained a good GPA of 3.2 out of 4—despite my many incompletes. The university required only thirty-two credits for a bachelor's degree, yet my distribution of courses did not meet the criteria for any single major. Having enough credits for a diploma, I asked for the university's clemency in granting my bachelor's degree, allowing me to conclude this interminable, bitter voyage before I left America. I knew my academic life was finished, and this was my very last chance to leave with something to show for my all effort and struggle.

Finally, I asked for the perpetuation of two crucial sources of support until I left for Israel in the late fall. One was permission to remain in the college dormitory until my departure, since my part-time wages were insufficient to pay rent anywhere else. Rabbi Farber kindly offered to be my campus sponsor to see to it that I would apply for seminary in Israel and vacate the college premises on time. And I asked the university to cover my student health insurance until I left, which would reduce the cost of my mental health medications and therapy. With my depression and PTSD severely exacerbated by the Latham ordeal, I reckoned it fair to ask the college to subsidize my health care for a few more months in compensation. After seventeen years living on my own and paying my own bills, I didn't know how I was going to keep a roof over my head anymore.

With the letter of explanation composed, and the chaplain's encouragement, I wrote to ask for time with Carla Lopez, Nina Musconi's new supervisor, forwarding the narrative detailing my experience with Nina and the Latham case conference members. I did not threaten a lawsuit, though I had been assured I had grounds for one. I was denied even a meeting with Carla Lopez; I imagine her children may have made paper airplanes out of my documents. Following my underwhelming reception

Cinder-*oy*-la!

from Carla Lopez, I set my sights on the ombudsman's office
with a mixture of determination and dread.

Chapter 25

*B*aruch Hashem (thank God), as I was to find out more than once in moments of great vulnerability, aligning one's life with God brings untold blessings. God weaved His love through the network of truly caring religious people surrounding me. Compelled to leave the Latham dormitory before my August meeting with the ombudsman, I was offered room and board with a Chabad family living in Newton in exchange for help with their children. The Tesslers knew I was saving up for a course of study in an Israeli seminary, and they kindly did not ask for money from me. I continued to take the train into Cambridge to try to mop up the oil slick I'd spilled at *Public Opinion Research*. And I was thereby able to put away enough money to fund several months of study in Israel.

My chief duty in the Tessler household was making six bagged lunches for the children every day. This one got sprouts with his hummus; this one got peanut butter; this one got homemade pizza with olives, that one, cheese and tuna. I felt a bit like Lucille Ball at the candy factory's ever-escalating conveyor belt as I tried to satisfy their fancies each morning. Two-year-old Noah—their youngest son—spent much of his day pushing a plastic table and chairs into and out of the kitchen, and I enjoyed how his parents cheered on his initiative despite its pointlessness. Adele Faber and Elaine Mazlish books occupied the top of the toilet tank in the Tessler home, as Karen and David endeavored to discipline their children with sensitivity and kindness.

In the beginning, I slept in the dank basement with a bare light bulb dangling above my head, but I was soon invited to share their oldest daughter's bedroom, and we struck up a warm bond. We spent many hours giggling under the covers with a flashlight after the rest of the family had gone to bed. Hannah was ten at the time, yet bore the maturity of a matriarch at the helm of a brood of six. It was Hannah who got me to begin using my given Hebrew name. She wrote "Miranda" on a piece of paper and tore it up in a bargain-style initiation ceremony: "There," she said definitively, as the pieces wafted onto the floor, "Miri is no more. You're Rebecca now."

Chabad children are raised to look at every Jew as a beloved child of God and merely to set an example of faith and piety. They dedicate their lives to redeeming the sparks of godliness in every Jew, but make no demands—giving everything while expecting nothing. They are gratified by witnessing the delight in the heart and soul of a Jew rediscovering her heritage, and I believe I was privileged to bring this satisfaction to many of my mentors. Hannah saw a ripe fruit, and she shook me loose so I would replant my seeds in holier soil. The roots took, and I began to introduce myself to new acquaintances as "Rebecca," just like that.

Since I had been born just before the annual synagogue Sabbath Torah reading of *Toldot*—featuring Rebecca's courageous procurement of her husband Isaac's firstborn blessing for their virtuous second son, Jacob—our family's Conservative rabbi suggested that my parents give me the Hebrew name Rebecca in addition to their preferred English name. Disreputable ancestry distinguished Rebecca, one of the four biblical matriarchs. She was credited by her choice to join the righteous family of Abraham and marry Isaac, despite being the daughter and sister of frankly evil men.

Judaism teaches that parents have a share in prophecy when they choose a Hebrew name for their child. I give thanks that my parents chose for me the identity of a strong survivor who maintained her goodness despite the waywardness of her birth family. Choosing the redemption of a spiritual life, Rebecca transcended her base roots, and I was trying to do the same.

At the Tesslers, I witnessed the ingenuity of kids who are not spoiled with too many material things. They were always engaged in playing out imaginary scenarios, such as an ice cream store, a pizza shop, a fire station—with each kid taking a role in an improvised plot. They were a lively bunch of kids, whose parents had to set plenty of limits, yet I saw a lot of parental love and pride taken in their creativity and exuberance.

Meanwhile, my research into Israeli seminaries for the newly observant brought several institutions into the frame. I was encouraged to enroll in a school offering in-depth textual study of primary sources since I sought understanding rather than superficial conformity. One institution's recruitment pamphlet featured young women bearing the distinct impression of academic and material prestige. Just looking at the brochure made me quiver. Fortuitously, the director of another institution was slated to give a recruitment speech in Boston in July, and I resolved to attend.

Ruth Bramowitz, the director of Aliyot (Ascensions) College for Women, was a large and mannish woman with a dramatic flair, a rich laugh bubbling up from the depths of her considerable innards, and an undeniable charisma. I enjoyed her lecture, though I didn't find it extraordinary. Yet I was hooked when I overheard Rebbetzin Bramowitz say to someone afterwards—in the meet and greet with the audience—"Yeah, we took a woman whose parents made the Adams family look presentable and literally turned her life around." She proceeded to kvell about the salvation they had brought this poor wretch.

Careful to observe the Jewish laws of speech that forbid gossip (the transmission of even true, derogatory information about others unless precise preconditions are fulfilled), both my mentors, Gabriel Rakover and Rabbi Yosef Goodman, gently tried to steer me away from her institution and toward another without spelling out their concerns. But I refused to be dissuaded. Spending two decades trying to achieve parity with the privileged at Latham University, I sought my peer group in Israel, which I determined was the second string. That Aliyot was reputed to be the home of the misfits, the disadvantaged, and the strays suited me just fine, as long as they would rescue me and find me a good home.

Against both of my mentors' advice, I insisted on attending Aliyot College: I still saw myself as a loser needing patronage. Inhaling an intoxicating whiff of Rebbetzin Ruth Bramowitz's grandiosity, I thought I could rely on her to save me, too. Unfortunately, I didn't see I was walking into my final trap.

Chapter 26

I wish I could say that once I decided to go forward with my complaint against Nina, I had a surge of confidence that never left me. Nothing could be further from the truth. But I did notice, as did my psychiatrist and Monica, my therapist, that every time I took a step toward communicating my grievance, my depression abated a bit. When too much time elapsed without progress, I sank into malaise again. It was as though Nina Musconi and I dwelled together in some psychic, dysfunctional family system, and choosing to hold her accountable meant I could displace the stain from myself. I so needed to restore my integrity—in my own eyes as well as everybody else's. Trembling though I was before the facade of power and authority, I turned to my mentors countless times for reassurance and encouragement.

During this period, I drifted in and out of an awful state called *dissociative flashback*, in which I experienced the physiological anxiety as if the traumatic abandonment were happening again—the racing thoughts, heart palpitations, hypervigilance, and extreme fear. It was a noxious brew of PTSD symptoms, which led me to wonder whether I would fall apart and be driven back to Refuge for relief.

I took myself to Recovery, Intl. meetings to release the tension pressing out of every pore, chanting slogans such as these that I learned there: "I don't fear the people I will have to speak to at Latham University, I fear the sensations I will have to bear and the thoughts and feelings I might have *while* I speak with them" and "The sensations are distressing but not dangerous; I can endure the discomfort until comfort will come." I rejoiced in the encouragement I got from the meetings' leaders, Alice and Emmett: she, a high-functioning schizophrenic, and he, a sufferer of severe obsessive-compulsive disorder, both of whom had better self-esteem than I had, reflected in their refreshing ability to laugh at themselves. I never pulled rank amongst them, grateful for support from any corner.

In early August, two weeks before my audience with the ombudsman, I stole a week's escape to a Lubavitch summer Torah study retreat in Rhode Island and was privileged to receive a dose of wisdom from Rebbetzin Adina Blau, my mentor from Chicago. She urged me to concentrate on the goal of being *heard* by the college administration, not on the outcome of gaining loan forgiveness or my degree. "If you focus on the outcome, you'll feel defeated and victimized again if you're denied your demands," she cautioned.

She also encouraged me to communicate my disappointment to the secondary players privately so as not to shame them, which is forbidden by the Torah. Adele Chertoff, Amy Seidenfeld, Paula Ferguson, and Phillip Yeager, MD, had seemingly taken their cues to abandon me from Nina.

Adina explained that the Torah commands us to *express* our frustrations and disappointments to others, but in a respectful manner, to avoid the sin of "hating your brother in your heart" through nursing a grudge. According to her, voicing my disappointment to those who did not act with malice might elicit genuine apologies, which would be healing for me. Torah laws of human relations were given to foster conflict resolution and communal peace, not martyrdom. Meanwhile, all my friends and mentors urged me to complete the application process for seminary study in Israel, so I could leave the Latham saga behind me, no matter the outcome.

Amidst the building tension and excitement, I welcomed a guest whose return seemed a sign of heavenly favor: the otherworldly light—what I believed to be some kind of message from God Himself—began to reappear during my sessions of prayer. I felt that God was reassuring me and reminding me that I was not alone in redressing these childhood wounds by seeking the discipline of one who abused her authority just as my mother had.

God was reminding me that I was traveling this dramatic passage so that I would finally forsake human redeemers and accept God as my savior. Bringing my life into alignment with His will, I would no longer need mortal protectors. I shared my exultation with Mendel, my Chabad rabbi, that God was once again making His presence evident in my life.

My initial intention had been to go with a chaperone to the ombudsman's office. However, by the time the long-anticipated meeting arrived, I was so tanked up with encouragement from my mentors and dry rehearsals in my imagination that I felt perfectly capable of going alone. Yet I was completely unprepared for what transpired there. Before a small, Gestapo-like woman with a black butch haircut and a tall, greying man who seemed half asleep and did not utter one word during the entire consultation to prove that it wasn't so, I began to explain my complaint against Nina Musconi, the Latham University Women's Center director.

I had barely gotten the words out before Dr. Frances Kilpatrick shouted at me, "How dare you tarnish that good woman's name! She's one of the finest public servants at this university! Who are you to believe you were entitled to anything? Your claims are preposterous. She never offered you anything, and you're delusional to think you had anything coming to you.

Get out of my office, and I don't want to see your face again. The nerve of taking our time with this nonsense!"

"You mean you won't even conduct an investigation?!"

"That's right, missus, and you're lucky I don't put a sanction on your record!"

Mortified, I did my best to try to assert and reassert my experience and insist on my right to a hearing, but it was clear that she hadn't the vaguest pretense of a listening ear. She was so convinced of my guilt and Nina Musconi's innocence that she refused even to look at the stack of evidence I had brought with me. With Dr. Kilpatrick's degrading personal attack, she determined to make sure I was far too frightened and ashamed to open my mouth in protest ever again.

I left the Office of the Ombudsman shattered and hollow. I wrote Dr. Madeline Fishbane, the Latham gynecologist who had been kind to me, in a fit of despair, assigning the players celebrity lookalikes: the satanic Ruth Gordon from Roman Polanski's *Rosemary's Baby*, hurling gratuitous accusations at me while her impassive husband stood there mutely abiding my psychic disembowelment…

I witnessed the university close ranks and pull up the drawbridge before this pesky upstart who sought to expose a blemish in the staff. This one covered for that one and that one for this one. Those who were compassionate were ultimately ineffectual. The closer I got to those who bore responsibilities to me, the more violent the rejection. Who was I to dare to complain? What made me think there would be genuine concern for the fate of students or that the ombudsman's office would represent an impartial body dedicated to investigating and resolving disputes in good faith? It appeared as if my naïveté was even greater than my bad luck. I was aghast to reach behind the curtain of the Wizard of Oz at Latham University to find a sinister person prepared to wound a student who'd already suffered so much. I had come to the end of the road with my great quest to achieve justice. I didn't find redemption but rather the coldest of shoulders. I was finished, or so it seemed. Sowing the seeds of my future in Israel was my saving grace.

With a heavy heart, I applied myself to gaining admission to my seminary of choice and appealed for a grant offered to Boston residents studying in Israel. With dejection and some shame, I entered biographical details to my application to Aliyot College, downplaying the emotional ramifications of my broken family. Yet I enjoyed rendering the spiritually heady events of the last year and a half into an essay that hinted coyly at my mystical experiences. The fact is, I had been traveling in spiritual overdrive and made up for in religious intensity what my observance lacked in duration. While my formal Torah learning was thin, my commitment to embracing a Torah-true lifestyle was thorough. Through dressing modestly, forswearing swearing, refraining from intimacy with men, eating kosher, and cleaving to God with every prayer and blessing that I uttered, I had become—through the oldest, most elite system of divinely ordained behavior modification known to humankind—a better person. My imminent *aliyah* reflected a genuine ascension in my spiritual standing. America, the land of the Big Mac, was no longer a fitting home for me.

I sent off my application to Aliyot on October 8 and heard the glad news two weeks later that I was welcome. Given the vague resemblance of Aliyot College for Women to a psychiatric hospital, they might have said I was "admitted."

On a Friday afternoon in November, before the Sabbath, my rabbi, Yosef Goodman, appeared with the gift of a new ArtScroll Hebrew/English prayer book autographed with a touching farewell from the family. It was a present to accompany my journey to Israel. For many months now, I had taken succor and reassurance from the psalms that comprise the bulk of the daily Hebrew prayers.

For reasons we can't fully understand, Jews, in their unique role as God's representatives in a godforsaken world, have been bequeathed the fate of prophets scorned—reflected poignantly in our liturgy. While my first psychologist had already dubbed me "Cassandra" for having a high level of insight, which had been denounced by my family, it turns out the whole nation of Jewry is granted special wisdom when we cleave to God. Yet I see the processes of self-deception and scapegoating manifesting even between different camps of the Jewish people. Unfortunately, we reflect the defects common to the human family. Although I was hurting over the outcome at Latham, I took comfort from my religious life, which promised me the security of dwelling among those who were striving to fulfill a higher code of human behavior.

To boost my mood and occupy my final weeks in America with something practical—in between saying my goodbyes—I combed my favorite stores for all the summer clearance clothes I could find that met Torah standards for modesty: at least three-quarter-length sleeves and skirts below the knee. Nothing gave me as much pleasure as finding superior garments at giveaway prices at the end of the season. Evidently, this is the genetic endowment of a Jewess, as King Solomon lauds his mother Bathsheba for her shopping acumen in the epic tribute "Woman of Valor," sung to Jewish wives every Friday night at the Sabbath table. I was determined to cut a different form in my new life in the Holy Land. Cognizant of how dressing like a waif had advertised my weakness to my nemesis, Simon, I adopted a classic, tailored image that proclaimed self-confidence and dignity before I could open my mouth and spoil the impression.

I also spent time with a profound self-help book with the regrettably crude title *Getting the Love You Want*, by Dr. Harville

Hendrix. Completing the exercises in the book allowed me to examine and contemplate how my attraction to Simon's materialism had grown out of my own self-denial, arising from my fear of resembling my avaricious mother. Dr. Hendrix explained that individuals seek wholeness; therefore, when we disown our legitimate needs, we will subconsciously seek out these qualities in a partner—often in an exaggerated form—in a quest for balance. I was now prepared to admit that I liked dressing well, but that didn't make me a princess.

Chapter 27

With about two weeks before my departure for Israel, dissatisfaction gnawed at my insides. I don't know what possessed me, but I simply wasn't prepared to accept my sorry fate at Latham University. If I didn't obtain a better outcome, I feared I'd be victim again and again. Chalk it up to a Jewish conscience: I knew in my gut that what I went through shouldn't go unpunished. And I didn't want to schlep this painful legacy with me to Jerusalem.

With nothing left to lose, I wrote an email asking for time with Carla Lopez's superior, Stephanie Wilson-Moore, and received another rejection letter. Urging me to take my concerns to Carla Lopez or to the ombudsman, Dr. Frances Kilpatrick, Dr. Wilson-Moore revealed she hadn't even read my letter, which explained that these two women were indifferent to me at best and abusive at worst. Doggedly, I sought the next higher superior in the published chain of command at the college, forwarding Dr. Wilson-Moore's rejection letter and my narrative about the case conference calamity to the deputy provost, Dr. Alex Reed, asking for an hour of *his* time with the executive director of Hillel, Rabbi Farber, in attendance.

I explained that I was leaving for Israel after eighteen years pursuing an undergraduate degree, and that I sought to inform someone in a position to protect students of a senior administration member who had behaved reprehensibly and posed a risk to other students. I added that I wasn't a threat to anyone and didn't understand why no one would listen to me. After three days of silence, I wrote again, pressing for an answer. The deputy provost wrote back that he was checking some background details and would get back to me. In wonderment, I received an email from his secretary the following day inviting the rabbi and me to a meeting with him that Friday.

In the deputy provost's office, knowing I had limited time, I concentrated on three main points. I told him I believed Nina Musconi had misused her power and authority, and argued that a grave danger to students exists if the Latham Women's Center director may pledge and revoke university aid to students, according to her personal whim. That she conducted her business with students without anyone's supervision left us at her mercy. I was speaking out about my experience because I felt duty bound to protect others. I gave the deputy provost a huge box full of documentation in the form of meeting notes, emails, and medical records, substantiating my narrative and its consequences, and urged him to take disciplinary action against her.

Secondly, I told him that although I knew it was unlikely that Nina would acknowledge her negligence, it came as a shock to me that the ombudsman's office would refuse to investigate my complaint. I was using proper channels to file a grievance, yet I was effectively threatened and bullied into withdrawing my complaint.

Finally, I shared that I was leaving the United States to study in a Jerusalem religious institution to put this sorrow behind me, and I asked the college for mercy in waiving one or two specific major requirements to grant me my bachelor's degree. Although I had labored long and hard at Latham University against many obstacles to obtain an education—including battling for sixteen years with an undiagnosed, untreated attention deficit disorder—the trauma I suffered at the hands of Latham staff had effectively put an end to my academic future. I was angry and deeply sad that this was how I was terminating my undergraduate studies, and I believed I deserved better. Forced to shoulder the pain, the financial debt, and the unfinished business, I had been left with a medically diagnosed case of PTSD that impaired my performance until this day.

While I was not given an apology—the deputy provost was not in a position to judge the truth of my claims at first meeting—he listened to me, with unmistakable compassion, and he seemed to believe me. It was the first time in several years that I was treated with respect. I found his reception incredibly consoling. I was utterly proud of myself for not giving up until I had a hearing, even until the last minute.

The deputy provost seemed appalled by the conduct of the ombudsman. In the week before I was set to fly to Israel, Dr. Reed offered to arrange a meeting for me with the dean of the College of Liberal Arts to investigate whether my graduation could be expedited, given the extenuating circumstances.

I felt a palpable relief leaving the deputy provost's office. While I was railing at the injustice of the grievance process back in August and ruing my list of unmet demands, my rebbetzin, Adina Blau, had tried to persuade me that what I needed most in order to heal and recover was not a successful outcome, but a completion of the grievance *process*. Whether the university admitted their error and met my demands was ultimately much less important to my healing than being heard. Having no control over the response of the college, all I could do was make the issues known to them, hoping they would do right by me and act to protect others.

While I was suffering and struggling, I couldn't see the merit in Adina's position. I was preoccupied with vindication and compensation. Yet I experienced the truth of her insight firsthand as I left Dr. Reed's office feeling unburdened, finally, and ebullient. I had made a decision to free myself irrespective of the university's response by leaving for Israel to pursue my spiritual life.

I had an extraordinary and profound experience within twenty-four hours after meeting the deputy provost that showed me just how much I'd gained. I spent this next-to-last Shabbat before leaving for Israel with the Goodmans in Brookline. It was my chance to say goodbye to all the precious people that I'd befriended in that religious community.

On Shabbat morning, after synagogue, I was walking with two friends down a busy Beacon Street toward the house of a third friend to have Shabbat lunch. Who should drive by but my *mother*, whom I had not seen in more than fifteen years! She was gaping at me with wide eyes and an open jaw as if I were a ghost. She was slowing her car down but wasn't stopping. She had a questioning look on her face, searching for a sign from me to tell her what to do. Instinctively, I motioned for her to pull over. She rolled down her window, gazed at me, and repeated the words, "It works, it WORKS, IT WORKS!"

"*What* works?" I asked. She told me that a rabbi with whom she had met urged her to light Shabbat candles and ask God for a sign that I was safe and okay. She had followed his advice for the first time the very night before.

What she didn't know was that the very same morning, I had reached the end of an ordeal that had nearly killed me. Since my meeting with the deputy provost, I felt "okay," possibly for the first time in my life. If she had seen me anytime during the years prior, she would have seen my frailty, my debility, and my weakness. I would have run from her. That God chose this particular moment to bring me face to face with my mother again was one more of His tremendous kindnesses. Standing up to Nina was a *tikkun*, a spiritual reparation for my helpless childhood. Because of my act of courage, I was ready to meet my mother again without cringing.

I motioned to my mother to get out of the car. She was using crutches, having twisted her ankle. She looked uncharacteristically frail and quite a bit older. I told her in absolute truth and sincerity that I was fine. And I told her that I was moving to Israel. "Will I ever see you again?" she asked, helplessly. "I don't know," I answered, in truth. I told her that I would pray for her well-being, and—not knowing what possessed me to say it—I told her that I forgave her, that however she had treated me, I knew it wasn't her intention to hurt me. My mother got a bit tearful when I said these words. We said goodbye and she drove off.

In retrospect, I believe my impulse to console her came from my growing understanding that my mother, too, was a victim. Cut off from her source of spiritual sustenance as a Jew by her parents who'd left Torah observance, she had unmet, vital needs for the glory of closeness to God, which she misguidedly turned to her husband and children, mere mortals, to fill. Only Heaven knows what else had been betrayed in her childhood.

Immediately, I began wondering why God had chosen to have us meet again at this particular time, merely a week before I planned to leave the United States forever. Realizing that Thanksgiving Day fell the following week, I wondered if perhaps I should spend it with my mother, knowing that she would probably be alone. I am eternally grateful that the pious women with whom I spent that Shabbat talked some sense into me. For these women, the commandment of honoring parents is sacrosanct. Each one is the antithesis of callous and unfeeling.

Yet without even knowing the details, they knew that I had suffered throughout my life from my mother's brutality, and they were not convinced that she had changed. One of them said to me, "It is *your* kindness and pity coming out, that you want to spend Thanksgiving with her, but you have to protect yourself. You know that as soon as you are alone with her, she will revert to her old ways. And you have to get on that plane strong and confident. You can't afford to risk your well-being." They were unanimous in their caution, and to this day, I know that they were right. I am grateful that they were there to help me restrain my naive wishes. What had trapped me throughout my life was the facade of kindness and gentleness in my mother, masking cruelty and violence that always took me by surprise.

God privileged me to have closure with my mother after I was restored to strength. Perhaps because I was right in my impulsive words—and she does mean well by me in her heart, no matter how devastating her behavior—God privileged her to hear that I forgave her and allowed us to say goodbye before I left America. I believe as well, that in His kindness and mercy, God wanted me to realize how much I'd grown. I have kept my vow to pray for her and the rest of my family. I know that their healing is in God's hands.

The following week at the university, my vindication gained speed. The deputy provost emailed me that he had forwarded a copy of my narrative to the director of the College of Liberal Arts, who agreed to meet with me about expediting my graduation. Rabbi Farber accompanied me to this meeting as well. Three staff members attended: the director of the college, an advisor who had once harshly rebuked me, and the faculty consultant for an interdisciplinary *humanities* major. The atmosphere in the room was one of palpable concern. It was clear to me that I was being regarded as a truthful witness and a worthy recipient of compassion.

Given my sufficient course credits and grade point average, I was asking them to waive a few requirements to grant me a bachelor's degree with my existing record of courses. Appealing to them for mercy, I let them know that I was leaving the country to heal from a traumatic ordeal about which they now knew the details.

The rabbi and I agreed afterwards that I was even more eloquent and persuasive in my second meeting with university staff. Ultimately, we came to a compromise that acknowledged my personal gain through this whole trial: I was promised my bachelor's degree after I finished the class on modern Judaism taught by my friend and mentor, Professor Rakover. My friendship with Gaby was among the handful I planned to take with me from the university, and I cherished the course material. In more fortunate Divine Providence, which would ultimately result in my fulfillment of this plan, Gaby and his family would also move to Jerusalem within a year or two.

I was treated with dignity and respect by the College of Liberal Arts staff, and I felt their compassion like a balm to my bruised soul. While I received none of my original requests, I spoke my piece, and I was believed. And as Adina Blau suggested, that ultimately meant everything to me. The loss of my reputation had been the gravest wound. Rabbi Shimon is quoted in the Mishnah: "There are three crowns: the crown of Torah, the crown of the priesthood, and the crown of kingship; but the crown of a shem tov [*a good name*] surpasses them all" (Ethics of our Fathers 4:17).

Before leaving the university, I emailed my exultation and gratitude to Madeline Fishbane, MD, the Women's Health director and sole staff member who had always been in my corner. To this day, I do not know whether any investigation or disciplinary action was taken against Nina Musconi, yet I left the college a winner. I have not looked back.

My eighteen-year odyssey at Latham University was over. Eighteen years, I realized, was heavy with symbolism: the Hebrew word *chai* (life) is comprised of the letters *chet* and *yud*, respectively valued in gematria as ten and eight, with a total of eighteen. That is why Jews often donate money in multiples of eighteen as a good omen for life. I had spent a lifetime in my struggle at Latham, coming in as a damaged and helpless daughter, yet leaving as a woman spurned who found redemption by turning to the one true Source of life itself. And now I was going Home.

At the end of two years of training, each Women About Change graduate was invited to design a T-shirt depicting her identity as a survivor. While my request to pay extra to receive a more modest, long-sleeved T-shirt was denied me, in every other way, my T-shirt bore witness to the Source of my newfound courage. At the top, I painted a Hebrew acronym which means "with the help of Heaven," written by observant Jews in the corner of every piece of writing. Below these Hebrew letters appears: "My name is Rebecca! Lord, please grant me healing, strength, and the courage to help others. My truth is my POWER and I will speak it with the help of God. No more Silence. No more Shame." I painted two images on my T-shirt: the biblical matriarch, Rebecca, is likened to "a rose among thorns" because of her wicked relatives. The thorns surrounding the rose drip the blood I shed in my years of suffering. And I painted a rainbow in between the mountain peaks from my unforgettable, prophetic dream at the beginning of my voyage to recovery.

While Women About Change's graduation ceremony took place two weeks after I left the United States, I schlepped in my limited hold luggage all the reading materials we were given—in tribute to the importance of what I learned there. True to the essence of a Jew—the Hebrew root for Jew means "one who gives thanks"—I sent WAC a check for $500 within my first year of marriage to credit them for their inimitable service.

Before I left America's shores, I gave away my extensive astrology library—three shelves full of the best books on chart interpretation and forecasting I could find, collected over twenty years. I had found more questions than answers in their pages, though they offered me insight. I called up Samantha Chadry, my local astrology guru, who had once given me some free guidance in a desperate phone call. We met and I gifted her with all but a handful of the books.

Sources in traditional Judaism corroborate the fact that the movements of the heavenly bodies influence human character and destiny. Judaism even sanctions using astrological insights to craft a constructive, meaningful life. In one salient example, the Talmud tells the story of a person born with a strongly placed planet Mars—regarded to be destined for violence—who is encouraged to become a "spiller of blood" in a *holy* manner, by becoming a surgeon, a mohel (a ritual circumciser), or a shochet (a kosher butcher; Babylonian Talmud, *Shabbat* 156a).

However, the Torah expressly prohibits examining the heavens for propitious times to perform deeds—in other words, for using the knowledge to play chess with God. Relinquishing my astrology books, I was following the Torah's injunction "to be simple with God," trusting Him completely with my future.

In Judaism, our performance of the commandments and our lifelong efforts to improve our characters should proceed independently of the prevailing and constantly changing astrological winds. In fact, the Jewish nation is promised to be "above the *mazal*"—liberated from the influence of the planets— as long as we follow God's will and fulfill the mitzvot. I have come to understand that it is precisely *because* we override our natural impulses in order to do the will of God—and thereby become better than our native selves—that we elicit the blessings that flow to us as a result. Sadly, when we spurn our birthright and our religious obligations, and behave like the non-covenanted nations, we become as predestined as every other people.

In our last meeting, Monica, my therapist—who had done her utmost to bathe me in unconditional love—presented me with a gift of a genuine crystal heart painted with a layer of pure gold. She teased, "This is for your evil twin," because I was always insisting that a beast lurked within me. She herself was truly a gift to me, as I have savored my memories of our bond.

In what surely appeared to the Tesslers—my Chabad hosts—as a concession to debauchery from which they tried to dissuade me, I spent my last night before leaving for Israel at the Brighton apartment of my old flame, Jacob Eisen, who had driven me to the Refuge Unit at Bournewood Hospital. Jacob had generously offered to take me to the airport with my luggage and to store the many boxes of papers and memorabilia I couldn't bring with me. While I was heedlessly violating Jewish law—which prohibits an unmarried man and woman from sequestering themselves alone together—I knew I had nothing to worry about. Jacob, like my other secular male friends, had grown accustomed to my passionate religiosity and regarded it as the nonnegotiable chastity belt it was.

Though my old friends regarded me as a complete anachronism, they respected my effort to live by my new principles. Yet I was not so principled that I was prepared to forgo transportation to the airport and free storage, or Jacob's magnanimous offer to front me the money for plane fare. Having met my family, Jacob was a willing Gabriel Byrne to my Bridget Fonda in *Point of No Return*. He was the sacrificial godfather who cedes the girl to her higher purpose and paves the way for her freedom. It was an unrequited romantic role custom-designed for a forty-three-year-old inveterate bachelor.

The following day, when Jacob came back from work to take me to the airport, he found me sitting on the living room floor amidst the flotsam of a shipwreck: half-open suitcases, guts splayed out across the carpet. How could I decide what I would and would not need — for the rest of my life? If it were not for the pressure of the clock, I would still be sitting there today.

Fortunately, Jacob's shock and apoplexy propelled me into action. I shoved whatever would fit into my bags and closed them with the help of his two-hundred-pound body. Off we raced to the airport.

My utter calm and conviction about the rightness of leaving America for the Land of Israel assuaged my anxiety about what I was doing. I was free from angst. I was leaving my erstwhile home, alone, with little more than a few hundred dollars and a few strangers' addresses in my pockets.

My serenity was uncharacteristic yet profound. I sat for the flight between a secular Israeli Jew from Canada and a Christian Arab from Jerusalem. As we landed, I gripped each of their hands. I was so ecstatic, the plane could have gone down in flames and I wouldn't have stopped grinning.

Chapter 28

I arrived at Aliyot College for Women in Jerusalem heady with the accomplishment of having shattered my own glass ceiling: I was thirty-five years old and six thousand miles from home. I had left my mother and father, Simon, and all my painful memories behind. I was living on sheer faith for the first time in my life. I didn't know what I would do when my money ran out, and I didn't have a plan. I knew I was being guided by an unseen force, but to where I wasn't sure.

There was poetry in arriving at an Orthodox Jewish seminary at the time of Chanukah. The miracle of the single day's cruse of oil that burned for eight days marked the wresting of the ancient Jewish Temple from the Greeks who had colonized Jerusalem and turned many Jews into idolaters, in 164 BCE. The Greeks worshipped the body and mind as human temples independent of God. And I had just renounced my slavish pursuit of secular academic study in favor of rediscovering the wisdom of my ancestors. Rejecting atheism and nihilism—the moldy fruits of the twentieth century—I was reconnecting once more to the Tree of Life of my forbears. What had preserved the essence of a Jew through every kind of calamity was the study of Torah, cast aside so recklessly by my kin.

Aliyot's study hall followed the classical style of Torah learning—built on teams of two students given the task of translating and analyzing a piece of Hebrew Torah text, followed by a lecture and discussion exploring the central points. Our curriculum drew from biblical and medieval Jewish literature. I was spending my days steeped in Jewish ethical precepts, freed from having to write long academic papers that bumped up against my ADD handicap. I was as happy as a cowgirl at a rodeo. Contributing enthusiastically to class discussions, I quickly made a positive impression on my teachers.

Having understood how I had perpetuated my own indignity in the past with my bohemian look, I now made every effort to "dress for success." Rebbetzin Bramowitz, the head of the institution, noticed me right away. Each student was encouraged to choose for herself a mentor and submit to guidance, having entered seminary voluntarily in order to bring herself, her character traits, and her conduct into alignment with Torah values.

Choosing Rebbetzin Bramowitz for a mentor, when I had others available to me, had everything to do with my parents. Though I didn't yet know it, Rebbetzin Bramowitz shared with my parents a signal trait—her narcissism (which distinguished my imago, in Harville Hendrix's ingenious construction)[1] — thereby drawing me like a siren into a dance that would ultimately lead to humiliation. Rebbetzin Bramowitz was a very large, charismatic woman who wielded her approval selectively, knowing that her winks, hugs, and conspicuous praise carried cachet for which most students were in competition.

---

[1] Hendrix defines the imago as a composite picture of the adult caregivers (usually parents) who influence a person most strongly in childhood. See Harville Hendrix, PhD, *Getting the Love You Want: A Guide for Couples* (New York: HarperCollins, 1988), 38.

While I was learning the most exquisite profundity in my daytime Torah classes, the Aliyot dormitories were a hothouse for insanity. When I first arrived in my dorm apartment, I was met by a pear-shaped vixen named Valerie who informed me curtly that my room was the small, dark one at the end of the hall. Her long tangle of red curls announced the hot, selfish temperament I would come to loathe. Faith, a pretty lawyer of almost forty, used to march over to a cluster of us and demand, "WHAT ARE YOU SAYING ABOUT ME!" when we were discussing replenishing the toilet-paper supply. The rebbetzin thought it savvy to house all the older singles together in one apartment, but that only made for especially concentrated neurosis—putting every overflowing estrus factory under one roof.

The next woman to arrive in our apartment was a tall British woman named Nicole. She was as skinny and hard as flint, and her total absence of body fat—despite ingesting massive quantities of junk food—matched her conspicuous lack of human feelings. She was the most difficult woman for me to adjust to. She had a caustic sense of humor and a maddeningly deceptive habit of thanking others constantly that I came to realize was only a cheap gesture to keep the favors coming.

A registered letter in official type came to our apartment every week for Nicole. I suspected she was running from something, either creditors or the law. She must have obtained some kind of legal deferment from her troubles while she was enrolled full-time in a program of religious instruction. Covered up and learning Bible by day, she went out at night wearing spaghetti-strapped skimpy cocktail dresses under her overcoat. She would come home and boast of the men who'd wined and dined her each night: married, single, young, old—anyone with a wallet. She hid her mercenary aspirations only in the study hall, where she claimed to be engaged in a spiritual quest. In the

257

dorms, she chain-smoked and walked around in a thong, cracking jokes about pedophilia. Although she confessed to hating children, she resigned herself to having them one day as the price for a man's favors.

I couldn't get a handle on Nicole: she sidled up to those in power, purring like a cat, flattering and humoring teachers and students alike, yet spoke contemptuously about them behind their backs. She railed in private that religious people were weak, but she elected to live amongst them and study their words and deeds.

The hostility beneath her charming smile came out only behind closed doors. If anyone dared to criticize her, she became enraged, the glint in her eyes betraying her sheer joy at having an opportunity to drop her "good girl" pretentions.

Nicole and I bore a certain fascination for each other, because she was dishonest, and she knew I was utterly genuine. She delighted in cornering me in acts of trivial hypocrisy: misunderstandings over whether identical yogurts in the communal fridge were mine or someone else's, tardiness in doing chores, or failure to be honest about my true feelings over others' crass behavior, which she seemed to intuit.

Nicole was simply too much for me to take. After Simon, my gaskets were blown by vicious human beings pretending to be virtuous. She even had Simon's habit of conspicuously confessing what a horrible person she was, inviting us to deny it. Like him, she bickered over every communal expense, yet hoarded the most expensive perfumes and cosmetics. This too-familiar snake in the grass upset my equilibrium. After two months of silent suffering, I found myself tattling on her, despite my reluctance to engage in *lashon hara*—bearing true tales about people. But when I went to Rebbetzin Bramowitz to share my concerns about Nicole, twice, I had them flung back in my face: I was too sensitive. I was too judgmental. I should loosen up.

It is true that I lacked a certain ability to fit in amongst the Aliyot student body. I was too serious, and I took my new obligations to behave in a Torah-true manner to heart. I solved my social problem by making friends outside the school, with women who'd been mitzvah-observant their whole lives. While I suffered from the ambivalently observant Aliyot social scene, I still loved the learning.

Yet I found myself confronting the gap between the rarified spirituality we were imbibing from ancient texts and the fickle practice in the catty, immature behavior of many of the students. One was Madison, a spoiled brat from Los Angeles with a compulsory French manicure, who whined her way to the best reference books and learning partners. She had an unmistakable way of sliding her lunch tray half over an empty place at the communal table when one of the less popular women or I would approach, only to yank the tray away when one of her sycophants appeared. Another was Cheryl, who couldn't muster a smile if you weren't a member of the same clique, ignoring my cheery "hello," while she conducted her morning round in bitter silence as if I weren't there. And these women were the favored students at Aliyot College.

Ironically, I found the best students were the ones who felt Rebbetzin Bramowitz's wrath. In my presence, Rebbetzin Bramowitz savaged a hard-working, genuinely good-hearted disabled woman from South Africa, accusing her of demanding that everyone placate her for her misfortune. I hadn't witnessed that living with this woman, but I did see that the more aggressive women expected the rebbetzin to back them in taking advantage of the socially weaker students. Judy, a roommate with whom I shared some kinship, told me confidentially, "If you want to get what you want at Aliyot, flatter the rebbetzin—that's her currency." *Where had I experienced this before?*

It was a school tradition at Purim for the students to put on comical plays to entertain the staff and one another. Nicole and I collaborated in the writing of a Purim spoof that pitted our minds in fruitful tension, yielding a play that was uproariously funny, yet so ribald that the rebbetzin forbade its production. She claimed that I would be ashamed I'd written it one day. But I felt victorious that I'd been able to match wits with my archenemy and emerge with a genuinely funny if totally irreverent Purim parody.

After three months of learning, Rebbetzin Bramowitz bestowed the gift that would keep me at Aliyot long after the institution would prove toxic to me: she elected to grace me with a five-month scholarship for tuition and dormitory fees. Rebbetzin Bramowitz declared that she believed I would give back to the Jewish people someday, and their investment in me would return to them. I was touched by her gift, even more so because I was cognizant of how my moral fastidiousness was making me a cipher among the women in the study hall. Yet the staff wanted me to stay.

When I stumbled upon a drug party held in one of the dormitories, I felt unfit to merge with a group too hip for me. I closed down emotionally, pulling into myself for fear of confrontation or risking coexistence with those whose habits and values I disdained. I hated myself for harboring such bitterness toward some of the students, particularly Nicole, but I couldn't relinquish my sense of propriety.

Suffering a raging case of *baal teshuvah*-itis (when the new revelation that the world has a Creator with expectations of us merges with a little Torah knowledge), I became so fearful of sin that I behaved like a monk. I had always been averse to telling tales, long before I became religiously observant. Learning that gossip was a sin, yet being woefully ignorant of the laws that not only *permit* the speaking of *lashon hara* but in certain cases make it mandatory, left me paranoid about causing anybody harm with speech. Even when that left me defenseless.

One day I could take the pressure no longer. I fled from the study hall and climbed atop the highest hill I could find, occupied only by wildflowers and an abandoned relic. There, as close as I could come to Heaven, I took my petition to God: Why was I suffering like this? I had come to Jerusalem searching for sanctity. Why had God made me dwell with decadence? What was this for? What was I to learn from this? I let my tears pour forth, knowing that I was safe to express myself with God as my only witness. I cried and cried, letting go of the burden of being above reproach in a godforsaken institution.

I was blessed to receive answers almost immediately. Though I didn't have visions of light anymore, on rare occasions I had such clear intuition that I knew it was Heaven speaking.

That day on the hilltop, God told me through my own conscience that I couldn't afford to think of Nicole in such bleak terms for my *own* sake—not for her sake. I had convinced myself that she was the devil incarnate, yet here I was, a shivering wreck in her presence. I had sacrificed my peace of mind obsessing over her devious nature. I had to pull myself together and let go of my silent campaign to discredit her. Because I'd kept my observations to myself, aside from seeking Rebbetzin Bramowitz's counsel, I had condemned myself to isolation and loneliness in addition to anguish.

Then I had a most comforting apprehension, which restored my morale: "Remember who *you* are," God seemed to reassure me, reminding me that He had shared with me unusual visions because I was indeed worthy and valuable. One who is privy to such a close relationship with God remains forever chosen and beloved; our bond was unshakeable. I felt sobered and fortified by these insights and realized that my duty was to remain true to my values, while relinquishing the obsession with Nicole and her admirers.

Aliyot had four study levels from novice to advanced, and I had started at the second. At the helm was a loose cannon called Rebbetzin Segal—a *baalat teshuvah* herself—who had not impressed me from the very beginning. She swung into class late on most mornings, dragging an overstuffed carpetbag and excusing herself on account of her ADD, on the days she didn't blame it on her narcissism. I found her exhibitionism immature, and I resolved not to expose myself unduly to her. Fortunately, with hard work and diligence, I placed out of her level early on and could limit my dealings with her.

Unfortunately, she ended up being the trigger for my comedown with Rebbetzin Bramowitz. Rebbetzin Segal saw me sitting alone in the study hall one day. She approached and asked me why I seemed so forlorn. I shrugged my shoulders, wary of her sudden interest in me. I wasn't about to unload to her—I had my standards.

"Rebecca," she dug in, "you're not doing anybody any favors holding everything in. It's a mitzvah to talk about it when something is troubling you. You could give yourself an aneurism holding in so much tension. What is it? Well, I see you don't trust anybody here. You think you're too good for us." She seemed to realize I was bursting at the seams and would buckle with a little pressure.

Cornered, I couldn't hold it in. I told her how troubled I was living with someone like Nicole. I despised everything she stood for and felt exquisitely uncomfortable in her presence. She reminded me of people, like Simon, who'd played a devastating role in my life, and I felt degraded by her. I'd tried to talk to the rebbetzin several times but she wouldn't listen, and I had built myself a life outside the school. I hadn't talked to anybody else about my feelings, and I felt quite lonely.

Rebbetzin Segal said nothing while I unburdened. She just listened. I went to the next class feeling deeply uneasy that I had exposed a fellow student and had no idea what Rebbetzin Segal thought about my words. The tension and self-rebuke were beginning to choke me.

In the lull after classes, I beckoned to Rebbetzin Segal: "What do you think about what I said? You didn't say anything while I spoke." It was getting dark, and she invited me to walk her home. We stopped off at a nearby park overlooking the lights of the city twinkling in the distance.

"Rebecca, you're a pious idiot," she said. "You aren't supposed to torture yourself with the laws of speech. They're there to support you. It took our staff months to discover what you recognized almost immediately about Nicole. It would have helped us a great deal if you had come forward sooner with your observations. We might not have poured so much into her, not realizing that she was a bottomless pit. Someone who studies Bible in my class for six months and then declares blithely that she doesn't believe in God has an agenda. I wish we hadn't been so naive."

"I remember in graduate school," she continued, "I had a fellow student like Nicole in my class, and I couldn't concentrate the entire semester. I was completely unnerved by this student and her duplicity. I couldn't understand why I was the only one who saw it. I felt very alone. Why did you suffer for so long without asking for help? Nicole is very slick. I can understand why she bothered you so much, hearing your history. But your perceptions are on target. You are absolutely right."

"You mean the staff has come to the same conclusions about her?" I asked.

"We have," she said, "I only wish it hadn't taken us so long!"

I shuddered realizing that indeed I'd been living with a snake, feeling a wave of bitterness that Rebbetzin Bramowitz hadn't reached out to me and didn't think to validate my feelings and offer me compassion, once it became clear that my judgment had been correct. I was angry. I had felt bereft for months over the loss of Rebbetzin Bramowitz's support, yet I wondered if something could be salvaged from our relationship now that my perspective had been vindicated.

I penned Rebbetzin Bramowitz an obsequious, flattering letter that nevertheless dared to express my disappointment that she hadn't reached out to reassure me or express concern for my welfare, once the staff had ferreted out Nicole and realized she was as deceitful and manipulative as I had claimed she was. Rebbetzin Segal had even called her "sociopathic." Yet I still felt abashed that I had allowed my distress over living with Nicole to dampen the joy I felt in actualizing a religious lifestyle.

But what happened next, I couldn't have foreseen. Rebbetzin Bramowitz yanked me into her office, angrily confronting me over the audacity of my letter. "This letter is outrageous. How *dare* you tell me how to run my school! I *like* Nicole," she declared. Noting Nicole's penchant for flattery, this shouldn't have surprised me.

"But Rebbetzin Segal told me the staff sees it now, too. I was right about Nicole. She told me," I sputtered.

"Oh, yeah, get her in here and see what she says," she commanded.

I searched the building for Rebbetzin Segal and summoned her to Rebbetzin Bramowitz's office.

"Tell her what you told me," I urged.

"What do you mean? I *listened*. I didn't tell you anything," she said.

"But you told me the staff believes that Nicole is sociopathic. You told me it would have helped you if I'd come sooner with my testimony."

"I told you it would have helped *you* if you'd come sooner—that we could have helped *you* with *your* anxieties and discomfort. I didn't tell you anything about Nicole or the staff. I don't know what you're talking about. You obviously *wished* I would have agreed with you," she dissembled.

Rebbetzin Bramowitz looked on with her arms crossed—gloating—a smile of satisfaction on her lips at my exquisite humiliation.

"You're selling me down the river to save your own skin," I hissed.

"You are paranoid, delusional, and ungrateful," Rebbetzin Segal declared.

Rebbetzin Bramowitz proceeded to rail at me—accusing me of hurling outrageous accusations at her, which she could not find in my letter when I challenged her to do so. She accused me of scapegoating her and Rebbetzin Segal for what she now called my "extreme social anxiety." She declared they'd never had a problem like me at Aliyot in her entire career. While I insisted my motivation in writing had been a sincere desire to rebuild our relationship—which had run aground over Nicole—she could not bear the suggestion that she might have let me down. Any intimation of mine of error on her part triggered the most ferocious aggression from this erstwhile "Torah personality." She threw pieces of my vulnerable family history at me in front of Rebbetzin Segal, which I'd shared with her confidentially months before, as evidence for what she now called my "hallucinations."

Exhausted from vainly trying to reassure the rebbetzin of my conciliatory motives, I pointed out that all these months, I hadn't campaigned for one student to join me in my assessment of Nicole, no matter my exquisite tension. She couldn't accuse me of harming anyone, only myself.

"That's the only reason we're letting you stay," she declared, "You can be sure of it. But you'd better watch your back." With that, Rebbetzin Segal left the room.

Before dismissing me from her office, Ruth Bramowitz vowed the words that shook me more than any other: "Don't let any matchmaker ask me for a reference about you. I can promise you my report will keep you single for life," she sniggered.

Matchmakers in the Orthodox world rely heavily on seminary teachers to recommend newly observant women, who are otherwise unknown to them. In the world of the newly mitzvah observant, evaluations by heads of Torah institutions are like SAT scores for the college-bound—they carry weight and cannot be dismissed. I knew that any guy who was "checking me out" would inquire at Aliyot. The institution where I'd chosen to spend my first seven months in Israel was now sinking my chances to build a future. And at almost thirty-six, my time was running out.

I careened out of the office and the study hall, too embarrassed to allow anyone to see my disgrace.

My dear friend and neighbor, Joyce, saw me huddled on the back steps of our building looking like my dog had just been run over by a tractor trailer. She begged me to confide in her, but I wouldn't. I didn't tell other students. I didn't tell other teachers. I didn't lead a mutiny. I just bore the pain of being framed. And perhaps, that is why, when my day came, I was able to give blessings that overturned the heavens for a posse of older single women whose fortunes changed after my wedding. One by one, they got married within the year—dropping like ducks in a shooting gallery. Our Sages say: Get a blessing from one who is humiliated and stays silent.[2]

Meanwhile, Judy, my lone remaining friend in the apartment, was becoming unglued over a romance gone wrong, after jubilantly dating for several weeks. Judy's romance was curdling owing to a common case of courter's cold feet. With proposals of marriage offered before secular couples would have learned one another's middle names, the drama of dating in seminary comes fast and furious—never mind that secular couples have mingled bodily fluids before they know one another's middle names. Marriage remains a remote, tepid threat in secular dating.

Judy thought she was getting married, and at thirty-something, this would have been a salvation. Instead she was being dumped. Judy began to take out her rage and bitterness on the hapless creatures that congregated on the refuse left on her dirty dishes, and me. She could be found at odd hours frantically spraying the cracks in the walls and floor with WD-40 to get rid of the termites. Only she was the only one who saw the termites. But she claimed they were everywhere.

She began leaving me notes accusing me of abandoning my responsibility to do my dishes when they were her dishes left in the sink. I knew better than to saddle any of these histrionic suffragettes with my responsibilities. For weeks, I quietly did her dishes and took over her household chores, while her paranoia continued to mushroom. It culminated one evening when she accosted me, shrilly accusing me of saying *lashon hara* about her to the rebbetzin, when it became apparent shortly thereafter that she had actually gone to the rebbetzin and complained about *me*.

---

[2] Babylonian Talmud, *Shabbat* 88b; *Midrash Eichah Rabbah*, petichta 24.

Fearful that I would tire of her irresponsibility and publicly cry foul, she made an offensive, defensive lunge and claimed to the rebbetzin that I was guilty of her neglect. It didn't matter that this was a lie. The rebbetzin bought it, and I was ejected from that apartment and placed in another one—sprung from one set of loonies and caged with another.

The second apartment had younger women who weren't as practiced in their dysfunction. There was even one young woman who'd grown up Torah observant but found herself lodged among those in the throes of molting from social decadence to purity. She was a delightful British lass named Dahlia—employed at Aliyot as a tutor—who became a lifelong, dear friend. Dahlia, ever so careful not to get embroiled in the petty apartment politics, tactfully offered me in private, "Rebecca, I think you'd be much happier at Mesorah."

Mesorah (Tradition) College was a much older institution that had pioneered education for the newly observant. It had a more stable reputation and mingled a central school for the very fresh with many satellite programs for those who had always been *frum* (religiously observant). I filed away that piece of grace and retrieved it when I was out of hope.

Why did I persist in staying at such an unhealthy institution, trying to exonerate myself? Why was I finding myself victimized yet again? It had something to do with fear: fear of the rebbetzin making good on her threats. Fear that she held the keys to my future; and therefore I must appease her in order to extract my pledge. Fundamentally, I lacked complete trust in the Creator of the World to be more powerful than those who would pretend to His throne. I still saw myself as defective, needy, and at the mercy of people with authority. I hadn't fully broken free from my past.

The picture was complicated by the fact that I adored some of the Aliyot teachers. We had rabbis in the afternoon who were all models of piety, compassion, and wisdom. I had been privileged to receive a lot of encouragement from Rabbi Meyers in my first half year at Aliyot. I found myself helplessly bawling like a baby when I learned he was leaving the school to obtain a PhD. I felt as if he were abandoning me to savages.

I had a morning Bible teacher named Debra Susskind whose specialty was the thought of Maimonides, the renowned medieval philosopher and codifier of Jewish law. She invited me frequently for Shabbat, and we cultivated a close relationship, nourished over intimate talks at her family's table. I had an inspiring teacher of the Torah laws of human relations who remained painfully aloof from me as she, Rebbetzin Bramowitz, and Rebbetzin Segal formed the central leadership triumvirate at Aliyot, and I'm sure she heard any number of lies about me. In a Purim send-up at Aliyot, the students cast me as this rebbetzin because they knew that I most shared her grace and tact. While some of the Aliyot teachers were godsends, I couldn't ignore the oedipal drama unfolding between the rebbetzin in charge and me.

A few weeks after my move to the new apartment, I came home from a trip to find the precincts in a crisis. Everyone was hysterical. Beth, one of the rebbetzin's favorites, was running a high fever, and she was staggering around, glassy-eyed. She couldn't stay on her feet, yet she was refusing to go to a doctor. She was frightening to look at, with her skin an inhuman grey next to her raging red eyes.

I persuaded Beth to let me take her temperature and suppressed a shudder when it registered above 103. I offered to accompany her in a taxi to Terem, the nearby urgent medical care center, and she agreed. However, someone in the apartment called an ambulance.

When Beth heard there was a medical crew at the door, she summoned a superhuman strength and barricaded herself in her bedroom, requiring a broken door and a brawl before Beth would submit to the medic's ministrations. It seemed as if Beth had had a forcible commitment in her past, and this event was triggering flashbacks.

Rebbetzin Bramowitz arrived, conducting herself exactly like a bull in a china shop. She glared at us and lit into us, taking sides like an Olympic boxing referee instead of reassuring and acknowledging the lot of us who were only worried about Beth and motivated by concern for her welfare. The rebbetzin couldn't manage the flock in her institution without a fight. In her mind, there were only those for her and those against her. I watched her operate, silently shaking my head in disbelief that she would castigate us for her pet's breakdown.

The following day, she blamed *me* for calling the ambulance, declaring that I excited Beth, and that without my interference, Beth would have lamely acquiesced to treatment. It didn't matter that she invented this out of whole cloth. I had nothing to do with the ambulance, but I certainly wouldn't have blamed the woman who called it for deliberately throwing a match to kerosene.

Unfortunately, the rules of the game at Aliyot were all too obvious: blame Rebecca, and the rebbetzin will buy it. I was the sharpshooter behind Lee Harvey Oswald in Rebbetzin Bramowitz's book, her enemy number one, and everyone knew it. Although the rebbetzin herself had just admitted to me, "For eight months, I didn't hear one complaint about you from anyone, and now I find out you are behind everything," she didn't question the dynamics driving her new assessment. She never asked herself if her tendency to publicly gossip— broadcasting her disdain for particular students—might have set me up to become the fall gal.

I might have been guilty of being too prim and proper, but I never insisted anyone share my scruples. I tried to be an angel at Aliyot because I thought that is what God expected of me. And yet I became the scapegoat. Not only because I had the chutzpah to expect righteousness from the head of my seminary, but also because I was still currying favor, fearing people instead of God. I should have had enough faith in God and myself to leave a corrupt institution and find a better one.

What happened next bore a touch of the supernatural. Our school was traveling to the South with the rebbetzin for a Shabbat out of town, which I ordinarily would have attended. Yet I began running an unexplained fever, which led me to stay home. That Sabbath morning, a member of the community visited me who had been asked by Rebbetzin Bramowitz to inform me that I was being evicted from the school. The sudden fever, which ended as mysteriously as it came, saved me from a demeaning Shabbat with the rebbetzin while clueless that she was planning to oust me.

But a freak accident the following week made my expulsion even more humiliating. Walking along a commercial boulevard near my home, I leapt over a low wall surrounding a parking lot in order to reach a store. Yet I underestimated the height—catching my foot and falling back onto the sidewalk. I knew when I hit the pavement on my right arm that I had suffered a grievous blow. Wincing with pain, I squeezed back a rivulet of tears. A passerby took me to the emergency room, where they casted my broken radius. Though I hoped that Rebbetzin Bramowitz would allow me to stay until I healed, I was informed I had to leave even sooner.

In a textbook example of a "lucky" break—scrambling to find shelter—I found myself a room in a home owned by a Sephardic widow named Mazal, who was the soul of my grandfather in female form. While I was casted, she gently washed my hair each morning in the sink and prepared me nourishing diced vegetable salads with the Moroccan grandmother's lightning speed. The limitations of our respective Hebrew-English language skills meant we could only go so deep in conversation, like my grandfather and me, but she, like he, was a tender nurturer. For 250 shekels a month, I considered myself extraordinarily lucky to be occupying one room in her downstairs that was a quarter the size of the tiny Cambridge studio where I first entertained mystical visions. Yet there were no crazy Anglo would-be religious women making my life a living hell, and I was living with someone whom I could trust. I only wished I had gotten away from Aliyot long before.

Aliyot College was not an abject disaster: I learned a lot of Torah there and cherished my enduring relationships with certain teachers. But I also learned, finally, to be so wary of signs of narcissism in others that I feel rather insulated from traumatic reenactments. At the institution where I transferred, I picked it up loud and clear from a certain rabbi who has a worshipful following. I listened to a few minutes of one lecture and felt its presence like a clammy grasp for adoration. He may do much good for those who are not destined to dangle too close to the web. But I refused to become one of his groupies. I never entered his classroom again. I realize I have such a native vulnerability to narcissistic people that I dare not expose myself to this allergen. In the footsteps of the narrator of Portia Nelson's immortal poem, "Autobiography in Five Short Chapters," I finally learned *to walk down another street.*[3]

---

[3] Portia Nelson, *There's a Hole in My Sidewalk* (Hillsboro, OR: Beyond Words Publishing, 1993).

Part Six

Redemption

And I will take you to Me for a people, and I will be to you a God; and you shall know that I am the Lord your God, Who brought you out from under the burdens of the Egyptians.

—Exodus 6:7

Chapter 29

Nursed by God, Mazal, and time, I got up my nerve to apply to Mesorah College, a much larger and more established women's Torah seminary in Jerusalem. I was almost out of funds, but luckily for me, I was in the right place: a central tenet of Jewish religious life is the concept of tzedakah (charity, from the root word *tzedek*, justice). The Torah commands Jews to furnish those without means with the wherewithal to conduct their lives with dignity. That secular Jews in modern times flock to communist and socialist movements is no accident: it is in our bones to give and share. However, donating generous charity, providing interest-free loans, and helping others find employment or open businesses are the Torah's answers to poverty, rather than income redistribution or socialism. Although there are plenty of poor in Israel, the number of organizations that provide for the needy is practically limitless.

I was gifted with two sources of tzedakah: Mesorah College accepted me as a full-time student without requiring me to pay a penny, and a philanthropic rabbi, who heard my biography and understood my quest to establish myself as an Orthodox Jew, agreed to provide me a small but meaningful stipend for living expenses for one year. Mesorah provided classes all day and a free hot lunch and supper. I signed an informal "moral obligation" agreement obliging me to pay back the whole tuition should I someday become able (which I in fact fulfilled when I could do so). I paid my modest rent and incidentals from part-time work folding laundry and washing dishes for an erudite American Torah teacher named Naomi, who became a close friend.

At Mesorah, I qualified for the program for somewhat learned women who had already committed themselves to living as mitzvah-observant Jews—receiving group Torah classes in the morning and afternoon lessons conducted one-on-one with tutors. The seminary curriculum included Bible, law, ethics, prayer, philosophy, history, holidays, and life-cycle studies. (Some women's seminaries include the study of mysticism, Chassidism, or Talmud.) I was thrilled. Although I still felt a bit odd as a thirty-five-year-old among mostly younger women, I made enough friends of all ages to keep me company, and I was fortunate to be paired with tutors with whom I shared wonderful rapport. No matter the social challenges I had encountered at Aliyot, I loved learning Torah and never doubted that I'd made the right decision to devote my life to it.

Mesorah had a more wholesome atmosphere and a decentralized administration, posing minimal risk of marginalizing a student because she failed to kowtow to someone in charge. A caring British rabbi who related to every student like a granddaughter headed my school. His wife, a renowned midwife, also ran a worldwide charity organization collecting for Jerusalem's poorest. Though this couple had no children of their own, they had shepherded thousands from the far-flung, remote edges of Jewish life to absorption within the Orthodox community.

Those who work in *kiruv*—the quest to bring nonobservant Jews back to the traditions of their forefathers and foremothers—share a profound delight in restoring a priceless legacy lost to Jews through no fault of their own. Children born to Jewishly uneducated parents are not held responsible in Jewish law for their lack of understanding or practice (at least during the time in history when access to Jewish learning was difficult).[1] Most Jews born in North America don't know that 125 years ago, European Jewish immigrants to America were largely traditional, but had left Jewish observance, mainly because of pressures to make a living. The Reform movement began in the 1800s in Germany, and later, spread to America. Jews born after the founding of various twentieth-century American denominations such as Conservative, Reconstructionist, and Renewal harbor the illusion that Judaism was always "denominational." It is as if they are led to believe that God provided Moses with three or four versions of the Ten Commandments when he ascended Mount Sinai: original recipe, reduced calorie, lite, and zero percent. One version requires keeping the Sabbath laws and three of the four dispense with them.

Simply contemplating that the 200 years since reformers diluted Judaism are but a blink in the *3,800 years of Jewish history*—during which time being Jewish always involved a unique, consecrated lifestyle—is enough to give contemporary liberal Jews pause. Yet most don't pause to contemplate, because they neglect to study Jewish history and learn Judaism from "denominational" teachers who smear classic Judaism with so many postmodern grievances. They are born into a milieu like mine, which frowned on belief in God and the Torah, holding its prophecies to be naive, superstitious, and backward. One need only behold the rebirth of the nation of Israel in her ancient homeland after two thousand years to see those "laughable" biblical prophecies fulfilled.

---

[1] Maimonides, *Mishneh Torah*, Mamrim 3:3.

With the full depth of Judaism arrayed before me, I set about dedicating myself to learning, as well as deepening the many friendships I was making in the city. I stayed in touch with some Aliyot teachers and was fortunate to be their Shabbat guest, even as I formed new bonds with teachers at Mesorah. I was still gaining emotional repair from all this caring, and I strove as always to repay the kindnesses wherever I could. My equilibrium restored after learning a few months at a nurturing Mesorah College, I began to anticipate the next, most vulnerable stage in my development as an observant Jewish woman.

Chapter 30

I had promised myself I would begin the search for a husband by the age of thirty-six. Like a pint of cottage cheese nearing its expiration date, I knew my appeal was at least partially determined by my freshness and the promise of fertility I could still offer. But I was loath to enter the market when I knew I would be scrutinized and forced to account for the breach between my family and me. In other words, what kind of self-respecting, normal Orthodox Jewish man would accept a woman who had made herself an orphan? How could I seem anything but a scoundrel? Because of the rival pressures of knowing my shelf life was dwindling, yet dreading the exposure that dating would require, I cried for three days straight before making my first appointment with a traditional matchmaker. Emptied of all the anxiety and grief my body could hold, I persevered and met my first *shadchanit* just after my thirty-sixth birthday.

Before meeting bachelor number 1, I consulted with Rabbi Feder—a rabbinic judge and my Jewish law teacher from Mesorah—who advised me to keep my romantic past to myself. He gave me a *psak halachah* (a ruling from Jewish law) that I could be much more circumspect about my family details than I was accustomed to, as well. According to Torah law, this history was irrelevant to my present conduct. He identified which facts I was obliged to tell a serious suitor and when. His guidance relaxed me about the matters over which I felt the most vulnerable.

Rebbetzin Esther Apfelbaum, the matchmaker and mentor to students at Mesorah College, cautioned me that at thirty-six, I would not have my pick of desirable mates. Older bachelors frequently bore more than a few nicks and blemishes. I vowed to myself to make it work with whichever man I was introduced to unless the effort proved untenable.

But I was not prepared for just how prescient her words would be. Halfway through my modest round of ten prospective suitors, I had been treated to the effeminate doctor who bore a deep dark secret, which he broadcast, adorned with sequins and rhinestones; the skeleton with no hair (not even eyebrows) who left me sitting at a table to chat for half an hour with the restaurant owner; and the mumbling, schizotypal son of a yeshiva dean, who paced and wrung his hands in the restaurant corridor in between courses. And I went out with each of these guys more than once! The only normal guy among them—a *baal teshuvah* whose nerdiness rejoiced me with its familiarity—shocked me by rejecting *me* after the first date. A straight-talking rival matchmaker told me he was searching for a cash cow who could fund his full-time Torah learning for years. It did not take long before my determination, forbearance, and hope turned into bitterness, resentment, and self-pity.

Yet somehow, this parade of deplorable options brought about a catharsis. After wallowing for a while in a swamp of "it's not fair," I volunteered to help my landlady and my kind-hearted female psychiatrist (a screwball scientist if ever there was one) clean for Passover. Wiping the doctor's greasy window blinds and shampooing Mazal's carpet refreshed my thinking and brought blessing in its wake. The divine reward and punishment system that lies at the core of our faith operates according to the principle of *middah k'neged middah* (measure for measure). Judaism, long before Buddhism, brought the concept of karma to the world: God reflects our deeds on earth with a heavenly mirror. I suddenly realized that God didn't *owe* me a husband. I had no right to feel bitter. Everything was a gift—everything. Fastening onto this realization and letting go of my expectations helped me to lighten up entirely about the quest for a husband. I accepted that God would or would not reveal my *bashert* on His timetable and concluded that I might as well enjoy my life in the meantime.

A week later, a former teacher of mine from Aliyot College, Sarah Margolis, called to invite me to a holiday meal on the last evening of Passover at her home. While I had a pleasant connection with Sarah, we didn't know each other well. I was thankful that the part-time teachers at Aliyot remained ignorant of the gossip, politics, and drama that occupied the full-time staff: not everyone at Aliyot knew I was a hazard to humanity. Two other older unmarried women were guests at Sarah's that evening, along with Sarah's cousin—a nice-looking single man seemingly in his forties. He was friendly and interesting, and I wondered if Sarah had invited the "golden girls" of Aliyot to find a match for her cousin.

Over sumptuous food, we discussed the shocking statistic that only one-fifth of the ancient Israelites left Egypt in the Exodus; the rest—trapped by their complacency—perished in the plague of darkness. I quipped, "Weren't there any Lubavitchers running around getting everyone to paint their doorposts red?" I noticed Sarah's husband, Aaron, laughing— sometimes these Torah discussions at the table can get rather stuffy.

With my more carefree attitude, I decided to call Sarah after Passover to thank her for inviting me and inquire about her cousin. Feeling more relaxed about dating, I also felt bolder. Sarah admitted that she had thought of matchmaking, yet deferred the proposal of introducing me to her cousin until she spoke to her husband. Meanwhile, she asked for the name of someone at Mesorah College who knew me well.

Unbeknownst to me, Sarah's mentor and my mentor were exactly the same person. Rebbetzin Esther Apfelbaum, the matchmaker at Mesorah College with whom I had processed bachelors one through nine, lived in Sarah's neighborhood, and Sarah consulted her on every major decision. She was a renowned *tzaddekes* (righteous woman) and the wife of one of the most eminent Anglo-born yeshiva deans in Israel. Rebbetzin Apfelbaum and I had forged a genuine attachment, and I was only too happy to provide Sarah with her name. A couple of days later, Sarah called me with a surprise. Her husband thought it would be worthwhile to introduce me to someone with whom she and Aaron were even closer than her cousin.

Michael Turov was the tenth man I was introduced to in my Orthodox dating career. His biography was nothing if not intimidating. He had been Aaron's own Torah study partner for the past twenty-five years. Members of Michael's extended family were illustrious rabbis in America and Israel, hailing from devout Lithuanian ancestry. His family name announced *yichus* (distinguished lineage, the equivalent of Orthodox Jewish royalty) to all who heard it, though I, in my ignorance, had never heard of his clan.

Michael had been observant all his life, had never married, and was wealthy enough to retire from a successful career as an electrical engineer—now spending his time caring for his widowed mother, learning Torah, and traveling the world. Sarah, my teacher, assured me that he was an original thinker, kind, and humble to boot.

The letters p-r-i-n-c-e danced in my head. I was surely in over my head. I would be surprised to find a man like him shopping at the same kosher supermarket, let alone sitting across from me at the dinner table. But such are the ways of Providence: the mighty walls of Jericho fall at the sound of faithful trumpets. Michael was calling me for a date, and there was no sense refusing to accept the lottery ticket. As I made ready for the date, I tried to quiet my restlessness—choosing a conservative outfit featuring a five-dollar vintage tweed blazer I had purchased with the charity money I ought to have received from Nina Musconi.

Michael picked me up next to the entrance of a building adjacent to Mazal's house, betraying his own nervousness by greeting me with "*shavua tov*" on a Thursday evening. "Shavua tov" (have a good week) is the traditional salutation Israeli Jews offer one another on Saturday evening, immediately after the Sabbath concludes, before the working week begins.

We drove to a local hotel and spoke in the lobby over fruit salad and cake for the next three hours. I was struck by how pleasantly and quickly the time passed. Michael was genial, amiable, and charmingly self-deprecating. I found myself smiling at him almost all the way through the date. I recorded in my journal that night that I had found something very appealing about his face: although streaks of silver hair reflected his approaching middle age, Michael's unlined complexion and apple-kissed cheeks radiated the kind of innocence found among the very pious.

I appreciated Michael's candor as he told me that—although indeed Zionist—his parents had chosen to live in Israel as much for the tax benefits as for idealism. Once his married sisters had settled here, his parents followed; then Michael joined them. We exchanged observations about *Jerusalem Post* newspaper columnists and our feelings about being a Sabbath guest.

I was impressed to discover that Michael's response to suffering too many slights as the "older bachelor" guest at other people's tables—such as being seated with the children or being handed the newspaper instead of being engaged in conversation—was to host family and friends at *his* Sabbath table even as a bachelor. Employing a technique from Shaya Ostroff's book *The Inner Circle: The Seven Gates to Marriage*, I chose an open-ended question to ask Michael: "How did you become interested in engineering?" which elicited the charming anecdote that as a precocious scientist at the age of six, he had staged a slippery experiment exploring what weighs more, hot or cold water.

When our conversation drifted to philosophy—with a grateful nod to my professor, Gaby Rakover—I ably discussed Mendelssohn, Hirsch, and Geiger, the intellectual forefathers of the struggle between reformers and those who remained loyal to Jewish tradition, which captivated European Jewry at the time of the Haskalah, the so-called Jewish Enlightenment. Michael's parents looked to a scion of their own family for inspiration, who favored a premier Torah education combined with secular learning—calling for the strictest adherence to Jewish law, while contributing to the wider world. America and Israel had provided the soil for many scholars of the family to develop, where they escaped Russian pogroms and the Nazis to study Torah, free from persecution.

Among a couple of the compliments he offered me on the first date, Michael confessed he liked my name, Rebecca, calling it "one of the nicest," since he admired my biblical namesake. At the end of the date, Michael asked if he could see me again. I told him I'd look forward to it. Our first date revealed an unexpected comfort and ease prevailing between two people whose backgrounds couldn't be more different if his parents had been Nobel laureates and mine had been aboriginal pygmies.

Michael called me the following day to invite me to have a bite and stroll on the *tayelet*, a sculpted promenade overlooking Jerusalem's Old City, on Saturday night—eliciting all the romance that night carries in the secular world. My *kishkes* began to churn: What does it mean that he's so interested? Why is he in such a rush? Isn't a man in a rush a sign of an obsessive or controlling personality? Had I found myself another troublesome character? Yet he seemed so nice, so normal, so wholesome. He was close to his family and had lifelong friends. I prayed to God to calm my nerves and help me perceive him frankly. To the date, I wore a black corduroy dress with girlish pink flowers—trying to escape a feeling of dawning responsibility.

On our second date, Michael asked how my family felt about my moving to Israel. I offered the script that Rebbetzin Apfelbaum had composed: a casually spoken "We're not so close. They're used to my independence." In the first of many miracles, Michael responded with the elaboration *I* had prepared in case Michael probed further: "Well, that's how it is in America," he offered. "You grow up, go off to college, move away, and see one another on Thanksgiving or Chanukah...and if they're not observant Jews, what customs do you really have in common?" Then he dropped the issue, free of suspicion or interrogation.

Since the restaurant was closed, we strolled and talked about his family, his musically talented mother and sister, his academic training. He asked suitably interested questions about my studies and my plans for the future. I noticed early on that the chemistry between Michael and me brought out my playfulness. I found myself asking him how he liked being "the filling in the cookie"—a son sandwiched between an older and a younger sister. We spoke about our musical interests and enjoyment of hiking. I tried hard to follow my rebbetzin's advice to "be light, have fun..."

On Saturday night, when Michael invited me out a third time, he asked me how soon I'd like that date to be. I suggested Tuesday: in a coy effort not to seem too eager, I mentioned a lecture I had wanted to attend on Monday night. I immediately felt foolish for hurting him for the sake of my false pride.

Before our third date, a daytime trip to Latrun, an outdoor military museum in Canada National Park, I prepared a surprise picnic lunch of rolls, feta cheese, tomatoes, hummus, cucumber salad, carrot sticks, and fruit. When I unpacked this small feast, Michael exclaimed, "Well, you have the quality of Abraham our forefather: you say little and do much." When he asked me if I had made the salad, I answered, "Tell me if you like it first." I found myself again feeling surprisingly playful in the company of a man whose background and breeding positioned him at an entirely different altitude from me. Leaving a darkened auditorium after watching a seductive army recruitment video, I quipped, "May I escort you to the Victorian petticoat exhibit now?" not wanting him to be swept away with patriotism and sign up for duty. Michael laughed appreciatively at my possessiveness, giving me much-needed encouragement.

As we sat talking on a bench at Latrun, I became acquainted with Michael's penetrating nature. While I was inclined to trust most people and take them at their word—unless I had been personally deceived—Michael took a sober, critical assessment of others. He began to sound off about one of his pet peeves—the burgeoning charity industry. Michael was convinced that the hard-sell marketing techniques recently embraced by fundraisers—such as sending glossy mailings, providing gifts to donors, and airing cloying radio ads—were making money for more than just the poor. Michael's response was to increase his giving from 10 percent to 18 percent of his income, just to make sure that the Torah-mandated 10 percent still made it into the hands of the needy. Although more or less *charedi* himself, Michael was critical of many of the sacred cows of the postwar ultra-Orthodox, for example the premise that husbands and fathers should study Torah full-time, while expecting God or the wealthy to make their ends meet. Michael's family believed in the value of work, yet held their religious duties to be their raison d'être.

On our way home from Latrun, as we passed an Arab village, Michael asked me if I'd felt afraid, given the recent spate of terrorist attacks. Feeling a sudden urge to shock Michael, I confessed that I had lived in Umm al-Fahm, an Arab village in the north of Israel, as a teenager. (I had chosen to spend my vacation week volunteering in the village, during my year on kibbutz.) I suppose I seized the chance to pique his curiosity.

Michael didn't request any details of this caper—only seeking reassurance that my youthful naïveté had been replaced with a more nuanced grasp of the complexities of the Arab-Israeli conflict.

After a l-o-n-g pause, he asked dryly, "Have you done any other astonishing things in your past you'd like to tell me about?"

Duly chastened, I muttered, "How did I get myself into this mess?"

We both knew what he was fishing for. As a *baalat teshuvah*, I felt my romantic past standing like a totem between us.

"Case closed," he offered, after an uncomfortable silence.

"*You're such a mensch*," I exclaimed in relief and gratitude that he was not demanding to know the vintage of this new wine in his glass.

"I hardly know you. I haven't got the right to ask you *anything*," he said.

When I got home, I tumbled in the door and spilled my excitement to Mazal: "He's a lovely, lovely guy. Gentle, kind, principled, and generous, with a sense of humor, too." I thought to myself, "It's *only* the astonishing things I've done that have granted me the grace to be introduced to someone as fine as you." I resolved to share this sentiment with Michael, if God would only bless me with the chance.

In contrast with the alienation and rootlessness of dating in the secular world—in which a woman never knows if she is bringing home Mr. *Goodbar* from a bar or a party—I had a gaggle of yentas coaching my every move in this once-in-a-lifetime shot at happiness: my friends, Naomi and Joyce; my teachers Sarah, Debra Susskind, and Rebbetzin Apfelbaum. Rebbetzin Apfelbaum laughed when I admitted I had told Michael I had done volunteer work in Umm al-Fahm: "You were a liberal Jew— you wanted to do good. Of course, you would do such a thing. But Jewish girls are abducted and held prisoner there, you should know," she chided me.

Sarah reassured me, "Michael doesn't want an old lady," when I anguished over wearing sneakers on a date for which Michael had worn a suit and tie. Both Sarah and Rebbetzin Apfelbaum cheered Michael's refusal to ask me prying questions about my past. Everyone advised me not to force Michael to face details about my family or myself that would cause him to question my worth.

To Sarah I confessed the anxieties pressing against my insides: I felt terribly ashamed that at thirty-six, I still hadn't graduated college and lacked essential life skills such as driving and cooking. If Michael didn't know what I had suffered, how would he understand how hard it was for me to progress in a conventional way? And if Michael didn't know how I'd distinguished myself amidst a cruel and disturbed family, how could he appreciate what was truly noble about me?

Sarah encouraged me to seek the validation I wished for from God or from my mentors but not from Michael. She reminded me that according to Judaism we become a new creation after committing ourselves to fulfilling the commandments of the Torah. Premature disclosures about my family would only alarm Michael and raise concerns about *my* emotional health. To her, that Michael was asking me out after every date was reassurance enough that he respected me.

On Thursday, Michael called to inform me that his mother had been admitted to the hospital for pneumonia, and he would most likely be spending the Sabbath by her side. He did not know how soon we would be free to see each other. Galvanized by the incipient crisis, I felt moved to offer aid. I called my good friend Tova who bakes delicious Sabbath challah and begged from her two choice loaves. I recruited my friend Aviva to drop them off in Mrs. Turov's hospital room on Friday afternoon with a succinct note wishing his mother a speedy recovery and his family a "Shabbat Shalom."

Immediately after Shabbat, when mitzvah-observant Jews resume using telephones, Michael called to thank me and invite me out for the next evening. I was relieved to discover that the electrodes in Michael's heart were wired naturally: whenever I extended myself, whether in kind word or deed, Michael responded straightaway with warm reciprocation. His soul was so different from those of other men I had known in the past.

On our fourth date, over kosher eggrolls and emperor's chicken, I learned more about Michael and his family. Michael's father had been an accomplished and demanding man to whom Michael had grown closer in the years before his death, when the vulnerability of aging had softened him. Nathan Turov had left Belarus for America as a teenager, apprenticed to a friend of the family in banking. With persistence and extremely hard work, Nathan managed to buy his parents and siblings refuge in the United States with his naturalization a few years before the Nazis, aided by the local police, slaughtered the entire Jewish community. Michael's grandfather, Samuel Turov, had been a noted religious scribe, whose works were in demand throughout the region. When the Soviet Bolsheviks banned Jewish religious articles, his scrolls were smuggled within Eastern Europe at great peril. Yet his ritual calling never generated a great income.

Michael's mother Rose had trained as a concert violinist under the distinguished Hungarian musician, Ilona Fehér. Rose's father was the leader of their Orthodox Jewish community in Hungary. After watching the Nazis abduct her frail, beloved grandparents—who were only to be murdered later at Auschwitz—Rose and her parents and brother were incarcerated in Bergen-Belsen for six months, before their liberation aboard the controversial Kastner transport. Since his mother had known gnawing hunger in the camp, she said the grace after meals for the rest of her life with devoted concentration.

Michael's father had only turned his thoughts to marriage when he had established his parents and siblings comfortably in America. At the suggestion of a family friend, Nathan flew to Switzerland where Rose and her family had been taken after their liberation. After two sober meetings, Nathan and Rose agreed to marry. By this time, owing to his drive and talent, Nathan had founded his own finance agency in the land of opportunity.

When Michael told me he was sent as a teenager to collect the debts of his father's clients, I suggested he must have had "steel *kishkes*." It was his dread of this assignment that discouraged Michael from entering the family business, to the great disappointment of his father. Michael did not know of the family's assets growing up, as Nathan never wanted his children to rely on his own wealth. They lived frugally and unpretentiously, yet rejoiced with their summer visits to the Swiss Alps, where the children reunited with their maternal grandparents.

Michael and his sisters grew up in New York in the shadow of their father's relatives, the celebrated rabbis of the family. Michael always felt exposed by the prying, ubiquitous question, "Which Turovs are *you*?" The answer—to him—could only be,

"We're the humble, unremarkable Turovs who only have merit by virtue of our kinship with the greats." Yet in time, Michael found out that his father had lent financial support to the more scholarly rabbis of the family.

Michael took over managing the family's assets for his mother and sisters when his father was too old to do so. With his inheritance, Michael was blessed to retire early from a career as an electrical engineer that had given him intellectual gratification but too much social stress.

Michael could not claim his father's natural talent for business; nevertheless, he managed the family's accounts—a time-consuming and nerve-racking task—because he felt the awesome responsibility to provide for his mother and sisters. He furnished them with quarterly statements of account in which each coin was accounted for, trying to invest the capital wisely—never taking a penny for serving as the family's accountant, broker, and financial advisor. Michael helped both sisters find their spouses and was a loving yet lonely uncle to all his nieces and nephews.

As we strolled after dinner through Yemin Moshe, a picturesque neighborhood with cobbled streets near the Old City, I sensed that our dates, though pleasant, were failing to become more intimate, because I was remaining so guarded. After disclosing his piquant views about the official Rabbinate in Israel, Michael accused me of being rather starry-eyed about Orthodox Jewry. He feared spoiling the fantasy if he shared his observations about the less than idyllic aspects of the Torah-observant world. I told him, cautiously, that I had suffered some share of disillusionment myself but had not let it discourage me. Michael asked me what I meant, and I realized I faced a choice. By refusing to trust him, I would deny him the opportunity to understand me. Our relationship would not deepen unless I was willing to become vulnerable and share with him some of the pain I bore within my bones. So I took a chance: I shared with him the debacle of Aliyot College for Women.

I was rather astounded by Michael's concentration. We sat on a stone wall while I shared with him all the sorry details of Nicole, Judy, Beth, Rebbetzin Bramowitz, and Rebbetzin Segal. Michael savored my every word. He didn't rush me or jump to specious conclusions. He looked for opportunities to champion my good judgment and integrity. For instance, after I confessed that my first impression of Rebbetzin Segal had been poor, he exclaimed, "See, you were right not to trust her!" when he learned how she betrayed me in the end. At each moment when he thought the persecution had reached its peak, he was aghast to hear that it became fouler. He was full of knowing sympathy and compassion. Not for one moment did I feel he suspected me of misrepresenting the facts or concealing my own guilt. He embodied the Torah commandment to be *"dan l'chaf zechut,"* to judge our fellow Jew charitably. He too had been a sincere and modest person who had suffered at the hands of power-driven manipulators in his youth. I believe he recognized himself in my story and felt comforted. "While I know the Torah world is teeming with unsung heroes, there are, regrettably, some among us who do not practice what we are obliged," I told him.

I shared with Michael the lesson I learned through the Aliyot fiasco: not to look for trials in life. That is, how foolish I was to stay at Aliyot College to try to restore my reputation when anyone else would have fled for more nurturing pastures; that I could take confidence from the knowledge that God knew my innocence and refuse to care what mortals thought about me; and, finally, to shun charismatic mentors with narcissistic and histrionic personalities. Although I am unconsciously drawn to them because they resemble my mother, I inevitably seek to reform them. I have come to understand that is God's job, not mine. I withheld from Michael that Rebbetzin Bramowitz had threatened to foul my efforts to marry by giving a poor report about me to prospective suitors. I had not yet learned the most fundamental lesson: not to fear people. Still vesting influence in earthly leaders, I was to learn that God overrules them all.

I experienced Michael's affirmation as a salve. Michael understood what it cost to be stubbornly idealistic in a world that is—even in an exalted Torah milieu—prone to corruption with imperfect people at the helm. He said, "I imagine you've told this story many times and each time you tell it you feel a little bit better." I said, "Actually, I have barely told anyone." It was precisely my aversion to exchanging gossip about others that had made me such an easy mark at Aliyot. He reassured me that he felt so much closer to me now and had a real window into my personality.

Michael softly asked, "Did you learn anything about me tonight?"

"I learned that you can listen as well as talk, and that you are worthy of my trust," I whispered.

We both felt a growing identification. I took a calculated risk in telling him the saga of Aliyot College, and I was very glad I did.

As we drove back to my neighborhood, there was a time that we rode in silence and I did not try to fill it. I knew I didn't have to. It was the deep silence of two souls beginning to dwell as one.

Not far from my home, he asked, softly, "When can I see you again?" I answered, "When do you want to?" I asked him if there was anything else I could do for his ailing mother. He responded, "Your prayers are incredibly valuable. I am sure the prayers of someone who is trying so hard to be righteous are very valuable indeed."

When Michael picked me up for our fifth date, he was trundling his sister's window blinds, which he had fixed, in the back seat of his car. He admitted shyly that he was the repairman in his family since he was handy with tools. I marveled at yet more evidence God was revealing of Michael's loyalty. My final altercation with my selfish brother Richard had taken place many years before *over window shutters*. Richard was a carpenter. Before buying some shutters, I had asked my brother if he would hang them for me, and he had agreed. After I bought them, each time I invited him to hang them, he made some excuse, until I returned the shutters to the store unopened—for lack of the skill or funds to accomplish the task myself. When I complained, Richard screamed at me in public, "I don't have to do anything for you. You're sick. You need a psychiatrist. Go get some medication and leave me alone!"

Though the shutters were a trivial disappointment amid a lifetime of cruelty, I was finally able to see the callousness of my brother without camouflage. Then and there, I renounced a lifelong devotion to him that had brought me only pain and humiliation. Yet here was Michael, serving his family cheerfully out of love and filial duty. I was moved to hear the hints of rectification that God was whispering.

Michael and I drove to the Jerusalem International Book Fair for a quick outing in between vigils Michael kept by his mother's hospital bed. Although she was improving, her recovery was slow. I was pleased that despite his preoccupation with her care, he was still making time for our courtship. As I slid into the front seat, I passed Michael a package, "For when you're bored at the hospital and have nothing better to do," with copies of the chapters I had edited for a local Jewish press and the college essay I had written for Gaby Rakover on the exalted Torah portion of the "Binding of Isaac." I wanted Michael to know that although I was soft-spoken, I was no intellectual featherweight.

I witnessed again Michael's essential frugality and intolerance for crookedness where money was concerned as we pulled into the convention center parking lot where the book fair was held. Michael drove past a parking meter, which offered him a ticket for a fee of five shekels an hour. He was infuriated to discover that the ticket was completely blank. "How will they possibly know what to charge me!" he protested indignantly. As he stared intently at the blank ticket, lost in consternation, I quipped, "Do you have infrared vision?" He laughed so hard at the absurd question that he bumped his nose against the steering wheel.

While we strolled the isles of the book fair, Michael burnished his heroic image by asking me each time I handled or pointed out an interesting book, "Would you like to have this book?" Though I demurred, I was touched by his apparent willingness to indulge my fancies. Michael drew my attention to a handsome coffee-table book of photos of the French and Italian countryside. "I can't look—it's too painful," I remonstrated playfully.

"But there's no reason to assume you'll never see these places for yourself," he ventured.

At the book fair, I was overcome with a sudden fear that I couldn't possibly keep Michael entertained or maintain the illusion of my wholeness. Who was I to imagine that I could sustain the interest of such a man? And how could I endure yet another rejection? I urged Michael to go on without me, claiming that I wanted to examine a book and would catch up with him later. I promptly lost him amid the crush of visitors. For ten minutes, I searched for him frantically until I found him at a stall called the Meeting Place. "I was about to have you paged," I confessed, as I witnessed him blush.

As we sat on a park bench after the fair, I felt Michael become romantic for the first time. "So how *are* you?" he asked tenderly. I thanked him for the effort involved in finding so many interesting venues for our dates. Although he appreciated the praise, he claimed it was undeserved: "Every time I open the newspaper something just jumps right out at me." He asked me if I'd like to go walking in my neighborhood to see the bonfires on the evening of Lag B'Omer, the Jewish holiday coming up in a few days' time, and I happily agreed.

We were both feeling a bit giddy on the eve of Lag B'Omer. Momentum was building in our relationship, and we were beginning to "talk business" as couples do in the Torah-observant world. We strolled around my Jerusalem neighborhood gazing at bonfires illuminating the night. Michael offered me an unusual personal compliment: "Rebecca, you dress beautifully."

"Thank you," I replied quietly.

"You really dress beautifully," he repeated.

"Thank you," I said. The third time he complimented me, I added, "It's nice to have someone to dress for." Michael followed up this unusually personal interchange with his first practical question: Did I want a TV in the home I would share with my husband (a departure from ultra-Orthodox custom) and what was my passport status? I received these questions with a glee bordering on the ecstatic.

Perhaps it was inevitable that some waves would rock our heretofore, idyllic romance, and these surfaced this evening. Michael probed to understand my relationship with my family. I only told Michael that I had encountered my mother unexpectedly in an unplanned farewell, days before I had left for Israel. We had not spoken for well over a decade before. "My mother was in the grip of evil spirits she could not put to rest. She was the most disturbed person in the family, but I believe she might have conducted herself differently had she been able. She must have suffered something terrible in her childhood, but I am unaware what it was," I explained. I shared with Michael what my mother had revealed about lighting Shabbat candles the very night before we met in Boston: "She must have done something to merit her prayers being answered so quickly. If nothing else, she has suffered," I acknowledged. "While I feel sorry for her, I simply cannot risk my emotional health," I said.

Michael accused me sharply of abandoning my family. "Heaven forbid," I retorted.

"So they abandoned you?" he suggested.

I responded, cautiously, "I understand that you need to know these things. I appreciate why you want to know these things." But I refused to elaborate. "I'm sorry; it's not the time..."

Michael retreated from this line of questioning with a calculated "Let's change the subject entirely. Let's sit on that park bench over there and you can tell me about your last great love."

"I most certainly will not," I declared. "Besides, if I'd had a great love, I'd be married!"

"Then perhaps your great love is yet before you," he offered. Armed with my rabbi's defense, I was sealed like a vault. I recoiled from his sudden scrutiny, bristling at his questions.

Stymied, Michael responded to my refusal to engage in "true confessions" by offering some surprising ones of his own. He proceeded to confess to me—unsolicited—an affair of the imagination he'd nurtured for six years with a married non-Jewish business associate who worked at the same engineering firm as he did, years ago in New York. He described himself as having been consumed with desire for her, until he finally concluded that she was evil for shamelessly flirting with him. He also told me of the woman he was once engaged to for six weeks. He described her as a high-powered Los Angeles interior designer with a six-figure salary. Yet she was not as invested in observing the Torah as he had been led to believe. He had proposed to her when he was just past the age his own father had married. Feeling the pressures of time and history, he had acquiesced to them when he proposed, not convinced, himself, that it was right. Michael broke off the engagement when her behavior confirmed his doubts about her spiritual sincerity.

I was quite shocked by these two stories and didn't know how to react to them. The image of my kind, gentle, and God-fearing Michael lusting after a married Gentile colleague was more than disconcerting. And he called it "love." The power and financial clout of his former fiancée also seemed to draw him. I couldn't help but wonder what these particular objects of desire revealed about the contours of Michael's own heart. If he could love these two women who sounded so different from me, how could he possibly love me? I was shaken by these revelations, and I was unable to conceal it. Michael felt embarrassed.

"I never touched a hair on her head!" he protested about the Gentile workmate. Yet he admitted that if she had ever turned up at his door, he couldn't be sure what might have happened.

As he took me home, I stammered, "I need some time to think—to digest everything that we talked about tonight. Don't worry. Have a good Shabbos, and I hope your mother gets out of the hospital soon." I knew I sounded cold, but I could not conceal my bewilderment.

Promptly the next morning, the benevolent hand of God interceded in the form of Debra Susskind, my favorite seminary teacher from Aliyot, with whom I maintained a tight connection. She knew I had been dating someone seriously and had called to ask me how it was going. I was so grateful to have someone with whom to appraise this sudden wrinkle in my joy.

Although I betrayed a confidence to tell Debra of Michael's secrets, I was so confused that I deemed it necessary. Debra's intellectual clarity sliced through my unease with the precision of a laser: "Nothing happened, Rebecca. That's the only thing that's important. Nothing happened. And furthermore, it's refreshing to hear that he has desire. With an older man who's been single for so long, sometimes you have to wonder if they've got any feelings at all. Men are essentially more physical than women are, and physicality independent of spiritual value can attract them. It's a fact about men. It's nothing to be threatened by. At least you know he's alive. It's actually *good* news." Debra's words staunched the flow from the scrape immediately. I was a bit ashamed that I had so easily lost faith in my hero.

For Debra, the real question was why Michael told me of these "affairs," of which he was clearly not proud. Although I suspected it was because Michael wanted me to feel safe in telling him about my romantic past, I came to understand that bracing candor and a tendency to confession were intrinsic elements of Michael's nature. With my tendency to worry and his aversion to camouflage, I had my concerns laid bare for me.

I came home early after Shabbat, but Michael didn't call. Sunday morning, I left word on his answering machine, and he called back immediately after his morning prayers. "Yes, we have some unfinished business," he said. I could hear dejection in his voice, and I assumed he concluded our romance was at risk.

To his relief, I reassured Michael that I was prepared to proceed with our dating, though I admitted to being somewhat mystified by his latest disclosures. His relationships with these two women, however stillborn, seemed so at odds with the impression he gave me of sensitivity, reverence, and piety.

To make amends, Michael invited me next to lunch at his apartment. "You're more than just a date," he ventured, "you're a peach, quite possibly, a plum."

"Just as long as I'm not a lemon," I replied.

Before my first visit to his home, I presented Michael with a jar of plum jam wrapped in tinsel.

I was quite touched that Michael grilled steaks for us and provided a complement of tasty side dishes. Being invited to his home heightened the romantic tension further, and I found myself quite enthralled in his company. So much so that I began asking Michael to keep the front door slightly ajar as we began to spend more time at his home. The Jewish laws of *yichud* prohibited our being alone together in a secluded place, being unmarried members of the opposite sex. But Michael felt it was sufficient to leave the front door unlocked and the blinds open.

Although Michael was sure that I had come under the influence of some overprotective Chassidic den mother, I assured him I was only responding to the signals my body was sending me. Spending so much time alone with a man I was clearly attracted to, and with whom I was developing more and more of an attachment, simply seemed unwise. Michael was tickled that I implied it was hard to maintain self-control while alone in his presence, yet he wondered what I was suggesting about my virtue.

Michael was troubled by the specter of my romantic past, because he feared that we might be visited someday by a venturesome former love, and because he wondered whether pain I might have suffered would compromise my ability to love him. I assured him that it was solely my family which had left the scars, but I believed I was whole, nevertheless. I refused to satisfy Michael's prurience, in accord with my rabbi's advice never to tell Michael anything that would cause him to lose respect for me. Even Mendel, my Chabad rabbi in Boston, once urged—when overwhelmed by my tendency to confess my every mistake— "You know the halachah also protects you: you shouldn't tell *lashon hara* about *yourself*, either!"

Neither of my rabbis was advocating deceit, just maintaining the best possible image before others. Since we all err, we needn't publicly indict ourselves for every misstep; privacy and dignity are fundamental Jewish values. While slights to others require acknowledgement and repair, we can atone for falling short of the divine image within us in the private sanctuary between man and God. Maintaining one's morale for the hard work of fixing one's flaws requires gentleness with the self—a posture I was still in a quest for.

On our next date, we shared a hike in a rural wood on the way to Tel Aviv, and Michael brought his camera along. We took pictures of each other, which we developed the same afternoon, and I tucked Michael's picture into my prayer book. (Snapping Michael's photo, I told him, "Say *Prince Charming*.") Now that we were safely past our first storm and back to being romantic, Michael felt safe in needling, "So, how many of your friends know I had a thing for a married woman?"

I told him, "Two and both were supportive of *you*."

On the drive home, Michael performed a superb rendition of Monty Python's parrot sketch. We found a station on the radio that played a pleasing blend of my favored folk and bluegrass and Michael's country-western—uncommonly compatible. Even Orthodox suitors could come tailor made.

Michael told me at night on the phone that he was beginning to remember what I looked like and sounded like when we weren't together. He confessed he had scanned my photo into the computer and blown it up until it filled a frame on his desk. He was prepared to concede, he now knew me "a little bit," but we would have to know each other "a great deal better" before he would be prepared to propose. I misinterpreted this remark to mean he wanted to know more about my family, yet each time I divulged a detail about them, I found myself flinching in embarrassment.

As soon as we realized how compatible we were, and how attracted to one another, each of us began our own dance of self-sabotage designed to ruin our own happiness. Even in this way, Michael and I were soulmates. Our relationship took on the characteristics of a seesaw, as we tested each other before emerging from each wobble on steady ground. Fortunately, God prevented a catastrophe.

For example, Michael began regaling me with vignettes from his contentious work history. Whereas Michael exhibited creative ingenuity and technical expertise in his field of electrical engineering, being an unmarried, older Orthodox male with genteel manners and uncompromising religious rituals often left him socially vulnerable at secular workplaces. His aversion to gossip put him at a disadvantage in firms where office politics would drive others to be quite vicious. In particularly intolerable cases, Michael resigned rather than work for someone whose ethics he despised—but not before a shouting match erupted between him and his about-to-be erstwhile boss.

Though Michael's peccadilloes might be explained by the difficulties a sensitive religious Jew encounters in the irreverent contemporary workplace, I chose to fret about the meaning of Michael's elitism and inflexibility, fearing I too might wake up to his letter of resignation one day when he found fault with me as a wife.

While Michael tainted his image with his less-than-storybook romances and quarrels with employers, I rocked the love boat by telling Michael the barest details about my past, against all my mentors' counsel. I admitted to Michael I had been in therapy half my life, yet I refused to claim that I had been abused. I didn't like these sensationalist labels: I was after his admiration, not his pity.

Owing to profound insecurity that I had something intrinsic to recommend me, I began to detail some of my exceptional life experiences. For instance, I revealed my father's occupational run-ins with the law, and that I believed I had discourse with the Almighty. I didn't put it exactly like that, but I did tell Michael of the visions of light that sustained me during the loneliest and most difficult time in my life. I was still too much of a rookie to realize that even deeply religious Jews could be skeptical of the mystical. There was another reason to withhold that information, and that was simply, modesty. Yet without crowing of the seal of God's approval, I felt too much of a failure. The fact is, a lot of my joy in living came from my experience of election, when the existence of God became indubitable for me. I was a newly born Jew, and I couldn't disguise the ecstasy this instilled in me.

Michael seemed unimpressed. In fact, he seemed worried. I might as well have admitted I was a professional snake charmer. I spent the next four dates trying to soothe Michael's nerves. We didn't discuss my biography, but he was noticeably aloof, and my confidence went south. I reproached myself for not heeding my mentors' warning against planting seeds of doubt about my background or my stability.

On our next date, as a comeback, I delivered a one-two punch to Michael's essential weakness of frugal pragmatism: with nothing but hope, I offered to make Michael dinner at his apartment. I hustled some recipes from my friend Joyce and sent him shopping for spices I'd never heard of, such as coriander and turmeric. The Lord Himself prepared that meal, because Michael concluded afterwards that I was a gourmet cook. Even I was astounded that each dish tasted succulent. Like a circus clown who keeps a dozen plates spinning in the air simultaneously, I managed to bring the contents of every pot to a perfect state of doneness at exactly the same time. I have to admit, I had made it look easy. This act of apparent competence appeased Michael somewhat about my wits. The fact that it was sheer beginner's luck, he didn't yet know.

However, once Michael sensed I was keen, he displayed new respect for the doctrine of caveat emptor. Hoping to uncover a controversy, Michael asked me how I felt about covering my hair after marriage. Without missing a beat, I answered, "I think it's a privilege." I'd once heard a rabbi illustrate a married woman's obligation to cover her hair by invoking the *parochet*—the embroidered velvet curtain that hangs in a synagogue before the ark holding the *sefer Torah*, our most sacred possession. The more valuable something is, the more it must be hidden, and the less it should be on display, he had said. A woman's enhanced status at marriage—as a potential giver of life—requires that a veil of modesty and holiness envelop her, of which head covering was a sign. I never had the reluctance of some *baalot teshuvah* to sacrifice their freedom of dress. Once I tasted the difference between holy and profane, I was only too eager to climb the spiritual ladder with all of its requirements.

On the same date, a picnic in the forest, Michael made a careless remark about my teeth: he claimed it was clear that my parents should have spent money to have my overbite corrected and had failed to do so. I cringed, he cringed, and I felt added anguish that this physical flaw had also troubled Simon, whose character was utterly beneath Michael's. Was our relationship also doomed by a man's fundamental superficiality? Later that evening I told Michael that his remark made me feel like a piece of merchandise on the discount rack. Validating my rebuke, he offered a heartfelt apology.

Nevertheless, Michael's new reticence manifested in obsessing over not feeling what he believed he should, and doubts that I could feel what I claimed I did. If I had never had a great love, he wondered, how could I be sure this was it? He insisted he was waiting for the lightning bolt—the feeling of exultation and exhilaration that should accompany falling in love and proposing marriage. He vowed not to hesitate once he felt it. He remembered his fever for the married woman from his past, and our warm bond felt bland by comparison. Yet he conceded my conjecture that his memory of "loving someone more than life itself" was a by-product of frustration and forbidden longing.

He granted me that by cross-examining him, I was showing him that I was indeed wiser than he was.

However, our courtship was running aground over differences in our expectations. Ironically, I was espousing the Torah's worldview, whereas Michael was betraying a secular sensibility. I praised our ease in communicating and our feelings of trust and comfort, while Michael pined for feeling "in love." I maintained that feelings of love arise between two people who behave lovingly. It seemed obvious to me that upholding the code of the Torah—which denied us physical contact—would put a ceiling on our passion. Yet for me this only heightened my desire.

Perhaps the reader wonders how I could seek marriage to a man without sampling our physical chemistry. Nothing could be more erotic than watching Michael sway under the trees as he supplicated the Creator of the universe when the time for afternoon prayer arrived, as I was privileged to many times. I needed a cold shower after watching him pray. I suspected this was evidence enough that I could trust my instincts.

I contended that what actually troubled Michael was the threat to his convictions—the breach of his deeply entrenched worldview. Someone had convinced Michael long ago that happiness in love was meant only for *other people*. He was so committed to this lonely fate that he was prepared to sacrifice a good relationship in order to preserve his safe solitude. Michael admitted that he'd long ago resigned himself that he was never getting married. He didn't know quite what to do with a nice girl who was prepared to marry him. Her presence disqualified his foundation.

Ultimately, shipwreck threatened our courtship because of Michael's fear. Given my background, shrouded in mystery, one could hardly blame Michael. Yet he and I both knew that this was not what held him back. Michael was an original thinker—not a follower—and he could look beyond the surface to recognize merit. That is why we had been dating for six weeks, when another man in his position might not have agreed to meet me at all.

As we sailed into stormy waters, I found myself stirring up a squall. Michael's hesitation, in contrast to his keenness at the beginning, was arousing my insecurity. If rejection was inevitable, I reasoned, I might as well bring it on myself. I found myself dragging my feet about turning in an editing test in my efforts to land a job. I was sleeping too late in the morning, feeling grim about the day.

But I took myself in hand and determined not to repeat past patterns. I would remain responsible and not give Michael an excuse to disrespect me. If he was yet another man who couldn't commit, I would not shoulder any of the blame.

As our relationship foundered, I obeyed the siren song. Like a salmon that swims upstream in order to spawn, I was determined despite the peril that Michael would know what was essential about me: that I had lost my beloved grandfather by my father's hands. He had to know where I stood in life and why I stood alone.

At the Western Wall, on our nineteenth date, I began to reveal my father's role in my grandfather's death, yet Michael stopped me when he saw me becoming too distraught. He anticipated what I couldn't bring myself to say and reassured me that he believed I was a stronger person because of everything I had been through. He insisted that understanding my past helped rather than harmed our relationship. Michael wrote in his journal that night, "Rebecca fought to save her grandfather, but no one would believe her."

To me, Michael quoted the Hebrew biblical verse that Boaz said to the Jewish convert, Ruth, when she offered herself to him on the threshing floor: "And now, my daughter, fear not. I will do in your behalf whatever you ask, for all the elders of my people do know that you are a virtuous woman" (Ruth 3:11).

Later, at the Sheraton Hotel, over cake and tea, we revisited our stalemate. Michael questioned whether he was a misanthrope who couldn't love or just a lonely man withered from too much neglect. I wondered whether in marrying me he might deem he had settled for less than he expected; perhaps he would respect me less than he should. He admitted he was worried that others might make catty remarks about my shallow Torah education. It was a wary, calculated conversation. Suddenly I offered a game-changing observation: I told Michael that it seemed both of us had suffered too much pain to dare to hope that our dreams might be fulfilled. To acknowledge the potential in our relationship—to trust in our love—was almost too frightening, lest we each suffer another heartbreak neither of us could bear.

Somehow this epiphany shook Michael's heart loose. He began to warm up to me and agreed that I had grasped the essence of what held him back. I knew Michael was sensitive and feeling: I had seen evidence of it each time his eyes welled up with tears over the virtue and self-sacrifice of our matriarchs, patriarchs, prophets, and kings. Michael was a true believer, who wanted neither counterfeit love nor second best.

I saw the tight lines in Michael's forehead soften. He looked younger and more joyful. "I dreamed about you again last night," he confessed. "Part of it was good, and part of it was *very* good." He suddenly ventured, "I want us to decide on a date for the wedding before we announce our engagement. I want to meet your friends and to socialize with them, and I expect you to socialize with my family." He proceeded to ask me how many guests I'd like at our wedding and for my impression of various wedding halls. He was saying everything except "Will you marry me?" but I didn't object. He seemed pleased I was letting him talk this way. My delight was so obvious that I had a smile on my face the length of the equator.

Now I remembered my rabbi's requirement that I inform Michael of one more crucial fact *before* our engagement—that I took medication for depression and anxiety. Yet he had caught me off guard with his surrender: I didn't know how to break the news to him at this point. Instead, I told him of the plot of *Turtle Diary*, a quaint film drawn from a Harold Pinter play about two lonely people who finally feel the stirrings of love at middle age but are afraid to succumb to them. Through their mutual and symbolic quest to free caged sea turtles from the London Zoo, they find connection and courage. Michael responded, "But you're not old, you're young. You look like someone in her twenties, and you are presently laughing like a sixteen-year-old. *I* am old. I will have to go back to the gym to get in shape to be able to keep up with you!"

Suddenly Michael stunned me with the following question: "Is there any mental illness in your family?" Rabbi Feder had warned me about *precisely this question*, and I received it with all its damning force. "Wha...what did you say, Michael?" I stammered, stalling for time.

Then I walked soberly into the gunsight, as I had been instructed to. My throat parched, I admitted, "Well...my only brother is a paranoid schizophrenic with a character disorder." I might as well have told him I was born to a flock of seagulls. Michael looked at me quizzically and said, "Oh, my sister's sister-in-law has a child with that diagnosis," and he casually drifted to another subject. He responded with the level of concern that might follow a confession that one of my family members suffers insomnia during the vernal equinox. The Talmud even cautions a man to inquire about a prospective bride's *brother*, if he wants a preview of the quality and character of his own children. I am convinced to this day that when *HaKadosh Baruch*

Hu (the Holy One, blessed be He) wishes two people to marry, He blinds them to the risks—sprinkling a kind of romantic pixie dust over them, which renders them impotent in the face of His will.

Heartened by Michael's aplomb, I told him, "There's something else you must know." Yet Michael insisted, "Tell me the next time. I'm too tired already." Thus I was spared the anguish my final secret might engender—and freed to savor his extraordinary acceptance of a far more alarming confession.

Michael proceeded to ask me if I'd like to live in Jerusalem together with him, and I said, "I'd love to." He asked, "Where would you like to live? Would you like to live in my apartment?" Though I eagerly nodded my consent, I shared one concern, that I needed a room of my own—a study or an office. He offered the use of the third bedroom in his house, while he suggested that I might like to change the decor. He thought the apartment would be sufficient until the first baby would come. We were feeling very giddy and romantic.

When I stepped out of his car by the curb to Mazal's house, Michael blew me a kiss, which I returned with wonder and gratitude. I managed to sleep only two hours that night. At dawn, I went to my friend Naomi's empty house to feed her birds. I contemplated my glorious fortune in the quiet of her home as a queen surveys her public. I could hear the heavens ringing.

Chapter 31

T he next morning, my elation was punctured by the rude announcement that Michael had woken up with sheer panic in the shape of a disabling pain in his neck. He canceled our date for the next day and informed me he was departing for America. Fleeing…for a week. He told me the East Coast sheltered three people who might help him make sense of his confusion: his first cousin, Abigail, a prominent family law attorney; and his best friends, Hindy and Martin Finkelstein. He said Hindy would give him "a stern talking-to" and then maybe he'd be able to make up his mind. Unbeknownst to me, he told Aaron, our matchmaker, that it was "probably over." He called me the next day from the plane, saying, "For a moment, I thought I could be young again, but now I'm not so sure."

Immediately, I reproached myself for revealing how my grandfather had perished. Rebbetzin Apfelbaum concluded, "God must have led you to say it, because everyone else told you not to." Sarah eased my regret when she told me that Michael had told Aaron the night before that I was his intellectual equal and his moral superior. Could this really have been my mistake?

Shelly Morgenstern, the local relationship doctor, who specialized in helping older singles get married, supplied practical advice for handling Michael's eventual reentry into the atmosphere.

She urged me to insist he face me to deliver the verdict and provided a script for me in the style of a flowchart:

No? "I'm disappointed." If because of fear, go see Shelly.

Not sure? "I'm willing to give it a little more time." Suggest he see Shelly. (Either way, she'd collect a hundred dollars.)

Yes? Well, we all know the odds of *that*.

She urged me to be as cheerful as I could muster until we met and he gave me his answer.

I was advised to provide Michael with no more than another month to come to his senses, if he hadn't already. If he couldn't propose by then, I was to surrender him to the dustbin of the *alter bachur* (older bachelor) who *never will marry* and get on with my life. I had a whole cadre of mentors and fans lined up to declare in unison: the collapse of this courtship was *not my fault*. Everyone assured me that I had conducted myself honorably and admirably dating Michael. Sarah rued that if Michael didn't marry me, he'd never again have as good an opportunity.

Rousing myself to be cheerful at his return was as difficult as swimming to the top of the ocean after I'd been on the sea floor for over a week. Although I began the week with sham cheerfulness and made an effort to keep to my routine, I slid into near catatonia by the end. I was miserable, and there was no denying it. Since I had never turned to the bottle, I didn't do so now, but I did mope, sulk, and moan, especially to my dear friend Joyce. The night before Michael returned, I penned him as moving a letter as I could, urging him not to let his vague fears about marriage and subsequent gossip steal his chance for love.

Michael's performance at the week's end, after a couple of extra days' recovery from jet lag, was nothing short of abominable. He sunk to new depths of disgrace. He overslept the date he arranged with me, and I had to wake him up with a phone call. He was reluctant to take me out but asked instead that I come again to his apartment, when this kind of intimacy—in the face of our imminent breakup—was clearly inappropriate. When he faced me across the table at a restaurant, he admitted he hadn't brought me anything from the States, simpering, "I know I should have." He wanted me to reveal how devastating my week had been, while he told me how exciting his trip was. Regaling me with the sights, he declared, "I know you would have loved it."

He proceeded with questions about wedding plans even before asking me to marry him, again. His neck took on the properties of Felix Unger's sinuses: each breach of the decision before us was accompanied by a neck spasm Michael declared immobilizing. "If my neck continues to spasm like this, I can't be expected to move forward with a proposal," he decided. He had the nerve to tell me a string of superlatives about a woman from his past whom he claimed he'd cried over for two months, after she became engaged to another man the very day he resolved he was going to pursue her. He acted like a guilty schoolboy—asking my forgiveness multiple times, while simultaneously justifying himself and gloating over his exploits. He was indulging himself at my expense, and I was disgusted.

However, we did have another extraordinary interchange, which revealed that the Lord hadn't abandoned this match. At the end of our date, I told Michael there was something else I was obliged to tell him. I explained that for two decades, I had taken medication for depression and anxiety, and I might have to take these medications for the rest of my life. Michael shrugged, nonplussed: "Do you know how many people take pills like these? They're more popular than aspirin." With that, he dismissed my confession. Only later did it dawn on him that the use of such medications might threaten a fetus, and he had reason to be concerned about their effect on my childbearing. Yet even this risk he was prepared to swallow.

Cinder-*oy*-la!

Michael agreed to see Shelly Morgenstern the next day. He told me he'd call me immediately afterwards. In the meantime, I consoled myself by composing a list of all the reasons to be happy if my relationship with Michael ended. Presently, I didn't have to search hard for Michael's flaws, but I knew I was only feasting on sour grapes. Michael was the kindest, most loving, refined, and loyal man I'd ever come across, and losing him would be nothing short of devastating. The only silver lining was the knowledge that, whatever pain I'd have to endure if this two-month episode of romantic, dignified dating ended without a proposal couldn't possibly match the agony of having spent years with a man and giving everything I had—body, soul, resources, and time—only to find out he couldn't and wouldn't marry. And worse yet, never had any intention to. This was some solace; but it wouldn't assuage my inestimable heartbreak.

Debra Susskind, my seminary teacher who had spin-doctored Michael's first indiscretions again saved the day: she concluded that Michael was punishing me for causing him so much distress—tempting me by his crudeness to end our *shidduch* and thereby sparing himself the need to summon the courage to propose. She urged me to be patient and understanding, reminding me that if Michael's behavior had been so self-absorbed all along, I never would have invested in this relationship. Michael had all the nobility and virtue I had come to expect, only he was facing his own fears and limitations, and this was causing him great embarrassment.

Michael called me promptly at one p.m. the next day, informing me that he had met Shelly Morgenstern: "She was very nice, but she can't make the decision for me either," he said. He pleaded with me for another week. He claimed he would spend it in Jerusalem, praying and learning Torah and doing nothing to distract his heart from the duty to make a decision. He promised me an answer in exactly one week. I agreed, even managing to

312

affirm that I was proud of him and that I believed he'd find his courage.

When I hung up, I felt it: a creepy, crawling feeling that started around my eyes, washed over my forehead and scalp, cascaded down my neck, shoulders, and back, picking up substance and gravity, only to lodge like a stone in my stomach. I had just signed up for another week of *hell*. I decided I would not endure it. I dialed Michael back.

"I'm sorry, Michael, I can't do it," I declared. "I will not wait for you. You can take all the time you need, but I am moving on. I am calling up matchmakers tomorrow. I want to marry an adult."

"You mean I might call you up next week and you might be dating someone else?" he asked.

"That's right," I confirmed.

"Well. That concentrates the mind, there's no doubt about it," he said.

When we hung up, he called Aaron and I called Sarah, Aaron's wife. I had to wait until he'd finished speaking before I could get through.

Michael told Aaron he had to make up his mind that day. Aaron said, "I think it's time to take you to see Rabbi Apfelbaum," Rebbetzin Esther Apfelbaum's distinguished husband.

Sarah congratulated me for taking care of myself and steeled me for the denouement—while I instantly regretted my ultimatum and yearned to call him back to say, "Of course I'll wait for you, forever...I love you!"

"You'll do no such thing," Sarah declared. "Let him come to his senses."

Rabbi Apfelbaum responded to Michael's terror with a professional disclosure. As a *rosh yeshiva* (yeshiva dean), he had conducted hundreds of weddings in his life in which he knew the grooms well as his students or members of his community. He told Michael, "In my experience, 20 percent of grooms come to the wedding canopy utterly confident that they are marrying the only woman in the world who's right for them. They know they have found their *bashert*, and they are composed, serene, even joyful. The other 80 percent of grooms arrive at the *chuppah* because the guests are waiting, the band is playing, and the hotel management and florist are demanding to be paid. And yet, even with these statistics, it works out for most of the couples. They are happy and have long, satisfying marriages."

"You mean I'm *normal*?" Michael asked timorously.

"It's the 20 percent who are not normal," Rabbi Apfelbaum reassured.

Michael felt released from expectations that he couldn't seem to satisfy. He could not claim to be unafraid, but according to Rabbi Apfelbaum, this anxiety in no way meant he was making an unwise choice. It was something to be endured until it dissipated with the promise of a new day.

Michael called me back and said he'd come to a decision. I could hear the lilt in his voice. He asked to see me the next evening, and for the name of my favorite perfume. I called my friend Miriam who had offered to lend me a lovely outfit for the occasion. Michael picked me up at eight p.m., and we drove back to Yemin Moshe, the site of our first truly meaningful date.

After securing from me a promise to join him for counseling if for whatever reason I was disappointed with him as a groom, he asked me to marry him. It was very heady being an engaged bride without as much as having clutched my intended's hand, yet this was another leg of the journey I was privileged to travel, and I relished its wonder and purity.

About six months after the passing of Michael's father, two years before we met, his late father's rabbi had told Michael, "Take heart, your father can still help you from Heaven." Michael knew the rabbi was addressing his loneliness—his lack of a partner in life with whom he could build a family of his own. Judaism teaches that the purification process a soul undergoes in Heaven yields blessing for the deceased's surviving kin.

After my grandfather's death, his best friend Alvin told me that my grandfather had confided in him that he didn't want to die because of me. "Who will take care of my Mirileh?" he had asked, plaintively. Michael is convinced that his father and my Pop-Pop cooked up our *shidduch* in Heaven. I believe it. The man whom my grandfather chose to take his place could not be more perfect.

"[God] raises up the poor out of the dust, and lifts up the needy out of the rubbish heap to seat them with princes, even with the princes of His people" (Psalm 113:7–8).

Chapter 32

In observant Jewish dating, people do the inconceivable: they determine over the course of a few hours, days, or weeks of *talking* to a prospective spouse whether they can commit to spending the rest of their lives together, raising children together, growing old together. In today's world, wherein no one invests more than a few evenings and sometimes only a few hours before enjoying the deepest intimacy—when the thought of marriage before living together seems reckless—this leap of faith is unimaginable. When you spend time together without the elixir of touch, nothing physical distracts from the essential questions: Do we share the same values, the same goals? Are we fortified or undermined by one another's presence? Do we bring out the best or the worst in one another?

What engenders the courage to make the most fateful of decisions with just hours of conversation? It is simple: God. Torah-observant Jews are raised with the conviction that for every person, God created a partner—like Adam and his custom-built Eve. We need only be alert to the signs that we have found each other. Jews raised with eternal Jewish values regard their obligation to marry and rear the next generation as paramount. To leave behind children who will joyously carry God's mantle aloft is considered the foundation of an accomplished life. To break the chain of heritage from Sinai to the Messiah is to fail the community and the heart. Therefore, the Orthodox date more ruthlessly than any do: if a date does not rate to be a lifetime partner, they swiftly move on.

Despite my fears—and my awareness of the gap between our upbringings—God erected a billboard in lights announcing, "You have found your *bashert*," in every remarkable act of grace in our courtship. All that remained was to convince Michael. With a *frum*-from-birth man who hadn't married by the age of forty-five, this was no cakewalk.

It turned out that Michael and I shared fears that we wouldn't be adequate and that, in marriage, we would be exposed—fears that Michael revealed just before he proposed. Michael delayed marriage for the same reason that I had once chosen an unsuitable partner who would never commit. Because, broken as I felt, I feared *I* could not sustain the intimacy that marriage required. Although more than two decades of unanticipated solitude had eroded Michael's self-confidence, he has proven to be a wonderful, natural-born husband.

I was swept to Jerusalem by a tidal wave of Divine Providence that carried me to safe harbor. The rebbetzin who had once threatened me was powerless before the parting heavens, which showered me with blessing when I became a bride and joined Michael's family. A teacher on her very own staff had introduced me to my groom! Michael's sisters, who'd waited decades for their beloved brother to take a wife, embraced me like a long-lost sibling. Rabbi Yosef and Rachel Goodman—and Rebbetzin Apfelbaum, who had moved with her husband to the United States by this time (so he could head a prestigious Torah institution)—flew across the world to attend our wedding, though I was only a stranger to them a few years before. I experienced firsthand how precious is the commandment to provide for an orphan bride in the eyes of the Torah community. I delighted in inviting and rejoicing with everyone whose kindness graced my life in my new land. Michael and I clasped hands for the first time after the blessings were recited and danced away from our wedding canopy.

More than twenty years have passed since those lonely days when my anchor to the world was nothing but heavenly light. With some chagrin, I admit I'm not on the level anymore where something like that would ever happen to me, but neither am I striving for it. I am not pining for the suffering that made that kind of exquisite epiphany possible. Gershom Scholem wrote in *Major Trends in Jewish Mysticism*, "Only when the soul has stripped itself of all limitation and, in mystical language, has descended into the depths of Nothing does it encounter the Divine."

Parenthetically, I am well aware that some, perhaps most psychiatric professionals, and laypeople, might regard those visions of light as a manifestation of deep depression and psychopathology. However, I maintain my faith that they were a comfort sent to me from Heaven. I believe this not only because I saw this extraordinary light for a couple of months *after* I had recovered from depression and was feeling profoundly joyful, but also because of the nature of a diary I kept at that time.

I was gratified to discover some similarity between the insights I recorded there and those found in our Book of Psalms, about the fickleness of humanity and the steadfastness of God (minus King David's sublime poetry). I was privy to painful truths about human weakness and limitation, which emerged from an uncommon despair. Yet my perception was never keener, my judgment never clearer, than during the time I first recognized that God was behind everything that had happened to me, as is true for all of us.

To those whose persecution prompted my epiphany, I might quote what the biblical Joseph said to his brothers, when they worried that he would avenge their cruel deeds after their father Jacob died: "As for you, you meant evil against me, but God meant it for good" (Genesis 50:20). However crushed I may have been at the time, the events were but a prelude to the swiftest and most remarkable change of fortune. In order to merit the precious gifts God had waiting for me, I had to be refined through suffering, and redirect my search for relief from people to God. I allow that if I *hadn't* sensed a Presence during that terrible time, I just might have gone crazy. Readers are welcome to draw their own conclusions.

Although I never again had visions of light, and never considered courting them, I have been privileged on very rare occasion to such astonishing and vivid Providence, that it was as if God was accompanying me, imperceptibly. Would that all of us would unmistakably experience God's fearsome and loving presence. Reverent Jews pray morning, noon, and evening for that day.

Typically, Providence is keen yet less dramatic in my life today. I experience God's presence in a subtle accord between time and space, when my fumbling virtue and God's beneficence coalesce to form a gently harmonious mechanism not unlike a clock whose simple face hides a delicate coordination. Such as the time I was preparing for Passover and just managed to finish cleaning and storing away my everyday dishes and taping the cupboard closed the moment that my boisterous children bounded through the door—preventing the chaos that would have erupted had they found me camped on the floor surrounded by breakable china. God is found in countless blessings of timing that reveal a divine protector. As an unrepentant self-improvement junkie, I am just as fiercely dedicated to *tikkun*, only the sphere has shifted to home and family, where most women meet their Maker.

The mitzvot of the Torah set the contours of my life, whether celebrating Shabbat and the festivals, hosting guests, studying Torah, or engaging in outreach with my fellow Jew. The discipline of an observant Jewish life gently, naturally calms the waves that trouble the depths of one with a family history like mine. Starting and ending each day with prayer, I am restored and renewed by my Creator, imperceptibly present amidst my loving new family and friends. I have plunged deep roots into a community that brims with kindness, faith, spiritual striving— the best of what humanity has to offer. Like the proverbial ugly duckling, I have found the nurturing clan where I belong: "Those who sow in tears shall reap in joy" (Psalms 126:5).

I wish to add that I did not decide easily to reveal what happened to me many years ago in one women's seminary for those returning to mitzvah observance, especially when the Orthodox Jewish world already suffers from flagrantly unfair press. I could not paint a falsely positive picture that returning to Torah observance means one never encounters unhealthy people. I believe it is especially crucial for teachers introducing Torah to the naïve who are searching after wisdom to exemplify a high standard of integrity, as so many do. I hope my disclosure of an incident that causes me some pain to this day encourages all of us to reflect on how we could do better.

While I have faced my share of trials, and will no doubt continue to do so, I live with confidence that each season of my life is custom designed to cultivate my potential. God has chosen us for a life of profound meaning and peerless value, which accords me serenity amidst every tribulation and a quiet but palpable joy.

Even my perverse experiences of persecution left me fortified to bear the excoriation and isolation of my adopted land. *Gam zu l'tovah* (this too was for the good). While Israel distinguishes herself in forbearance, mercy to her enemies, and faith amidst adversity, she is blamed, scapegoated, and shunned by the ignorant and the wicked, worldwide. This is the lot of the Jewish collective, forever destined to bear the burden of reforming the world—starting with ourselves.

A few years after I began living as a Torah-observant Jew, I came across a statement in a book that offered me solace for the years I had endured a rare punishment and ostracism at the hands of others, starting with my own family: *the national history of the Jewish people unfolds in the personal life of the Jewish mystic.* Although I searched fruitlessly for the source later, a university scholar of Judaism assured me that the concept is found in the Zohar.

The experiences that I had twenty-two years ago hardly made me a mystic, but I believe they were mystical, despite the tendency of others to be skeptical. I regard my life as a kind of parable, a microcosm of the experience of the Jewish people. Whereas my affliction reflected a mere taste of our people's tortured history, God's mercy and kindness to me—following my *teshuvah*—reveals our destiny. Since no earthly justice can account for the suffering that was my lot for the first thirty-six years of my life, I conclude that God wishes me to make known my unusual story of persecution, revelation, and liberation to help gather in His children.

As the pitch of worldwide anti-Semitism escalates, I bid the reader to find in my path of return the route to our freedom, salvation, and redemption. My reversal of fortune offers a paradigm for the contemporary Jewish people, estranged from our identity, our purpose, and God. According to Jewish mystical wisdom, my soul freely chose to endure the events I have described—even choosing my own parents. I suspect that my soul elected to accomplish this healing so that I might be a catalyst for *you*. Nothing would give me greater joy than helping to bring a beloved Jew closer to God.

If you are single and longing to be married, if you are a woman yearning to be a mother, if you wonder why you feel a stranger to your mate or your children; if you are lonely, unfulfilled, anguished, frightened, or ashamed, let my story guide you. Begin with prayer in your own words. Then bring your life into accord with the divine will, and let my blessings be yours.

Afterword

A couple of years ago—long after my marriage and the birth of our beloved children—I was given an opportunity to close a circle and thereby, closed two. Bumping into my favorite Judaic studies professor from Boston on the Hebrew University campus, I felt ready to finish my degree, and we met to discuss the parameters. My professor offered me a tantalizing proposal: "Read over the course material, and we'll meet to discuss it once a week in the outdoor library atrium over the course of the summer. No exams to take, no papers to write, and you'll have your Latham University degree." But within a couple of days, I knew this was a bum deal.

When I backed out of the arrangement before our first meeting—and insisted I wanted to write papers instead and submit them over the internet—my professor became angry and tried to talk me out of it, repeatedly. Although his intentions were prima facie undoubtedly honorable, he still sought the attention of a fawning student. Struggling for more than a year to write several university-quality papers after fifteen years out of academia—including a thirty-page final research paper that my professor reluctantly admitted was "a very good paper"—I felt he punished me in his demeanor and evaluation of my work for my decision to keep our relationship more distant.

In retrospect, I realize my teacher represented a falsehood about Judaism in our course so many years ago. He claimed that Judaism only prescribes what you do, not what you think. Yet there are examples throughout the Tanach and Talmud that reveal God's yearning for our hearts even more than rote obedience. Sincere intention is indispensable to genuine prayer, for example.

My professor and I have always had a special chemistry. But as a married woman, I didn't even want to think impure thoughts. Unfortunately, as frail human beings, we are prone to such things. Boundaries matter.

The Torah teaches that holiness is achieved only by giving up something desirable for the sake of God. While I lamented having to keep my former mentor distant, I knew it was the right thing to do. And I believe it was that choice—to fear God, not people, even at the price of alienating my favorite professor—that finally won me the character strength to write this memoir and the heavenly help in its publication. By passing my signature test, I gleaned wisdom worth sharing.

The unintelligible Latin "Latham" University bachelor's degree on my wall after forty-eight years, though no longer economically necessary (my husband generously repaid my student loans), speaks eloquently of the irrelevance of much of what the Western Jewish man and woman pursue: Man plans and God laughs, a Yiddish proverb.

I have come to understand my journey to faith and its vicissitudes—the suffering, the return, the revelation, and the redemption—as the voyage the Jewish people must undertake to be free of the pain of exile. When Jews learn to love and fear God above all, they will assume, as I have, their place of spiritual royalty. By virtue of the unbreakable covenant between God and the Jewish people, every Jewish man and woman is a prince or princess by destiny, a beloved child of the sacred marriage between Israel and the King of kings. Graced with the humility and crowned with the confidence of fulfilling our true role in the cosmos, we will fear no one. When God's treasured, chosen nation seeks His approval before anyone else's, *according to God's word with which He has gifted us,* we will have healed ourselves. Then, we will help God heal the world.

Acknowledgments

First and foremost, I acknowledge "my Michael" for the spiritual inspiration he has given me by his humble, kind, and righteous example and for his extraordinary generosity of heart and resources. Without his love and support, I could never have achieved my purpose. Secondly, I thank my precious children for their encouragement of their mother's mystery project, their acceptance of its confidentiality, and their respect for my privacy. I pray that any merit earned by this effort be their inheritance.

I thank each of the spiritual mentors disguised in this book, whose kindness and example shepherded my own growth. I thank the beloved circle of family and friends in whose shelter I have nourished and prospered these many years. I also thank the canny women whose review of this manuscript enhanced its clarity and style, as well as the exemplary staffs of Dartfrog Books and Booklocker.com: Evan Green and Angela Hoy merit special mention. Moreover, I have been extraordinarily blessed by the support of Rabbi Dr. Yisrael and Myra Levitz, Rabbi Nechemia and Dina Coopersmith, Judy Gruen, Sherrie Mandell, Lori Palatnik, Tova Mordechai, and Chaya Weisberg. I couldn't have done it without every one of you! Thank you for your generosity and kindness.

I also thank you, the reader, for bearing with me on this journey. If you have been touched by something I wrote, I would be so grateful were you to take the time to write an Amazon or Goodreads review, encouraging others to gain from it, too. Good reviews are invaluable to a new indie author hoping to gain a readership, and every one touches me personally. Additional comments or questions you would like to post to my website are welcome, at www.mirandaportnoy.com.

While I tend to thank the Lord privately many, many times a day, I cannot conclude this gratitude list without acknowledging that absolutely everything I am, have, and enjoy comes from Him. I am incredibly blessed to be a member of His chosen people. I pray that this effort brings Him spiritual delight.

Reader's Guide

*Cinder-oy-la! How a Jewish Scapegoat Becomes a
Princess* by Miranda Portnoy

Suggested Group Discussion Questions

1) How does the choice of title frame the story?
2) How does the cover complement the memoir?
3) What may the two epigraphs (quotations) that precede Miranda Portnoy's memoir mean to the author? What do they mean to you?
4) Before she embarks on her spiritual journey, Miranda paints a troubling portrait of the Jewish community, based on her experience with its members. What are the elements of this portrait? Do you think her portrait is fair? Why or why not?
5) Miranda made two startling discoveries in adult life. At thirty-two, she learned she had always had Attention Deficit Disorder and at thirty-three, she discovered there was a God in the world. What surprises have you discovered about yourself or the world that changed the course of your life? How did you come to discover them? What changes did you make as a result?

6) What do you think about Miranda's mystical experiences? Do you find them authentic, or do you think she was simply mentally ill at the time? On what do you base your view?

7) At several points in the story, Miranda gives up things she desires and enjoys to refine herself spiritually. How do you view her choices? When have you sacrificed something you desired for a higher purpose? How did you do it? What was the outcome?

8) In Chapter 19, Miranda presents a synopsis of Jewish philosophy, providing an explanation for the suffering we bear as humans. What are the strengths and weaknesses of such a philosophy? Do you agree or disagree with it and why?

9) In chapter 21, Miranda examines the consequences of reduced responsibility in casual sex. What are your thoughts about her analysis? What do you notice about gender relations in your world? What are the pros and cons of acknowledging our duties to a Higher Power in the sexual realm?

10) What do you think Miranda owes her parents and brother? Was she right or wrong to sever her ties with them?

11) What do you think about the way Miranda handled the betrayal by two women in charge of her first religious seminary in Israel? How would you have handled it and why?

12) What were the key decisions in Miranda's healing and emancipation?

13) What are some of the lessons in Miranda Portnoy's experience? What lessons might you apply to your own life, if any?

14) Where can individuality be found within a divinely ordained code of human behavior? What are the advantages and disadvantages of embracing such a code?

15) How did reading this book expand or change your perception of the subject matter?